Psychotherapies for the Psychoses

Throughout the world, access to psychotherapeutic and psychosocial treatments for the psychoses varies significantly, with many people diagnosed with psychotic disorders receiving only medication as treatment. *Psychotherapies for the Psychoses* considers ways that this gap can be bridged through theoretical, cultural and clinical integration.

The theme of integration offers possibilities for trainees and experienced mental health professionals from diverse orientations and cultural perspectives to strengthen alliances for tackling the gap in availability of treatments. In this volume contributors discuss:

- Theoretical integration across the psychological therapies for psychoses
- Global perspectives on psychosocial approaches for psychoses
- Integrating psychotherapeutic thinking and practice into 'real world' settings.

Psychotherapies for the Psychoses explores different approaches from a variety of theoretical perspectives, providing significant encouragement for mental health practitioners to broaden the range of humane psychotherapeutic possibilities for people suffering from the effects of psychosis.

John F. M. Gleeson is a Clinical Psychologist and Associate Professor across the University of Melbourne and NorthWestern Mental Health.

Eóin Killackey is a Clinical Psychologist and Senior Research Fellow in the Department of Psychology, University of Melbourne and ORYGEN Research Centre.

Helen Krstev is a Psychologist with PACE at ORYGEN Youth Health, and works in private practice in Melbourne.

Psychotherapies for the Psychoses

Theoretical, cultural and clinical integration

Edited by John F. M. Gleeson, Eóin Killackey and Helen Krstev

Routledge
Taylor & Francis Group

LONDON AND NEW YORK

First published 2008
by Routledge
27 Church Road, Hove, East Sussex BN3 2FA

Simultaneously published in the USA and Canada
by Routledge
270 Madison Avenue, New York NY 10016

Routledge is an imprint of the Taylor & Francis Group, an Informa business

Typeset in Times by
RefineCatch Ltd, Bungay, Suffolk
Printed and bound in Great Britain by
TJ International Ltd, Padstow, Cornwall
Paperback cover design by Hybert Design

British Library Cataloguing in Publication Data
A catalogue record for this book is available from the British Library

Library of Congress Cataloging-in-Publication Data
Psychotherapies for the psychoses : theoretical, cultural, and clinical integration / [edited by] John F. M. Gleeson, Eóin Killackey & Helen Krstev.
     p. ; cm.
   Includes bibliographical references and index.
   ISBN 978-0-415-41191-2 (hbk) – ISBN 978-0-415-41192-9 (pbk.) 1. Psychoses–Treatment. 2. Psychoses–Treatment–Cross-cultural studies. 3. Psychotherapy. 4. Integrated delivery of health care. I. Gleeson, John F. M. II. Killackey, Eóin. III. Krstev, Helen, 1973–
   [DNLM: 1. Psychotic Disorders–therapy. 2. Psychotherapy–methods. WM 200 P975 2008]
   RC512.P84 2008
   616.89′14–dc22   2007024122

ISBN: 978-0-415-41191-2 (hbk)
ISBN: 978-0-415-41192-9 (pbk)

The ISPS book series

The ISPS (the International Society for the Psychological Treatments of the Schizophrenias and other Psychoses) has a history stretching back some fifty years during which it has witnessed the relentless pursuit of biological explanations for psychosis. The tide is now turning again. There is a welcome international resurgence in interest in a range of psychological factors in psychosis that have considerable explanatory power and also distinct therapeutic possibilities. Governments, professional groups, users and carers are increasingly expecting interventions that involve talking and listening as well as skilled practitioners in the main psychotherapeutic modalities as important components of the care of the seriously mentally ill.

The ISPS is a global society. It is composed of an increasing number of groups of professionals organized at national, regional and more local levels around the world. The society has started a range of activities intended to support professionals, users and carers. Such persons recognize the potential humanitarian and therapeutic potential of skilled psychological understanding and therapy in the field of psychosis. Our members cover a wide spectrum of interests from psychodynamic, systemic, cognitive, and arts therapies to the need-adaptive approaches and to therapeutic institutions. We are most interested in establishing meaningful dialogue with those practitioners and researchers who are more familiar with biological based approaches. Our activities include regular international and national conferences, newsletters and email discussion groups in many countries across the world.

One of these activities is to facilitate the publication of quality books that cover the wide terrain which interest ISPS members and a large number of other mental health professionals, and policy makers and implementers. We are delighted that Routledge Mental Health have seen the importance and potential of such an endeavour and have agreed to publish an ISPS series of books.

We anticipate that some of the books will be controversial and will challenge certain aspects of current practice in some countries. Other books will promote ideas and authors well known in some countries but not familiar to others. Our overall aim is to encourage the dissemination of existing knowledge and ideas, promote healthy debate, and encourage more research in a most important field whose secrets almost certainly do not all reside in the neurosciences.

For more information about the ISPS, email isps@isps.org or visit our website www.isps.org

Brian V. Martindale
ISPS series editor

International Society for the Psychological Treatments of the Schizophrenias and Other Psychoses Book Series
Series Editor: Brian V. Martindale

Titles in the series

Models of Madness: Psychological, Social and Biological Approaches to Schizophrenia
Edited by John Read, Loren R. Mosher & Richard P. Bentall

Psychoses: An Integrative Perspective
Johan Cullberg

Evolving Psychosis: Different Stages, Different Treatments
Edited by Jan Olav Johanessen, Brian V. Martindale & Johan Cullberg

Family and Multi-Family Work with Psychosis
Gerd-Ragna Bloch Thorsen, Trond Grønnestad & Anne Lise Øxnevad

Experiences of Mental Health In-patient Care: Narratives from Service Users, Carers and Professionals
Edited by Mark Hardcastle, David Kennard, Sheila Grandison & Leonard Fagin

Psychotherapies for the Psychoses: Theoretical, Cultural and Clinical Integration
Edited by John F. M. Gleeson, Eóin Killackey & Helen Krstev

Dedicated to the memory of
Wayne Fenton
24 March 1953 – 3 September 2006

Contents

Contributors

Andreas Bechdolf, Consultant Psychiatrist, Early Recognition and Intervention Centre for Mental Crises (FETZ), Department of Psychiatry and Psychotherapy, University of Cologne, Germany. Email: andreas.bechdolf@uk-koeln.de

Lesley Berk, Research Clinician, Mental Health Research Institute and Barwon Health, University of Melbourne, VIC, Australia. Email: lesley@jc.com.au

Michael Berk, Professor of Psychiatry, Barwon Health and The Geelong Clinic, University of Melbourne, VIC, Australia. Email: MIKEBE@BarwonHealth.org.au

David Castle, Professor of Psychiatry, St Vincent's Hospital, Melbourne, and Mental Health Research Institute, University of Melbourne, VIC, Australia. Email: David.CASTLE@svhm.org.au

Grace Couchman, Senior Lecturer, School of Psychology, Psychiatry and Psychological Medicine, Monash University, Melbourne, VIC, and Clinical Psychology Centre, 239 Clayton Road, Clayton 3168, VIC, Australia. Email: Grace.couchman@med.monash.edu.au

Sarah Davenport, MSC, FRCPsych, Consultant Psychiatrist in Rehabilitation Psychiatry, Lancashire Care NHS Trust, PO Box 457, Northwich, Cheshire, CW9 7XX, UK. Email: sarahdvnpt@aol.com

Shona M. Francey, Research Fellow, Department of Psychiatry, University of Melbourne, and PACE Clinic, ORYGEN Youth Health, Melbourne, Australia. Email: shonaf@unimelb.edu.au

Jim Geekie, Clinical Psychologist, First Episode Psychosis, Auckland Healthcare, New Zealand. Email: jgeekie@adhb.govt.nz

John F. M. Gleeson, Associate Professor, Department of Psychology, University of Melbourne and NorthWestern Mental Health Program, Parkville, VIC 3052, Australia. Email: jgleeson@unimelb.edu.au

Lori Hassall, MSW, Clinical Coordinator, Prevention and Early Intervention Program for Psychoses, London Health Sciences Centre, London, Ontario, Canada. Mailing address: Prevention and Early Intervention Program for Psychoses (PEPP), WMCH Building, 392 South Street, London, Ontario, Canada N6A 4G5. Email: Lori.Hassall@lhsc.on.ca

Traceyanne Herewini, Maaori Cultural Adviser for the Youth Early Intervention Service and East Community Team (YEIS), 13 Green Lane Clinical Centre, Private Bag 92 189, Auckland 1142, New Zealand. Email: TraceyanneH@adhb.govt.nz

Eóin Killackey, Senior Research Fellow, ORYGEN Youth Health, Locked Bag 10, Parkville, VIC 3052, Australia. Email: Eoin.Killackey@mh.org.au

Helen Krstev, Clinical Psychologist, ORYGEN Youth Health, Locked Bag 10, Parkville, VIC 3052, Australia. Email: Helen.Krstev@mh.org.au

Tor K. Larsen, Professor of Psychiatry, Regional Centre for Clinical Research in Psychosis, University of Stavanger, Psychiatric Clinic, Armauer Hansensv. 20, p.b. 8100, N-4068 Stavanger, Norway. Email: tklarsen@online.no

Steven B. Leicester, Psychologist, PACE Clinic, ORYGEN Research Centre and ORYGEN Youth Health, Melbourne, Australia. Email: sbl@unimelb.edu.au

Andrew J. Lewis, Clinical Psychologist and Psychoanalyst, Senior Lecturer in Psychology, Faculty of Health, Medicine, Nursing, and Behavioural Sciences, School of Psychology, Deakin University, Geelong, Victoria 3217, Australia. Email: andrew.lewis@deakin.edu.au

Joanne McCormack, LCSW, Social Work Program Coordinator and Clinical Interviewer, Zucker Hillside Hospital, Glen Oaks, New York, USA. Email: JMcCorma@lij.edu

Craig Macneil, Senior Clinical Psychologist, ORYGEN Youth Health Research Centre, Locked Bag 10, Parkville, VIC 3052, Australia. Email: Craig.Macneil@MH.org.au

Rahul Manchanda, MD, Associate Professor, Department of Psychiatry, University of Western Ontario, and Medical Director, Prevention and Program for Psychoses, London, Ontario, Canada. Mailing address: Prevention and Early Intervention Program for Psychoses (PEPP), WMCH Building, 392 South Street, London, Ontario, Canada N6A 4G5. Email: maryellen.amaral@lhsc.on.ca

Frank Margison, MD, FRCPsych, Consultant Psychiatrist and Medical Director, Manchester Mental Health and Social Care Trust, Gaskell Psychotherapy Centre, Swinton Grove, Manchester, M13 0EU, UK. Email: Frank.Margison@mhsc.nhs.uk

Brian V. Martindale, Consultant Psychiatrist, South Tyne and Wearside Mental Health NHS Trust, Monkwearmouth Hospital, Newcastle Road, Sunderland, SR5 1NB, UK. Email: Brian.Martindale@stw.nhs.uk

Rachel Miller, MSW, PhD, Research Social Worker, Child Psychiatry Branch, National Institute of Mental Health, Building 10 (Room 3B24), 10 Center Drive, Bethesda, MD 20892, USA. Email: mrachel@mail.nih.gov

Anthony P. Morrison, Professor of Clinical Psychology, Department of Psychology, University of Manchester, and Associate Director, Early Detection and Intervention Evaluation (EDIE), Bolton, Salford and Trafford Mental Health NHS Trust, UK. Email: anthony.p.morrison@manchester.ac.uk

Sharon Scott Mulder, Manitoba First-Episode Psychosis Family Support Group, Box 3697 RR#1, Gimli, Manitoba, Canada R0C 1B1. Email: slsm@mts.net

Ross M. G. Norman, PhD, Professor, Departments of Psychiatry and Epidemiology and Biostatistics, University of Western Ontario, London, Ontario, Canada. Mailing address: Prevention and Early Intervention Program for Psychoses (PEPP), WMCH Building, 392 South Street, London, Ontario, Canada N6A 4G5. Email: rnorman@uwo.ca

Lisa J. Phillips, Lecturer, Department of Psychology, University of Melbourne, Australia. Email: lisajp@unimelb.edu.au

John Read, Associate Professor, Department of Psychology, Auckland University, New Zealand. Email: j.read@auckland.ac.nz

Ishita Sanyal, Consultant Psychologist, Regional Director, NAMi, India and Founder Secretary Turning Point, 27 Jadavpur East Road, Kolkata 700032, West Bengal, India. Email: ishitasanyal@hotmail.com

Serge Sevy, MD, Assistant Professor of Psychiatry and Behavioral Sciences, Albert Einstein College of Medicine, Bronx, New York, and Research Psychiatrist, Zucker Hillside Hospital, Glen Oaks, New York, USA. Email: ssevy@lij.edu

Brenda Wentzell, BA, BEd, Family Support Group, Prevention and Early Intervention Program for Psychoses, London, Ontario, Canada. Mailing address: 405 Sparling Court SW, Edmonton, Alberta, Canada T6X 1C5. Email: brenda.wentzell@shaw.ca

Gina Woodhead, BApp Sci (Occ Thy), BEd, MA, Coordinator of Psychosocial Recovery/ORYGEN Group Programmes, Early Psychosis Prevention and Intervention Centre (EPPIC) and ORYGEN Youth Health, VIC, Australia. Email: Gina.Woodhead@mh.org.au

Foreword

This new book springs out of the Fourteenth International Society for Psychotherapy in Schizophrenia (ISPS) Conference, held in Melbourne, Australia in September 2003. The theme of the conference was different perspectives in 'understanding' and 'treating' psychosis. Even the use of these two terms is arguably contentious and will no doubt land me in hot water!

The book represents a broad church with contributions from those with a cognitive-behavioural perspective, those adopting a more narrative approach and those operating from a psychodynamic approach. There are frequently tensions between proponents of these various approaches. The book attempts to bring together these different theoretical perspectives in a meaningful way. Material is examined from a theoretical perspective, a global perspective and an integrative perspective. The last specifically deals with integrating psychological interventions into 'real life' settings.

In the third section, the various approaches appear to take their beginnings from the patients themselves, recognizing the different needs of the first-episode patient group and their unique characteristics including developmental phase. The importance of the treatment alliance and collaboration is pivotal to working with this patient group; if one cannot engage these individuals, obtain some shared understanding, then there can be no therapeutic progress. One of the lessons learned from psychodynamic approaches has been the primacy of the therapeutic alliance – something to my mind traditionally denied by behaviourists and given some but insufficient attention by the first generation of cognitivists. In psychotherapy the patient is an 'active' collaborator rather than being the recipient of action initiated by an external referent, the therapist. 'Experience', 'Understanding' and 'Collaboration' are key constructs.

It is pleasing to see that there is a major focus on families in this book. The family has traditionally been vilified, excoriated or neglected since the 1950s. There is a renewed focus on working with families to better understand their problems including their need for support and assistance in living with and 'assisting' the client. Equally importantly, there is a need to prevent morbidity in family members and isolation of families from their own social network.

Another line of work concerns individuals in the pre-psychotic or 'at high risk' phase. This work is perceived differently by some clinicians: is it damaging and unethical to treat such people – only a percentage of whom will go on to develop psychosis of any type – or is it neglectful and unethical not to treat them? There are different views on this issue and we need to accept the merits of the arguments mounted by proponents of both sides of the debate.

A clear strength of this book is a willingness to entertain different perspectives and to examine the similarities and commonalities in approaches or at least commonalities in aspects of the various theoretical approaches, i.e., the focus on the individual or the family; on attempting to engage and form alliances with them; to understand the client's story – how do they perceive themselves and their 'mental illness'; the developmental tasks and challenges they face. Conciliation and tolerance are words that I would argue come through in this book but also a commitment to evidence of different kinds.

The book includes contributions from researchers and clinicians from various countries and this reflects a real strength of ISPS – it is a truly international organization. Two international contributions – one from New Zealand and one from India – provide descriptions of the cultural context for understanding psychosis and the delivery of psychotherapy for individuals with psychosis.

Two important figures, Professor Ian Falloon and Dr Wayne Fenton, died in 2006 and both had been involved in ISPS at different times. Born in New Zealand, Ian Falloon held a number of academic-clinical positions in the United Kingdom, USA, New Zealand and Italy. Ian was a seminal figure in developing psychoeducational family programmes to assist patients and families alike, in developing behavioural interventions for clients in the community and for his work in examining pre-psychosis clients. Often controversial, and sometimes confrontational in professional fora, Ian did believe passionately in helping clients and families to the best of his ability.

Wayne Fenton was at the time of his death involved as a senior figure in the National Institute of Mental Health in the USA and was a wonderful advocate for sufferers of schizophrenia and their families. I first became aware of Wayne's work in academic psychiatry when he emerged as a collaborator of Professor Tom McGlashan at Yale University and Chestnut Lodge. It is tragic that Wayne seemingly died at the hands of one of his clients and this dreadful event made the news world-wide. This is something that Wayne would have deeply regretted. He was concerned about improving patient outcomes and decreasing the community stigma that patients faced, so the manner of his death is ironic.

So how do we move forward from here? First, this book indicates that psychosocial approaches to understanding and treatment are alive and well. We are addressing significant issues in our collective work, e.g., relapse prevention, the subjective experience of clients, maintaining integrity of the self, stigma, vocational recovery, complex comorbidity and early detection. Our approaches form an important counterbalance to the prevailing biological perspective fuelled by significant funding opportunities and the financial rewards to be made in pharmacotherapy treatments, notwithstanding their efficacy. We have a harder row to hoe, though we must be equally careful in the claims we make for our therapies and not appear to be overly zealous or dogmatic in proselytizing our psychosocial approaches. We need to continue to show a strong commitment not only to the plight of our clients and their family members but also to the science of our approaches and the significance of our empirical findings. Both Wayne and Ian would have seen these two aspects as absolutely core (essential) to their own practice and advocacy.

Henry Jackson
May 2007

Preface

This book began in September 2003 when the Fourteenth International ISPS symposium was held in Melbourne, Australia. In the months following the meeting, Brian Martindale, the editor-in-chief of the ISPS book series, quietly, but persistently, urged the Melbourne-based group at ORYGEN Youth Health, via Patrick McGorry, to take responsibility for gathering key papers from the meeting into this volume.

Initially we were somewhat overawed by the challenge of capturing the volume and diversity of papers into a coherent book and, although our backgrounds include both the psychoanalytic and cognitive behavioural perspectives, we knew that many of the papers were beyond the scope of our range of theoretical orientations, which made the task of adequately representing the meeting seem near impossible. In our early editorial discussions, we found ourselves returning to the topic of the debate at the meeting which was entitled: 'Can biological and psychological interventions be integrated in the treatment of psychosis?' All three of us were somewhat surprised and challenged by the avid defence by some of the negative position. We shared an experience of working in a public sector mental health context where psychosocial interventions were strongly supported and we knew that our clinical and research colleagues at ORYGEN Youth Health shared our aspiration of integrated treatments. I believe we also shared with many delegates at the meeting a sense of dissatisfaction and frustration with the narrow terms of the debate, and we found ourselves motivated to expand upon the theme of integration.

We started to recognize that the debate, or more specifically the issue of integration, could serve us well as an organizing theme for this volume. With Brian Martindale's encouragement we steered away from attempting to record a belated set of conference proceedings, and set about the task of thinking more broadly about integration. In reviewing the conference abstracts we mapped out three aspects to this theme. So, the end result is that by using the narrow question of the debate as our starting point, this volume progresses through other critical themes, including theoretical integration across the psychotherapies in psychoses, cross-cultural perspectives in psychotherapies for psychoses, and integrating psychotherapies into public sector practice.

In addition to integration, another theme, or perhaps tension, is apparent throughout this volume – that between optimism and pessimism. On the one hand we see that the theme of integration, in its broadest sense, offers hope to the sufferer with psychosis and their family, because their experience is often characterized by fear, confusion, suffering and *disintegration*. On the other hand, one cannot help but feel overwhelmed by the gaps in the availability of psychosocial interventions in real world settings, and by the scarcity of integrative theoretical discussions in the field of psychosis. To write about and to reflect upon the efforts of others in addressing these gaps has been in many ways both a labour and a privilege which has had the transforming effect of heightening our awareness of the need for more effective and responsible advocacy across the globe for the availability of psychosocial treatment and related research.

We hope that this collection offers possibilities for experienced psychotherapists and for trainees from diverse orientations and cultural perspectives to strengthen alliances for tackling this gap. It is our belief that the process of striving for integration promotes constructive theoretical dialogue and stimulates the development of sustainable innovations in practice within contemporary public mental health settings. Our aim is that this text will stimulate the reader, and assist them to encourage colleagues, to creatively integrate psychotherapeutic thinking and practice into specific treatment settings.

John F. M. Gleeson, Eóin Killackey and Helen Krstev
Melbourne

Chapter 1

Integration and the psychotherapies for schizophrenia and psychosis

Where has the 'new view' of schizophrenia taken us?

John F. M. Gleeson, Helen Krstev and Eóin Killackey

Chapter overview

In this introductory chapter we have undertaken a selective review of contemporary integrated aetiological accounts of psychosis. We include a detailed description and critical analysis of the stress vulnerability models (SVM) of psychosis. We acknowledge their limitations, but argue that these models have provided a valuable theoretical platform for the development of integrated treatments in psychosis and for multidisciplinary research efforts which could expand our understanding of psychosis beyond classical linear models of aetiology. However, we lament the gap between the vision, offered in the 1970s, via the so-called 'new view' of schizophrenia and its translation into both practice and research. We conclude that more needs to be done, especially by the leaders of psychosocial research, to actualize the vision of integration.

Levels of integration

Before providing an account of the history of recent integrated perspectives of psychosis, it is worthwhile to consider the possible levels at which integration can occur in relation to treatment. One conceptual framework was provided by Norcross and Goldfried (2005) in the second edition of their edited volume on integration in the psychotherapies. They suggested that integration can be achieved, first, at the micro-level of technique (i.e., technical eclecticism); second, by considering the interactions and synergies between separate treatment approaches (e.g., psychotherapy *and* psychopharmacology); or third, by blending theoretically diverse approaches into integrated models of therapy (e.g., cognitive analytic therapy or dialectic behaviour therapy). An integrative 'perspective' in the psychotherapies has also been described, which has been characterized as a flexibility and inclusiveness in attitude to treatment approaches. Additionally, the term 'integrated approaches' has been used as a collective description for all of these efforts (Greben, 2004).

Integration in schizophrenia and the psychoses

Attempts to integrate aetiological explanations and treatments in schizophrenia have an extensive history. These efforts appear to be underpinned by a belief that interdisciplinary research endeavours provide the best hope for furthering the understanding of psychoses, and, that patients and their families will achieve substantial benefits from integrated treatments. We believe that these efforts can be broadly described as consistent with the 'integrative perspective'. Additionally, we can point to some examples of technical eclecticism contained in individual psychotherapeutic interventions described in the research literature (Hogarty et al., 1995). However, it is noteworthy that so little consideration has been given in the psychosis literature as to *how* to integrate across treatment approaches (Gabbard, 2006), and that examples of coherent, theoretically blended models of psychotherapy in psychosis are so rare (Kerr et al., 2003). As an illustration of this state of affairs, it is noteworthy that Norcross and Goldfried's (2005) extensive volume does not contain a single reference to the application of integrated psychotherapy to psychosis or schizophrenia.

The Melbourne ISPS debate: our starting point for a focus upon integration

At the Fourteenth International ISPS symposium in Melbourne in 2003, a panel of psychiatrists and psychologists, including Professor Henry Jackson, Dr Brian Martindale, Dr John Read, Professor Richard Bentall, Dr Wayne Fenton and Dr Ann-Louise Silver debated the question: 'Can biological and psychological interventions be integrated in the treatment of psychosis?' This discussion provided a starting point for this chapter, and the volume. Arguing for the affirmative Dr Brian Martindale argued:

> the simple answer to the debate is that they can be integrated. However the most important point is that psychological therapies are very rarely offered to any substantial degree and are usually done in such a skewed fashion dominated by biology.

Although on the opposing team Dr John Read opened his address also arguing that integration was desirable but that political and economic realities actively worked against it. He went on to argue that:

> The claim that we already have integration is frequently made, with reference to the 'stress-vulnerability' or 'stress-diathesis' paradigm. This is often equated with the so-called 'bio-psycho-social' model. This model, as currently applied, is actually a colonization of the psychological and the social by the biological.

These arguments lead us to an examination of the history of the 'stress-diathesis' paradigm in psychosis – specifically to reconsider its appropriateness as an integrative theoretical perspective, and to a consideration of the 'application' of the 'new view' of psychosis.

The 'new view'

The thirtieth anniversary of Zubin and Spring's (1977) 'new view of schizophrenia' is an appropriate vantage point from which to reflect upon its impact. Having emerged contemporaneously with Engel's (1977) broader critique of reductionistic biomedicine and his alternative 'biopsychosocial' model, Zubin and Spring's (1977) model remains the most influential example of an integrated model of the aetiology of schizophrenia – nearly 700 citations of their article at the time of writing is indicative of its popularity within the international research community.

Few contemporary leading researchers in the field of psychosis would argue for a unifactorial account for the aetiology of schizophrenia. Unfortunately, this consensus and enthusiasm for integrated aetiological explanations has not been translated into access to integrated treatments – we would concur with Brian Martindale and John Read that even across wealthy industrialized nations treatments are too often narrowed to biological options, or psychosocial interventions are adjunctive afterthoughts to antipsychotic medication. Data from our own country, Australia, provides a case in point. A national prevalence survey of people diagnosed with psychotic disorders revealed that less than 40 per cent of individuals with psychotic disorders reported receiving counselling or any form of psychotherapy over the previous year (Jablensky et al., 2000). Not surprisingly, this evidence provided a basis for cogent arguments for a redistribution in Australia of mental health resources for the treatment of psychosis towards psychosocial treatments and community supports (Neil et al., 2003). As also pointed out by Brian Martindale in the ISPS debate, there is compelling evidence that, despite the empirical support for their effectiveness (Pilling et al., 2002), family based interventions are rarely implemented into routine care (Fadden, 2006). From the perspective of the patient and carer, it has to be concluded that much of Zubin and Spring's (1977) vision remains unfulfilled.

The history of the stress vulnerability frameworks: an integrative perspective on psychosis

During the twentieth century a range of theoretical orientations strongly influenced explanations of the development and course of psychosis, including psychoanalytic theory, family systems theory, learning theory, and a range of biological models (Perris, 1989). Elsewhere, these have been classified in terms of theories focusing on environmental factors, learning and development theories, and biological models. The problem, according to Zubin and Spring (1977), was that none of these met the criterion for an adequate aetiological explanation for the onset and course of schizophrenia (Zubin and Steinhauser, 1984). This was the starting point for their macro-theory or 'heuristic framework' for psychosis.

The original model offered the promise of providing an integrated aetiological account of schizophrenia which could break the empirical logjam attributed to the competing unifactorial explanations, and was promoted as a theoretical framework for integrating psychotherapeutic and biological treatments.

The popularity of the SVM can also, in our view, be understood as a reaction to the pessimism of the Kraepelinian disease concept of schizophrenia, which others have argued was underpinned by nineteenth century ideas of *degeneration* and *disintegration* with implicit assumptions of inevitable deterioration (Barrett, 1998a, 1998b). This pessimism was countered by a series of long-term follow-up studies conducted in the 1970s and 1980s, which highlighted the prevalence of an episodic course amongst the population diagnosed with schizophrenia – at odds with Kraepelin's assumptions regarding prognosis. Although not entirely new, these data provided important grist for the SVM mill (Zubin et al., 1992).

The basic assumption of stress vulnerability models

The shared assumption of SVMs is that psychotic episodes result from an interaction between stable or *distal* factors (e.g., genetics *or* personality variables) and transient or proximal factors (e.g., life events, interpersonal conflict). The proponents of the stress vulnerability models agreed that interactions amongst these factors can result in acute psychotic psychopathology via the activation of latent vulnerability (Ciompi, 1989; Nuechterlein et al., 1992; Perris, 1989; Strauss et al., 1985; Zubin and Spring, 1977). Furthermore, as far as we know, all proponents subscribed to the notion that acute symptoms can be prevented or ameliorated by some combination of the individual's personal resources, the emotional support of close others, and by biological treatments. However, further analysis reveals that a diversity of models emerged with varying fundamental assumptions. Some examples of these variations are outlined next, followed by a description of their evolution.

An overview: from 'triggers' to 'integrated developmental perspectives'

According to Perris, the SVMs inherited older conceptualizations of *individual vulnerability* conveyed in the ancient Greek *diathesis* and in psychoanalytic accounts of the neuroses dating from the time of Freud (Perris,

1989). Perris also suggested that stress vulnerability proponents are indebted to Jaspers for linking hereditary predisposition (*Anlage*) and environment in his theory of the genesis of psychopathology (Jaspers, 1913, cited in Perris, 1989).

Paul Meehl's (1962, 1989, 1992) theory of *schizotaxia* was perhaps one of the first aetiological arguments for an interaction between an underlying latent propensity for schizophrenia and environmental contingencies based upon empirical research. Citing findings on neurological soft signs, Meehl (1989) argued that *schizotypes* inherit an integrative defect of the central nervous system (CNS) which he labelled *schizotaxia*: 'it is something wrong with every single nerve cell at all levels from the sacral cord to the frontal lobes' (Meehl, 1989, p. 936). He conjectured that schizotaxia, with the addition of variable social reinforcement schedules, led to the development of schizotypal personality organization, characterized by anhedonia, cognitive slippage, ambivalence, and interpersonal alienation. Meehl hypothesized that approximately 10 per cent of so-called *schizophrenes* developed schizophrenia via a range of potentiators, including invalidating social relationships.

Zubin and Spring's stress vulnerability model

The stress vulnerability nomenclature was introduced by Zubin and Spring (1977). They emphasized the episodic course of schizophrenia, as opposed to a continual disease process, arguing that individual episodes were triggered by endogenous and exogenous *challenging events* which exceeded the patient's vulnerability threshold. Zubin and Spring conceptualized vulnerability as either a genetically *or* environmentally acquired level of risk for developing the disorder, which could be offset by coping capacities, and by an ability to learn from previous episodes.

Zubin and Steinhauser (1984) added the concept of *etiotypes* to the model, i.e., heterogeneous pathways leading to the development of schizophrenic vulnerability with equivalent behavioural and symptom outcomes. It was argued that *aetiological life events* could produce various etiotypes through genetic, biochemical, neurophysiological, developmental, or learning mechanisms. In other words, many pathways potentially led to vulnerability and ultimately psychosis. We would argue that these theorists foreshadowed the trauma-vulnerability pathway highlighted more recently by Read and colleagues in their traumatogenic model (Read et al., 2001).

These early versions of the SVM model were criticized on several fronts. The main concerns were that they failed to stipulate schizophrenia-specific aetiological pathways to vulnerability and that the conceptualization of stress within the model overlooked subjective appraisal of life events (Nicholson and Neufeld, 1992). Others criticized the model for its characterization of remission from positive symptoms as a state of equilibrium, because it failed to account for deterioration in other symptom domains, such as negative symptoms (Carpenter, 1981). For some, this formed the basis for a rejection of the SVM in favour of a synergetic account of the psychosocial ecosystem (Dauwalder and Hoffman, 1992).

The UCLA model

Nuechterlein and Dawson (1984) incorporated Zubin and Spring's model into their *heuristic conceptual framework*. Drawing tentatively upon putative vulnerability factors, they attempted to outline the processes leading from stable, trait-like vulnerability to transient intermediate states (i.e., prodromal psychosis), and eventually to psychotic behaviours. They proposed that deficits in information processing were central to enduring vulnerability. They described interactions between these deficits and autonomic hyperactivity, and social competence and coping skills. When this interplay between enduring vulnerabilities became engaged in a vicious feedback loop with the social stressors and unsupportive social networks, transient intermediate states purportedly resulted. They argued that these states were marked by processing capacity overload, hyperarousal and deficient processing of social stimuli. In accordance with Zubin and Spring's (1977) model, unless the cycle was broken, psychosis resulted. Zubin and Spring's (1977) concept of a *threshold* for psychosis was also incorporated into the UCLA model of relapse, which entailed the hypothesis that maintenance medication raises 'the threshold for the appearance of psychotic symptoms' (Nuechterlein et al., 1994, p. 63). Nuechterlein and Dawson's (1984) initial working model evolved to later incorporate the concept of personal and environmental protective factors which buffered the individual from personal vulnerability factors and *environmental potentiators* (Nuechterlein et al., 1992).

Systemic stress vulnerability models

The paradox of the SVM discourse, in our view, is that in attempting to provide a macro-level, humanistic explanation of psychosis, the language is often sterile, with explanations built upon metaphors which seem to disallow the actual human experience of psychosis to be conveyed, in the way, for example, that seems more permissible in the consumer recovery literature (Corrigan, 2006). If Kraepelin's *dementia praecox* was underpinned by language and concepts belonging to degenerative infectious disease processes (e.g., general paresis), then perhaps the concepts underlying stress vulnerability models were influenced by physiology, reflected in the discourse of *thresholds, feedback loops, triggers* and *equilibrium*.

The metaphor was made explicit in Claridge's (1990) argument for a *systemic disease model* of schizophrenia. Claridge proposed, like Eysenck (see Eysenck and Eysenck, 1976), that there was a continuity of schizotypal personality variables, which was implicated in vulnerability, from the normal

population to the identified patient population, although the clinical population was situated at the extreme end of the distribution. This was compared to the diagnosis of hypertension because blood pressure levels are
continuous from the healthy to the clinical population. This argument is
maintained of course by contemporary researchers (Myin-Germeys et al.,
2003).

A second example of a systemic illness model was provided by Ciompi
(1989). Like Zubin and Spring (1977), Ciompi (1989) was concerned with
the competing unifactorial conceptualizations of schizophrenia which he
believed were analogous to multiple perspectives of the same mountain
peak. His theory aimed to bridge explanations from biological and psychosocial perspectives. Ciompi, consistent with the UCLA group, argued that
information processing deficits, associated with hyperarousal and increased
sensitivity to stress, were implicated in premorbid vulnerability. However, he
emphasized more strongly the interplay of biological and psychosocial processes over three stages, including the evolution of vulnerability, the onset of
active psychosis (which he termed *psychotic decompensation*), and beyond
(i.e., chronic states, remission or residual symptoms).

Ciompi's links between environmental processes and biological substratum
were constructed from four theoretical components. The first was stress
theory, which for Ciompi was important in linking environmental adversity
(overburdening the vulnerable information processing channels) to hyperarousal resulting from secretion of adrenaline and noradrenaline, which, he
pointed out, produced modifications in the central nervous system (Ciompi,
1989). This enabled Ciompi to hypothesize about the impact of a conflictual
family environment upon the development of the *vulnerable premorbid terrain*
and course of illness.

The second mediator described by Ciompi was neural plasticity, i.e., the
finding that neurons react to repeated stimuli both functionally and anatomi-
cally, consolidating the organization within neural networks. For Ciompi this
system of *privileged pathways* constituted the psyche (Ciompi, 1989, p. 17).
Plasticity, affected by environmental *and* biological processes, enabled him to
link neural functioning and structure to affective and cognitive patterns
which could be implicated in schizophrenic vulnerability.

Third, Ciompi referred to theoretical models of dopamine pathways, which
he argued associated basic arousal and attentional processes with higher
order executive functioning. Ciompi argued that excessive dopamine levels
resulted in a disturbance in the interaction between emotions and cognitions
in patients with a premorbid vulnerability. Finally, he drew upon the theory
of dynamics of complex systems, which originated from thermodynamics, to
account for shifts between equilibrium and active psychosis. This theory pos-
tulates that catastrophic structural changes (called *dissipative structures*) can
result from a rapid redistribution of excess energy within a system, producing
a *cascade effect* when the point of no return is reached. Ciompi pondered the

utility of this theory for the development of mathematical models of the course of schizophrenia. We would argue that Ciompi's set of theories provided an enriched view of the genesis of vulnerability and the connections between stress and vulnerability, incorporating both biological and psychosocial factors.

Brenner and collagues also attempted to close the explanatory gap between vulnerability and specific phenomenology (Brenner et al., 1994). Consistent with the UCLA group, Brenner's model emphasized an interaction between biological processes, cognition, and psychosocial stress. Drawing upon findings from a range of neurobiological methodologies (i.e., computerized tomography (CT), magnetic resonance imaging (MRI) and neuropathological studies) Brenner's group argued that deficits in information processing stemmed from premorbid damage to the paralimbic structures. They posited that early damage to these structures, when followed by psychosocial stress and/or spontaneous physiological processes, lead to a breakdown in critical integrative functions, producing the phenomenology of psychosis. This theory formed a basis for Brenner's Integrated Psychological Therapy (IPT) with a focus upon compensatory improvements in information processing.

Interactional-developmental models

Carlo Perris' *constructivistic and interactionistic developmental perspective on vulnerability* (Perris, 1998, p. 29) entailed a broad conceptualization of vulnerability (Perris, 1989, 1998). Like other stress vulnerability proponents, Perris assumed that schizophrenia subsumes a group of heterogeneous syndromes which have heterogenous aetiological pathways.

Perris' model of vulnerability differed from other SVMs in a variety of ways. His first point of departure was his conceptualization of vulnerability. Perris assumed that information processing deficits reflected largely unconscious dysfunctional working models (or schemas) of the self and the environment. Perhaps more radically, Perris assumed that vulnerability was generic in nature, becoming differentiated and expressed in specific psychopathological form – thus psychosis was only one possible manifestation. Reframing Zubin and Spring's (1977) thesis, he wrote: 'Each of us is endowed with a degree of vulnerability that under suitable circumstances can express itself in a psychopathological disorder. Such a disorder may assume the characteristics of a schizophrenic syndrome' (Perris, 1998, p. 27). This conceptualization of a *generic* vulnerability is consistent with the *dynamic vulnerability formulation* proposed by Nicholson and Neufeld (1992).

The trajectory of Perris' vulnerability also differed from the earlier models. Although others also emphasized the interplay between vulnerability and stress (see Nicholson and Neufeld, 1992), Perris proposed that vulnerability evolved across the lifespan through dialectical transactions between the person and the environment. These commenced with inherited genetic propensities, then incorporated child–parent interactions from an attachment perspective, and allowed for a continuing effect of the environment, as well as traumatic life experiences. For Perris, the individual was not a passive incubator of vulnerability, but was perceived in line with Bandura's (1978) notion of *reciprocal determinism*. This overlapped with Strauss and colleagues' *interactive developmental model* of schizophrenia (Strauss and Carpenter, 1981), which emphasized both the development of vulnerability and the individual's strengths, 'frequently in the direction of human development' (Strauss et al., 1985, p. 290).

Perris also reflected on the transition from vulnerability to active psychosis. Critical of the threshold concept, because of its inelegant fit with a multi-dimensional view of vulnerability, Perris, like Ciompi (1989) and Dauwalder and Hoffman (1992), believed *catastrophe theory* (Thom, 1975) could be applied to understanding onset and relapse. Perris argued that catastrophe theory's account of dramatic change following a slow build-up of disparate but interacting forces, offered a useful heuristic account of the emergence of psychopathology.

Finally, Perris' discussion of stress shifted the emphasis from *triggering* events to an ongoing interactional process of subjective appraisal of the environment and subsequent action. This could in turn precipitate certain events which may be more or less stressful, and which can also be *buffered* by protective factors. For Perris, the importance of stress lay in its potential for activating automatic dysfunctional thoughts, which serve to sustain core dysfunctional cognitive schemas, thus completing the transaction between stress and vulnerability. Perris' model remained a macro-theory which fell short of explaining how generic vulnerability becomes manifest in specific psychotic phenomenology, such as hallucinations and delusions.

The contemporary stress vulnerability models

Since the mid 1990s, a shift away from the development of macro-level theories of psychosis and schizophrenia has occurred, with greater emphasis upon micro-level aetiological accounts of individual symptoms. However, the SVM framework has been maintained as a basis for psychoeducation within cognitive behaviour therapy for psychosis.

In addition, the influence of the SVM models can be seen in what we consider to be the recent 'rediscovery' of social factors in the development of vulnerability within recent epidemiological research which has been focused upon social adversity, and the role of developmental trauma and abuse (van Os and McGuffin, 2003). This has taken fullest manifestation of course in the traumatogenic model of John Read and colleagues (Read et al., 2001). The influence of Perris' model is clearly discernible in more contemporary macro-level explanations – especially Freeman and Garety and colleagues who have strongly emphasized the role of early adversity, schema, and the role of emotions in mediating and maintaining psychotic symptoms (Freeman and Garety, 2003).

Toward the actualization of the vision splendid of the stress vulnerability models

The period from the 1970s to the mid 1990s witnessed the development of a rich theoretical discourse, which provided a platform for the development of integrated approaches to treatment and research in the psychoses. However, we would argue that this vision has failed to be realized.

There are of course many reasons why integration has not been implemented in practice. Some of these were covered by proponents in the Melbourne ISPS debate. Richard Bentall, for example, pointed to the fundamental differences in aetiological assumptions held by pharmacological practitioners and psychotherapists, John Read pointed to the political and economic forces of 'Big Pharma', which he argued have minimized the research and understanding of social and psychological factors within the stress vulnerability framework.

We would assert that there are other factors which maintain this state of affairs, which are more within the control of psychosocial researchers and practitioners. As argued by Fadden (2006), many clinicians working in contemporary mental health services may lack the training in fundamental counselling skills let alone skills in psychotherapy or family work specific for psychosis. We would also assert that the frequently large case loads in public community mental health settings are often not conducive for psychotherapeutic interventions, and that funding systems are overly focused upon expediting 'throughput' – i.e., early discharge to the primary health system. Where specific training has been accessed, ongoing supervision structures are often not in place to allow for wider dissemination. Managers of public mental health services may perceive these interventions as adjunctive or add-on options which mean that the structure of roles within public mental health facilities do not allow for it. In research endeavours, funding cycles and research benchmarking require rapid turn-around of publications – the testing of linear models of aetiology and evaluation of pharmacological interventions are arguably much easier routes to building a research track record than devising, funding and evaluating psychosocial interventions.

However, for those of us interested in pursuing Wayne Fenton's assertion at the 2001 debate that 'biological and psychological treatments must be integrated if we are to properly discharge our responsibilities as clinicians and psychotherapists', it is important to redress the pessimism, and consider what might sustain efforts and move us closer towards actualizing the vision of SVM proponents.

First, we would argue that further theoretical discourses are required around integration. Dialogues which focus upon theoretical integration and the development of integrative treatment modalities and methods of training in integrated approaches, although beginning via ISPS, have not become clearly articulated goals in the field of psychotherapy for psychoses. And yet, curiously, these discussions have a rich history spanning a wide range of other disorders. Why has this not occurred in relation to psychosis? Greater integration across specific theoretical orientations will in the end, we believe, aid consumers and families in getting access to psychosocial treatments.

Second, we would argue that research paradigms that test dynamic and interactive paradigms are much needed in psychosis research. The paradigm of epigenetics, for example (Petronis, 2004), provides a rich source of hypotheses examining the interaction between genetic and environmental variables. The contemporary 'stress' paradigm, foreshadowed by Ciompi, is another paradigm that stretches across the silos (Phillips et al., 2006).

Third, psychosocial researchers need to build richer international networks and collaborations to sustain viable psychosocial research programmes. This is an extremely challenging task – psychosocial interventions are notoriously expensive to mount relative to pharmacological treatments, and recruitment of participants is painstaking, and maintaining quality assurance (e.g., treatment fidelity and quality) is a resource-intensive endeavour. The aims of psychosocial treatments often require long-term follow-up measurement of outcomes, the pathway to publication is often tortuous, and impact factors for psychosocial studies are frequently of a lower order. We would assert that larger scale international collaborations are an important way forward.

The translation of 'boutique programmes' into routine practice is a fourth critical, but as Fadden (2006) highlighted, highly fraught endeavour. The national networks of organizations such as the ISPS could play a substantial role in advocating for greater access to integrated treatments. Psychosocial practitioners, although in our experience usually uncomfortable with the notion, need to become more effective at advocating for effective interventions and programmes. In our opinion they need to be more mindful of promoting the benefits of psychosocial interventions to the wider community – i.e., promote the fact that psychosocial interventions have been shown to improve quality of life in the *present*, rather than just offering the *promissory notes* of basic science. The aims of advocacy need to extend to include not only achieving greater flexibility from research funding bodies, but also working more effectively alongside consumer and family advocates in the task. The international early psychosis movement is a case in point – the effect of optimism and a saleable message of prevention has been critical to its success.

Finally, we would argue for the more radical notion that to truly implement integrated treatments consumers and family members have to be more involved in selecting the research questions to be addressed, and determining the priorities for integration. In this way the priorities can move beyond those set by academics and the pharmaceutical industry. We believe that once consumers are systematically involved in framing these priorities, then researchers and practitioners can more effectively work alongside each other across international communities, in advocating for integrated treatment approaches. In this way, the likelihood of unveiling a truly new view of psychosis and its treatment will be significantly enhanced.

References

Bandura, A. (1978). The self system in reciprocal determinism. *American Psychologist*, *33*, 344–358.

Barrett, R. J. (1998a). Conceptual foundations of schizophrenia. I: Degeneration. *Australian and New Zealand Journal of Psychiatry*, *32*, 617–626.

Barrett, R. J. (1998b). Conceptual foundations of schizophrenia. II: Disintegration and division. *Australian and New Zealand Journal of Psychiatry*, *32*, 617–626.

Brenner, H. D., Roder, V., Hodel, B., Kienzle, N., Reed, D. and Liberman, R. P. (1994). *Integrated psychological therapy for schizophrenic patients (IPT)*. Seattle, WA: Hogrefe and Huber.

Carpenter, W. T. (1981). Commentary on 'How to break the logjam in schizophrenia: A look beyond genetics' by Joseph Zubin and Stuart Steinhauer. *Journal of Nervous and Mental Disease*, *169*, 495–496.

Ciompi, L. (1989). The dynamics of complex biological-psychosocial systems: Four fundamental psycho-biological mediators in the long-term evolution of schizophrenia. *British Journal of Psychiatry*, *155* (Suppl. 5), 15–21.

Claridge, G. (1990). Can a disease model of schizophrenia survive? In R. P. Bentall (Ed.), *Reconstructing schizophrenia* (pp. 157–183). London: Routledge.

Corrigan, P. W. (2006). Impact of consumer-operated services on empowerment and recovery of people with psychiatric disabilities. *Psychiatric Services*, *57*, 1493–1496.

Dauwalder, J. P. and Hoffman, H. (1992). Chronic psychoses and rehabilitation: An ecological perspective. *Psychopathology*, *25*, 139–146.

Engel, G. L. (1977). Need for a new medical model: Challenge for biomedicine. *Science*, *196*, 129–136.

Eysenck, H. J. and Eysenck, S. B. G. (1976). *Psychoticism as a dimension of personality*. London: Hodder and Stoughton.

Fadden, G. I. (2006). Training and disseminating family interventions for schizophrenia: Developing family intervention skills with multi-disciplinary groups. *Journal of Family Therapy*, *28* (1), 23–38.

Freeman, D. and Garety, P. A. (2003). Connecting neurosis and psychosis: The direct influence of emotion on delusions and hallucinations. *Behaviour Research and Therapy*, *41*, 923–947.

Gabbard, G. O. (2006). The rationale for combining: Medication and psychotherapy. *Psychiatric Annals*, *36*, 314–319.

Greben, D. H. (2004). Integrative dimensions of psychotherapy training. *Canadian Journal of Psychiatry-Revue Canadienne de Psychiatrie*, *49*, 238–248.

Hogarty, G. E., Kornblith, S. J., Greenwald, D., DiBarry, A. L., Cooley, S., Flesher, S., et al. (1995). Personal therapy: A disorder-relevant psychotherapy for schizophrenia. *Schizophrenia Bulletin*, *21*, 379–393.

Jablensky, A., McGrath, J., Herrman, H., Castle, D., Gureje, O., Evans, M., et al. (2000). Psychotic disorders in urban areas: An overview of the Study on Low Prevalence Disorders. *Australian and New Zealand Journal of Psychiatry, 34,* 221–236.

Jaspers, K. (1913). *Allgemeine Psychopathologie.* Berlin: Springer.

Kerr, I. B., Birkett, P. B. C. and Chanen, A. (2003). Clinical and service implications of a cognitive analytic model of psychosis. *Australian and New Zealand Journal of Psychiatry, 37,* 515–523.

Meehl, P. E. (1962). Schizotaxia, schizotypy, schizophrenia. *American Psychologist, 17,* 827–838.

Meehl, P. E. (1989). Schizotaxia revisited. *Archives of General Psychiatry, 46,* 935–944.

Meehl, P. E. (1992). Factors and taxa, traits and types, differences of degree and differences in kind. *Journal of Personality, 60,* 118–174.

Myin-Germeys, I., Krabbendam, L. and van Os, J. (2003). Continuity of psychotic symptoms in the community. *Current Opinion in Psychiatry, 16,* 443–449.

Neil, A. L., Lewin, T. J. and Carr, V. J. (2003). Allocation of resources and psychosis. *Australian and New Zealand Journal of Psychiatry, 37,* 15–23.

Nicholson, I. R. and Neufeld, R. W. J. (1992). A dynamic vulnerability perspective on stress and schizophrenia. *American Journal of Orthopsychiatry, 62,* 117–130.

Norcross, J. C. and Goldfried, M. R. (2005). *Handbook of psychotherapy integration* (2nd ed.). New York: Oxford University Press.

Nuechterlein, K. H. and Dawson, M. E. (1984). A heuristic vulnerability/stress model of schizophrenic episodes. *Schizophrenia Bulletin, 10,* 300–312.

Nuechterlein, K. H., Dawson, M. E., Gitlin, M., Ventura, J., Goldstein, M. J., Snyder, K. S., et al. (1992). Developmental processes in schizophrenic disorders: Longitudinal studies of vulnerability and stress. *Schizophrenia Bulletin, 18,* 387–424.

Nuechterlein, K. H., Dawson, M. E., Ventura, J., Gitlin, M., Subotnik, K. L., Snyder, K. S., et al. (1994). The vulnerability/stress model of schizophrenic relapse: A longitudinal study. *Acta Psychiatrica Scandinavica, 89* (Suppl. 382), 58–64.

Perris, C. (1989). *Cognitive therapy with schizophrenic patients.* London: Guilford Press.

Perris, C. (1998). Defining the concept of individual vulnerability as a base for psychotherapeutic interventions. In C. Perris and P. D. McGorry (Eds.), *Cognitive psychotherapy of psychotic and personality disorders: Handbook of theory and practice* (pp. 21–36). Chichester: Wiley.

Petronis, A. (2004). Schizophrenia, neurodevelopment, and epigenetics. In M. S. Keshavan, J. L. Kennedy and R. M. Murray (Eds.), *Neurodevelopment and schizophrenia* (pp. 174–190). New York: Cambridge University Press.

Phillips, L. J., McGorry, P. D., Garner, B., Thompson, K. N., Pantelis, C., Wood, S. J., et al. (2006). Stress, the hippocampus and the HPA axis: Implications for the development of psychotic disorders. *Australian and New Zealand Journal of Psychiatry, 40,* 725–741.

Pilling, S., Bebbington, P., Kuipers, E., Garety, P., Geddes, J., Orbach, G. and Morgan, C. (2002). Psychological treatments in schizophrenia. I: Meta-analysis of family intervention and cognitive behaviour therapy. *Psychological Medicine, 32,* 763–782.

Read, J., Perry, B. D., Moskowitz, A. and Connolly, J. (2001). The contribution of early traumatic events to schizophrenia in some patients: A traumagenic neurodevelopmental model. *Psychiatry: Interpersonal and Biological Processes*, *64*, 319–345.

Strauss, J. S. and Carpenter, W. T. (1981). *Schizophrenia*. New York: Plenum.

Strauss, J. S., Hafez, H., Lieberman, P. and Harding, C. M. (1985). The course of psychiatric disorder. III: Longitudinal principles. *American Journal of Psychiatry*, *142*, 289–296.

Thom, R. (1975 [1972]). *Structural stability and morphogenesis: An outline of a general theory of models* (D. H. Fowler, Trans.). Reading, MA: Benjamin.

van Os, J. and McGuffin, P. (2003). Can the social environment cause schizophrenia? *British Journal of Psychiatry*, *182*, 291–292.

Zubin, J. and Spring, B. (1977). Vulnerability: A new view of schizophrenia. *Journal of Abnormal Psychology*, *86*, 103–126.

Zubin, J. and Steinhauser, S. (1984). How to break the logjam in schizophrenia. *Journal of Nervous and Mental Disease*, *169*, 477–492.

Zubin, J., Steinhauer, S. R. and Condray, R. (1992). Vulnerability to relapse in schizophrenia. *British Journal of Psychiatry*, *161* (Suppl. 18), 13–18.

Theoretical integration

Chapter 2

Integrating approaches to psychotherapy in psychosis

Frank Margison and Sarah Davenport

Introduction

There is a well-established evidence base for specific psychological treatments for psychosis, particularly those based on cognitive behavioural methods in individual and family settings. However, many practitioners do not align themselves to one particular model, but see themselves as integrationist in approach (Margison and Mace, 1997). Integration is a term that is often misunderstood or confused with related terms such as 'eclectic'. In this chapter the basic tenets of integration are explored. There is an emphasis on understanding how different levels of need can be conceptualized and then used to 'adapt' (Alanen, 1993; Alanen et al., 2000) treatments in an integrated way to meet those needs in an individual. The needs are then incorporated into an integrated treatment formulation.

One approach to integration is to combine key features from two models, for example in cognitive analytic therapy (Ryle and Kerr, 2002). Another is to take 'successful' factors from various therapies, but this can lead to a muddled and tactical rather than strategic approach. An alternative is to focus on important 'common factors' (Frank, 1973). However, following the latter approach to integration to its limit would ultimately lead to one undifferentiated therapy.

Integration can occur between different pragmatic treatment models or between the theories that underpin them. It is simple to justify the coexistence of different practical interventions, as it is rare for a model of therapy to actually preclude any other approach. Typically, in research, models are defined by what therapists actually do. Indeed this is the basis for most adherence scales. Demonstrating integration at a theoretical level is much more difficult, as few theories are sufficiently developed to allow true integration. In place of integration is a 'Rosetta stone' approach: different therapists label the same phenomenon in different ways consistent with the underlying theory. Where observed events seem to be described in two languages it is often assumed that there must be a common basis in theory, even if that theory has not been developed. A more parsimonious approach would be to say that one set of explanatory descriptions is wrong, and that the alternative terminology is more accurate.

These themes are explored in more detail later. This chapter reviews some integrationist ideas and gives examples from practice, emphasizing the role of social inclusion as an essential component of successful treatment integration.

Integration in service provision

In contrast to integration of approaches within a therapy, it is possible for whole service delivery systems to use integration as an organizing principle. Scandinavia has played a key role in developing integration between social, psychological and physical treatments into a coherent whole. Alanen et al. (2000) developed the Finnish integrated model for treating psychosis and, as will be described later, they developed the 'need-adapted' approach to treatment of psychosis. Cullberg et al. (2000) in Sweden have followed-up programmes involving the integration of psychosocial treatments with low dose neuroleptics, and Johannessen et al. (2000) carried out a multi-centre study of early intervention which relied on an integrated approach to treatment.

These Scandinavian developments in treatment integration have been mirrored internationally with significant developments in Melbourne (McGorry, 2000). This chapter deals with a specific aspect of treatment integration: the integration within a psychological treatment of different models, but the overall context still concerns the integration of a whole treatment system.

Integration versus 'brand names'

Integration is in constant opposition to developing distinct 'brand names'. The huge growth in these brand names for psychotherapy has been balanced by attempts to bring together diverse approaches (Albeniz and Holmes, 1996; Bateman and Margison, 2003).

Integration can be seen as a spectrum including several steps (Albeniz and Holmes, 1996; Beitman, 1989; Margison, 2005) as summarized in Table 2.1. The steps are not wholly distinct, and a particular therapy may exhibit several degrees of integration of different elements.

For schizophrenia and other psychoses, psychological treatments are at a relatively early stage in development, at least as empirically based treatments, and so the tendency to separate into distinct 'schools' is still evident (Margison and Mace, 1997). Bachmann et al. (2003) provided an overview of many of the distinct approaches to psychological treatment for psychosis. They also stressed the need for pragmatic, cost-effective and easy to teach methods of psychotherapy to deal with the enormous potential demand for psychological treatments.

Table 2.1 The spectrum of integration

Integration theme	Description
Rapprochement	Increasingly cordial relations between schools
Accommodation	Incorporating favoured parts of other models
Convergence	Increased common ground
Common factors	Different terminology increasingly seen as describing the same key themes
Eclecticism	A pragmatic approach drawing on elements of any therapy which might help
Assimilation	Full integration of outside concepts into the mainstream beliefs of a model
Integration of methods	As seen in therapies that explicitly combine distinct models
Full integration	The distinctions between original models become unimportant as a new fully integrated approach becomes distinct

Conceptual models of integration

A different approach to integration is seen in the work of Fenton (2000). He developed a method described as 'flexible psychotherapy'. This approach relies on a hierarchy of tasks and the therapist draws on a variety of therapeutic strategies to assist the patient to achieve each stage. The tasks include clarifying diagnosis, ensuring safety, reducing symptoms, mobilizing social support, assessing social care needs, encouraging acceptance, promoting strengths, teaching how to manage stress, preventing relapse, promoting the highest level of social functioning, encouraging activities that promote self-esteem and quality of life and finally, integration of the psychotic experience into the self.

One of the strengths of this approach is that integration is akin to project planning in that the therapist holds in mind a potential for the person to achieve wholeness by addressing specific areas of difficulty. The integration within the therapy has much in common with case management in that different approaches are brought in at appropriate times when the patient is ready. Fenton and Schooler (2000) summarize this approach and its evidence base:

> Current evidence-based recommendations and guidelines support a comprehensive, individualised treatment approach that integrates advances in psychopharmacology, practical oriented case management and individual psychotherapy, family psychoeducation, and community support and rehabilitation.
>
> (Fenton and Schooler, 2000, p. 3)

Arieti (1975) took a quite different approach to integration. He brought together the interpersonal domain through his principle of 'establishing relatedness' as the primary task. He also described treating overt symptoms (often using precursors of cognitive behavioural strategies), understanding and analysing conflict, and attempting to increase participation in the patient's life. This can be seen again as integration at the level of goals and methods with only passing attention to the integration of theory.

A third example of an integrative model is that of Hogarty's Personal Therapy (Hogarty et al., 1995). This approach is planned over three years and focuses variously on cognitive and emotional responses to stress with the intention of strengthening the individual by increasing the capacity to 'buffer' stress and enhance coping strategies. As with Fenton's approach, progress follows pre-set stages around goals specific for the individual. So, the first phase concentrates on internal coping and social skills training; the second adds relaxation and reframing; and the third brings in vocational and social activities with criticism management.

All three of these approaches have much in common with the 'Recovery model' now widely accepted as a less stigmatizing and more individually focused approach than earlier models. All three systematically identify the person's remaining strengths and resources and develop a shared vision with the person of what they can become.

Threats to integration

Integration can be seen at four different levels of the care system, each or all of which can be compromised and reduce the effectiveness of the system as a whole. The four key factors are the healthy *individual, carer and family*, the healthy mental health *team*, the healthy *organization* and the healthy mental health *system*.

Work on psychosis needs all four levels to be addressed if it is to be effective. The first level assumes that loss of integration within the individual's own psychological function affects family members, carers and others in the immediate network of the individual. The extensive work on the high levels of critical expressed emotion from family members can be seen as an effect of this level of integration breaking down (Leff and Vaughan, 1985). High levels of negative expressed emotion are best seen as a consequence of the family pressures experienced when a family member develops psychosis.

Less commonly discussed are the effects of integration or otherwise within the mental health team and its parent organization. Individual team members are subject to intense pressures, and dysfunctional forces within the organization may amplify the individual's defences. Davenport (1997) drawing on the work of Menzies Lyth (1988) described how these disintegrative forces lead to attempts of team members to use defences characteristic of organizations under stress; detachment, denial, ritualized task performance and avoidance of change. These defensive processes can interact in an unhelpful way with the fragmentation and splitting that underpins many psychotic illnesses. There is then a third component when the psychosis coexists with a history of abuse, adding into the dynamic interaction the characteristic dynamics of abusive relationships. These include boundary difficulties, revictimization, and difficulties with power relationships.

The combined effects of institutional defences, psychotic defences and effects of abuse can make it difficult to maintain a therapeutic inpatient milieu. Jeffcote and Travers (2004) discuss the utility of models of practice, but conclude that this 'one size fits all' approach does not work well in a forensic setting with women patients, but they do describe the usefulness of looking primarily at *relational* models to understand the difficulties within a secure woman's setting. When approaches to patients become dehumanized for the reasons described earlier there is a failure of effective care. This level of threat to integration can apply at a ward or team level. At this level it is difficult, but can be managed, especially when someone can stand back from the emotional intensity and bring in appropriate help.

At the organizational level the dysfunction may be less intense and there may still be pockets of good practice. But there is less ability to recognize and deal with this level of failure of integration. Sometimes it may be manifest in a culture of bullying or neglect, which will have an effect, direct or indirect, on the quality of care provided.

Integration within the wider system

Describing the lack of integration at a whole system level is extremely difficult as it involves the top level of policy making and implementation in a region or nation. It is also difficult to spot because the ideas are often expressed in popular language and vague, so being difficult to challenge. An example is patient 'choice', which almost everyone would agree is a 'good thing', but the mechanisms for increasing patient choice may be effective or cause dislocation between the values of the general workforce and the policy. Tension is not in itself bad, but the difficulty with this level of integration is that there is no obvious perspective from which to say that there has been a breakdown in integration.

Although there are significant differences and social contexts in different countries, a common pattern is to separate the responsibilities of commissioners from those of providers of care. Even when the other threats to integration are managed skilfully, a failure at this level of organization can have a damaging effect on the care of psychosis. Attempts to pull together key components of a mental health system have been tried in several countries. An example is the expectation in England that every health area should have specialist teams covering crisis resolution or home treatment, assertive outreach and for early intervention in psychosis as well as generic community mental health teams. This was initially laid out in an overall national plan for the whole National Health Service (NHS) and then in a National Service Framework for Mental Health. A review (Appleby, 2003) showed variable success across England, promising only partial delivery of the required funding for such a fundamental overhaul. Integration between these specialist teams is crucial in avoiding dislocation of the care pathway experienced by individual patients. The specialist teams are expected to incorporate relevant psychological approaches, such as concordance therapy to improve the take-up of concurrent medication.

Attempts at theoretical integration

In the introduction it was noted that it is easier to introduce integration at the level of practice than at the level of theory. This section describes some attempts at theoretical integration. Some influential models do exist that pull together different aspects of the causal chain leading to a psychosis. Some are attempts to integrate biological factors, psychological factors and the wider social environment. Indeed the dominant model in mental health is probably the biopsychosocial approach. As McGorry (2000) has pointed out, the biopsychosocial approach does at least deal with the potential for reductionism in some biophysical explanations. Biopsychosocial approaches show how there can be lawful interactions between early predisposing factors (including amongst others genetic predisposition, early exposure to pathogens, birth order, birth experience, date of birth, early physical trauma, neurodevelopmental delays, delays in neuronal maturation, psychological trauma and a myriad of other factors) and later precipitating and adult vulnerability factors.

It might be assumed that all of these levels of causation could be considered as equal contributors, but it is common to see the psychological and social factors as mediating variables affecting the expression of a biologically determined condition. The biopsychosocial model has led to a rapprochement between different schools of thought, but the integration is often at a very superficial level, as witnessed by polarized views on the role of medication. In practice non-physical treatments are often seen as 'adjuncts' to the main protagonist in the treatment plan, the 'silver bullet' of a precision drug that affects precisely the right neuronal pathways. Care systems do not put equal weight on the three legs of the tripod and differential investment in research leaves non-drug treatments in a disadvantaged position.

One specific version of a biopsychosocial approach is seen in the stress vulnerability model (Zubin and Spring, 1977). Essentially this proposes, as discussed in Chapter 1 of this volume, an interaction between underlying vulnerability and the expression of that vulnerability depending on social, psychological and environmental factors. The original hypothesis simply states that there is a lawful interaction between the two with the product of vulnerability and later stress determining the probability of breakdown into illness. Although this is not intrinsic to the stress vulnerability model, the theory is widely seen as similar to the relationship between a genotype and a phenotype, i.e., the root cause is at a molecular biological level and the basic picture can then be 'coloured in' by environmental factors.

The analogy with tuberculosis is telling: group treatment, as originally developed by Pratt (1908), was shown to be an effective treatment, at least according to the research standards of the day (Yalom, 1975), but these findings were effectively jettisoned when the role of mycobacteria in causation was demonstrated. By analogy, psychosocial influences are seen as vague and imprecise when compared to the assumed precision of biological markers.

Whatever the arguments about causal direction, neuronal activity clearly coexists with emotional experience, including the intense emotional experiences of psychosis. It is also clear that these interactions occur within a social system, and are modified by the social system. We relive past experiences of relationships in the present, in some form, and the different forms of memory can be seriously disrupted by traumatic experience (Meares, 2000, 2006; Read and Ross, 2003). At the very least patterns of social interaction and attachment style influence the content of a psychotic illness but may also determine its course and outcome.

Social inclusion, integration and needs assessment

A quite different approach to integration is found in the assessment of need as a basis for formulating the best approach to mental health problems. Some of the principles have been incorporated into the concept of a *needs assessment* that will produce a profile of actions needed to maintain (or restore) mental health. There are several approaches available for systematic needs assessment, for example, the Camberwell Assessment of Need (CAN: Phelan et al., 1995). The model described in Table 2.2 has six main categories, each of which are broken down into more specific areas. To some extent this model draws on an implicit hierarchy of needs, as the later goals are jeopardized if the simpler needs are not met (Margison, 2005).

From a purely psychosocial model of need it might be assumed that remedying any deficits in need would automatically restore the person to full social functioning. This is not necessarily true, as, according to the stress vulnerability model, these psychological and social needs can also be understood as 'buffers' against the neurocognitive changes brought about by stress. More buffering is needed if stress is unduly high, *or* if the individual's intrinsic vulnerability is high.

Some theories of causation merge vulnerability factors with likelihood of stress. For example, in considering the strong association of urbanization with incidence of schizophrenia, Van Os (2004) concedes that even a powerful

Table 2.2 What promotes mental health?

Safety and security	Physical health	Good, secure relationships	Sense of community	Occupation	Identity and self-esteem
Food	Overcoming disability	Attachments	Sense of belonging	Fulfilment	Valued role
Shelter	Freedom from pain	Friendships	Social support	Purpose	Ethnic and cultural identity secure
Physical security	Attention to basic health	Family ties	Access to community resources	Security	Lifestyle choices
Access to resources	Positive health and well-being	Sexual relationships	Religious and cultural needs embedded in the local community	Reward	Feelings of mastery and success
Freedom from exploitation and abuse		Connectedness	Access to community resources	Being valued	
Freedom from threat			Someone to advocate on your behalf	Being recognized for your role	

and replicable effect such as urbanization does not lead to a good explanation of what constitutes the 'toxin'. Many theories abound, including the association with social deprivation, increased availability of illicit drugs, and increased levels of traumatic stress through crime. Other factors, however, such as social drift have been shown *not* to account adequately for the phenomenon (Pedersen and Mortensen, 2001).

Given the imprecision of our causal hypotheses in individual cases, we are pushed to increasing reliance on generic models of how needs relate to underlying causes. The pioneers in this field in Scandinavia (Alanen et al., 2000) suggested the phrase 'need-adapted care'.

Alanen (1993) states that:

> Need-adapted care comprises:
> (a) Therapeutic treatments planned individually to meet the needs of patients and of the people nearest them.
> (b) The psychotherapeutic attitude, with efforts to try to understand what has happened and happens to the patient and those nearest them, characterises the treatment.
> (c) Different therapeutic activities should support, not counteract, one another.
> (d) The treatments are all part of a developmental and interactive process.
>
> (Alanen, 1993; cited in Pylkkanen, 1997, p. 242)

These principles have been described in detail in the well-established work in Finland, but they can be applied in other settings.

The role of case formulation as an aid to integration

Case formulation in working with non-psychotic problems has become routine practice, but it is relatively recently that formulation methods have been used systematically with psychosis. The development of a formulation shared between the client and the inpatient staff team has still not been incorporated into routine practice. Davenport (2002) and colleagues developed such a method using psychodynamic interpersonal principles embedded within a generic formulation that was shared with all team members, clients and often their families. The key features of the team formulation identify the patient's core self-schemas and beliefs, summarize dysfunctional attitudes and behaviours, and then identify likely staff and family responses. The desired therapeutic attitudes, responses and goals can then be built into the formulation. Specifically, the client's strengths were spelled out to promote self-esteem. The formulation was then shared with staff, patient and family to be used like an interpersonal 'map'.

A key feature of this type of formulation was that it was built around the actual conversations with the client, using as far as possible the client's own words. The shared formulation allows clients, staff and carers to quickly identify part of a cycle being enacted at any moment and the strategies to minimize the effects, or even use them beneficially. All involved need to know where they are in such a complex environment. By stressing coping capacity and how to increase this the client feels more in control.

The formulation approach can be used in a wide variety of models. Fowler et al. (1998) give an example in a chapter summarizing cognitive therapy for delusions. Their example emphasizes the importance of *containing* anxiety that is developing between patient and therapist:

> Andrew presented in a fearful state, saying, 'Everyone is against me, I see evil around in people everywhere, they look at me. People are influencing me. I can feel it in my body, they are changing the sensations in my stomach.' Andrew looked suspiciously at the therapist; it was a major task to keep him calm. The challenge in the initial stages of working with Andrew was simply to contain his severe anxiety and prevent spread of fear to the therapist.
>
> (Fowler et al., 1998, p. 133)

Cognitive behavioural approaches are probably the best researched approaches (Orlinsky et al., 2003) to psychosis, but advocates of cognitive behavioural therapy have followed a tactical approach in addressing very specific aspects of problems through pragmatic trials with relatively little attention to underlying mechanisms, although Bentall et al. (2001) have attempted to develop an overarching theory of delusion formation and paranoid thinking.

The integration of these different theoretical strands into a coherent whole is beyond the scope of this chapter, but it is noticeable that there has been a rapprochement between practitioners who are identifying similar phenomena and ways of addressing the consequential distress from related perspectives.

However, the underlying question of integration has not been resolved. The models described in this chapter, though having distinctive features, have much in common, and these common properties are incorporated to a degree in cognitive behavioural approaches, psychodynamic and systemic approaches. If this logic is followed through to its conclusions we would end up with one model constituted of 'common therapeutic factors' (Frank, 1973). This approach has much to commend it, and there probably are some principles that can and should be applied across all models of therapy. But, in practice, these approaches are extremely difficult to research because some of the common factors, such as maintaining a positive therapeutic alliance can be seen as 'micro-outcomes' rather than processes. In other words, a good alliance may be a marker of a good therapy but not necessarily a *cause* of a good outcome. The risk of moving too far towards an integrationist approach is that there is a loss of figure and ground. Some therapies see the relationship as the foreground. The behaviour is the practice that embeds the learning from the therapy. The opposite view is equally compelling: changing behaviour is the primary outcome, but attention to the relationship may overcome blocks to progress.

There are still some pragmatic questions: would the benefits of combining the features of different therapies outweigh the difficulty in maintaining coherence and focus? These questions are rarely asked. The nearest is when a particular model incorporates a specific element and the addition of this component is evaluated, but even this is rarely seen.

Therapies can be seen as bases from which the biopsychosocial model can be examined from somewhat different, though overlapping, perspectives. In doing so, a more fundamental issue is raised about the optimal extent of eclecticism. This tension between the pressure to take the best aspects of several therapies and the need to delineate a new, differentiated approach runs through any discussion of integration in psychotherapy.

For psychosis, there is the additional complication that any integration needs also to take into account the different needs of the patient at different stages of the psychosis. As discussed earlier, several integrative models build in different approaches at differing stages of the psychosis.

Social exclusion and mental health

The opposite of integration could be said to be social exclusion. The exclusion of certain groups from access to opportunities, advantages and rights given to others in civil society is still present in the twenty-first century. People with chronic mental illness have multiple factors that hinder social inclusion: they tend to be poor, socially isolated, inadequately housed, unemployed and at risk of victimization. People from ethnic minorities are over-represented in this group and so priority has been given to developing health care systems that embody an awareness of these particular needs and difficulties.

Other service providers in the fields of housing, arts and leisure and supported employment are required to engage with health and social care providers to ensure that meaningful social inclusion and community participation occur but few countries have developed relevant performance indicators to sustain such a huge cultural shift. An example within the British health system came from the National Institute for Mental Health in England (NIMHE, 2003a).

A linked report called *Inside Outside* (NIMHE, 2003b) highlighted the need for change in the way in which black and minority ethnic (BME) communities gain access to mental health services and for changes in the way in which services are delivered to them. This report identified institutional racism and discrimination towards BME citizens. Keating and colleagues have highlighted the experience of black people using mental health services as degrading and alienating, rather than empowering and inclusive (Keating, 2002; Keating et al., 2002).

The recovery movement

The recovery movement has brought about integration between individual needs-based approaches and social inclusion. The recovery approach involves building on the personal strength and resilience of individual service users, and building positively on their cultural and racial characteristics, whilst recognizing that there are many diverse routes to recovery. The recovery movement recognizes that 'psychological wellness' is not defined by the absence of symptoms of mental illness, but by the presence of valued roles and relationships and the satisfactory fulfilment of basic human needs. Two sets of needs are considered to be essential in pursuing healthy relationships among individuals and groups: these are, first, respect for diversity, which ensures that an individual's unique identities can be affirmed by others, and second, collaboration and democratic participation. These enable community members to have a voice in decisions that affect them, and promote both empowerment and social inclusion.

The characteristics of those who have recovered include hope, empowerment, social connectedness and a subjective experience of having regained control over their own lives. So, mental health services should promote community participation, opportunities for empowerment, support for diverse capabilities and freedom from discrimination. Integrating these principles into services requires considerable vision. Also, the principles need to be incorporated into individual therapy. How can social inclusion be built into an individual approach where roles are so asymmetric? Some models pay explicit and detailed attention to the nuances of the interpersonal conversation (Conversational model: Hobson, 1985; Meares, 2006). Others (such as cognitive analytic therapy) use specialist tools to look at how recurrent patterns are manifest in the relationship between therapist and patient (Kerr et al., 2003; Ryle and Kerr, 2002). However, neither approach goes beyond showing respect and humanity in a relationship that illuminates lifelong patterns. Important as these are they do not actively encourage social inclusion. It may be that social inclusion and psychotherapy are co-travellers: psychotherapy allows reflection and self-learning but the opportunities for improving inclusion have to occur in the real world.

The political climate is currently positively oriented towards recovery, social inclusion and sensitivity towards BME issues, so there is a great opportunity for mental health services to be flexible in responding to the needs of those who have been socially excluded.

What is needed to make a socially inclusive, integrated recovery?

Roberts and Wolfson (2004) suggested four themes, as outlined in Table 2.3, that are necessary to promote social inclusion.

Table 2.3 Prerequisites for social inclusion

1 Promoting self management
2 The patient as expert – empowerment
3 Valuing ethnicity and diversity
4 The value of employment (or something to recover for)

Promoting self management

There is increasing awareness of the value of self-management strategies that empower an individual to take control of their lives (Repper and Perkins, 2003). The Wellness Recovery Action Plan (WRAP: Copeland, 2002) is one of the most popular and established recovery tools. The individual user identifies actions, thoughts and behaviours that from personal experience are associated with staying well and reducing symptoms. These 'personal wellness tools' are then incorporated into a written plan that includes daily maintenance, triggers and how to avoid them, warning signs and how to respond to them, and a crisis plan.

The patient as expert – empowerment

There is a progressive move across the NHS to value patients as 'experts in their own experience' (Department of Health, 2001), but an associated need to reconcile the preservation of autonomy, with a duty of care for some of the most vulnerable people in society. A recovery-based service would centre staff training on the lived experience of service users, but would still need to find safe and respectful ways of addressing the issues raised by reduced capacity. Learning from individual expert patients promotes a focus on life rather than illness and greater emphasis on what patients value most: safe and satisfactory accommodation, sufficient money, supportive relationships, work and meaningful activity.

Valuing ethnicity and diversity

The New Zealand approach, particularly in the context of Maaori people (Lapsley et al., 2002; O'Hagan, 2001), has illustrated the importance of valuing a person's cultural origins and personal meanings as reference points around which to combat stigma and support their citizenship. Recovery is based on 'knowing who you are, and where you come from, and re-integrating yourself with your own people in your own way'. Rehabilitation services need to find diverse routes with their service users into culturally appropriate recovery pathways.

The value of employment (or something to recover for)

People with chronic mental illness have much higher than average levels of unemployment, and are already socially excluded as a result of their mental health problems. However, 30–40 per cent of people with enduring mental illness are capable of holding down a job (Ekdawi and Conning, 1994). Many wish to be in some form of employment, but few services for people with chronic mental illness have supported employment services with sufficient capacity or flexibility to engage them. Work is one route to social inclusion. Being in work enhances quality of life (Hatfield et al., 1992; Hill et al., 1996). Expansion in supported employment is supported by evidence.

A systematic review (Crowther et al., 2001) of the ways of supporting people with severe mental illness to obtain work, confirmed that supported employment schemes were more likely to get people back into competitive employment than pre-vocational training.

Work is a powerful route towards social inclusion. Helping people to gain and sustain employment should be considered a valid 'treatment' in its own right (Posner et al., 1996). It also achieves many of the targets set for mental health services in terms of social inclusion and makes a contribution to recovery.

How can we make socially inclusive and recovery oriented rehabilitation services actually happen?

It is important to emphasize the importance of training in transforming services. *Rehabilitation and Recovery Now* (Royal College of Psychiatrists, 2004) set out a vision for the recovery-oriented user-focused rehabilitation service of the future. Paying attention to the culture and the values of rehabilitation and recovery practice and providing high quality training will be crucial to bringing about integration between the world views of services and service users.

Conclusions

A common theme runs through the chapter of integration of treatments through addressing the needs of the patient and adapting the theoretical approach to fit. The analysis of needs, as summarized by Alanen et al. (2000), introduces a personal perspective to the work of the therapist and the experience of the patient. The theoretical weakness of integration is also exemplified in the chapter: it is never clear when the optimal balance between integration and differentiation is reached. The point of balance may also be different at different stages in the trajectory of illness and recovery. Pragmatic research may help us to know whether the addition of a particular component makes a treatment more effective, but the complexity of carrying through research on all combinations is daunting.

Also, different types of research tend to favour different degrees of integration. Efficacy research tends to favour discrete, carefully defined and theoretically coherent approaches; whereas, effectiveness research tends to adopt the ways therapies are delivered in practice, and will therefore include a degree of eclecticism. This bias acts in favour of higher effect sizes for discrete treatments, as these are the ones exposed to the research methods with the highest internal validity. On the other hand, effectiveness studies with their greater tolerance for 'real world' conditions allow greater variation in treatment delivery and hence approximate to the 'noisiness' of actual therapy, but with somewhat lower effect sizes reflecting the greater imprecision of measurement.

In routine practice it seems appropriate to allow therapists to integrate different areas of skilled intervention, but the risk is in allowing eclecticism to mask imprecise case formulation. Possibly using inherently integrative approaches, which follow their own internal logic, gives a good balance in practice by allowing some therapists to use appropriate quality control when working with complex patients. The weaker evidence base offsets this benefit for the newer, integrative approaches compared to established unimodal approaches.

Recovery and social inclusion principles are crucial to an integrative approach. The work with black and minority ethnic groups demonstrates an increased prevalence of severe mental health problems in these groups and a solely biophysical approach is clearly inadequate to account for the observed differences. It is unlikely that mental health care systems alone will reverse the observed differences. However, culturally sensitive interventions integrated into a health system may reduce the impact of social exclusion.

Acknowledgements

The work on formulation of treatment in psychosis was carried out with the late Dr Robert Hobson.

References

Alanen, Y. O. (1993). Skitsofrenia. *Syst ja tarpeenmukainen Hoito*. Juva, Finland: WSOY.
Alanen, Y. O., Lehtinen, V., Lehtinen, K., Aaltonen, J., and Räkköläinen, V. (2000).

The Finnish integrated model for early treatment of schizophrenia and related psychoses. In B. Martindale, A. Bateman, M. Crowe, and F. Margison (Eds.), *Psychosis: Psychological approaches and their effectiveness* (pp. 235–265). London: Gaskell.

Albeniz, A. and Holmes, J. (1996). Psychotherapy integration: Its implications for psychiatry. *British Journal of Psychiatry, 168*, 563–570.

Appleby, L. (2003). So, are things getting better? *Psychiatric Bulletin: Journal of Psychiatric Practice, 27*, 441–442.

Arieti, S. (1975). The psychotherapy of psychosis. In S. Arieti (Ed.), *American handbook of psychiatry* (4th ed.) (pp. 627–629). New York: Basic Books.

Bachmann, S., Resch, F., and Mundt, C. (2003). Psychological treatments for psychosis: History and overview. *Journal of the American Academy of Psychoanalysis and Dynamic Psychiatry, 31*, 155–176.

Bateman, A. and Margison, F. (2003). Psychotherapy: A new era. *Australian and New Zealand Journal of Psychiatry, 37*, 512–514.

Beitman, B. (1989). The movement towards integrating the psychotherapies: An overview. In J. Norcross and M. Goldfried (Eds.), *Psychotherapy integration*. New York: Basic Books.

Bentall, R. P., Corcoran, R., Howard, R., Blackwood, N., and Kinderman, P. (2001). Persecutory delusions: A review and theoretical integration. *Clinical Psychology Review, 21*, 1143–1192.

Copeland, M. E. (2002). Overview of WRAP: Wellness Recovery Action Plan. *Mental Health Recovery Newsletter [United Kingdom], 3*, 1–9.

Crowther, R., Marshall, M., Bond, G., and Huxley, P. (2001). Helping people with severe mental illness to obtain work: Systematic review. *British Medical Journal, 322*, 204–208.

Cullberg, J., Thorén, G., Åbb, S., Mesterson, A., and Svedberg, B. (2000). Integrating intensive psychosocial and low-dose neuroleptic treatment: A three-year follow-up. In B. Martindale, A. Bateman, M. Crowe, and F. Margison (Eds.), *Psychosis: Psychological approaches and their effectiveness* (pp. 200–209). London: Gaskell.

Davenport, S. (1997). Pathological interactions between psychosis and childhood sexual abuse in in-patient settings: Their dynamics, consequences and management. In C. Mace and F. Margison (Eds.), *Psychotherapy of psychosis*. London: Gaskell.

Davenport, S. (2002). Acute wards: Problems and solutions. A rehabilitation approach to the in-patient environment. *Psychiatric Bulletin: Journal of Psychiatric Practice, 26*, 385–388.

Department of Health (England and Wales) (2001). *The expert patient: A new approach to chronic disease management for the 21st century*. London: Department of Health.

Ekdawi, M. and Conning, A. (1994). *Psychiatric rehabilitation: A practical guide*. London: Chapman and Hall.

Fenton, W. S. (2000). Evolving perspectives on individual psychotherapy for schizophrenia. *Schizophrenia Bulletin, 26*, 47–72.

Fenton, W. S. and Schooler, N. R. (2000). Evidence-based psychosocial treatments for schizophrenia. *Schizophrenia Bulletin, 26*, 1–3.

Fowler, D., Garety, P., and Kuipers, E. (1998). Understanding the inexplicable: An individually formulated cognitive approach to delusional beliefs. In C. Perris and P. D. McGorry (Eds.), *Cognitive psychotherapy of psychotic and personality disorders: Handbook of theory and practice* (pp. 129–146). Chichester: Wiley.

Frank, J. D. (1973). *Persuasion and healing: A comparative study of psychotherapy*. Baltimore, MD: Johns Hopkins University Press.

Hatfield, B., Huxley, P., and Mohamad, H. (1992). Accommodation and employment: A survey into circumstances and expressed needs of users of mental health services in a Northern Town. *British Journal of Social Work*, *22*, 61–73.

Hill, R. G., Hardy, P., and Shepherd, G. (1996). *Perspectives on manic depression: A survey of the Manic Depression Fellowship*. London: Sainsbury Centre for Mental Health.

Hobson, R. F. (1985). *Forms of feeling: The heart of psychotherapy*. London: Tavistock.

Hogarty, G. E., Kornblith, S. J., Greenwald, D., DiBarry, A. L., Cooley, S., Flesher, S., et al. (1995). Personal psychotherapy: A disorder-relevant psychotherapy for schizophrenia. *Schizophrenia Bulletin*, *21*, 379–393.

Jeffcote, N. and Travers, R. (2004). Thinking about the needs of women in secure settings. In N. Jeffcote and T. Watson (Eds.), *Working therapeutically with women in secure mental health settings*. London: Jessica Kingsley Publishers.

Johannessen, J. O., Larsen, T. K., McGlashan, T., and Vaglum, P. (2000). Early intervention in psychosis: The TIPS project, a multi-centre study in Scandinavia. In B. Martindale, A. Bateman, M. Crowe, and F. Margison (Eds.), *Psychosis: Psychological approaches and their effectiveness* (pp. 210–234). London: Gaskell.

Keating, F. (2002). Black-led initiatives in mental health: An overview. *Research Policy and Planning*, *20*, 9–19.

Keating, F., Robertson, D., McCullough, A., and Francis, E. (2002). *Breaking the circles of fear: A review of the relationship between mental health services and African and Caribbean communities*. London: Sainsbury Centre for Mental Health.

Kerr, I. B., Birkett, P. B. L., and Chanen, A. (2003). Clinical and service implications of a cognitive analytic therapy model of psychosis. *Australian and New Zealand Journal of Psychiatry*, *37*, 515–523.

Lapsley, H., Waimarie, L. N., and Black, R. (2002). *Kia Mauri Tau!: Narratives of recovery from disabling mental health problems*. Wellington: Mental Health Commission.

Leff, J. and Vaughan, C. (1985). *Expressed emotion in families*. New York: Guilford.

McGorry, P. D. (2000). Psychotherapy and recovery in early psychosis: a core clinical and research challenge. In B. Martindale, A. Bateman, M. Crowe, and F. Margison (Eds.), *Psychosis: Psychological approaches and their effectiveness* (pp. 266–292). London: Gaskell.

Margison, F. (2005). Integrating approaches to psychotherapy in psychosis. *Australian and New Zealand Journal of Psychiatry*, *39*, 972–981.

Margison, F. and Mace, C. (1997). Psychosis and psychotherapy: Elements for integration. In C. Mace and F. Margison (Eds.), *Psychotherapy of psychosis* (pp. 1–10). London: Gaskell.

Meares, R. (2000). *Intimacy and alienation: Memory, trauma and personal being*. London: Routledge.

Meares, R. (2006). The conversational model. In S. Bloch (Ed.), *An introduction to the psychotherapies* (4th ed.) (pp. 287–305). Oxford: Oxford University Press.

Menzies Lyth, I. (1988). The functioning of social systems as a defence against anxiety. In I. Menzies Lyth (Ed.), *Containing anxiety in institutions* (pp. 43–85). London: Free Association Books.

NIMHE (2003a). *Respecting diversity, black and minority ethnic (BME) communities*. London: National Institute for Mental Health in England.

NIMHE (2003b). *Inside outside*. London: National Institute for Mental Health in England.

O'Hagan, M. (2001). *Recovery competencies for New Zealand Mental Health Workers*. Wellington: Mental Health Commission. Also at http://www.mhc.govt.nz.

Orlinsky, D. E., Rønnestad, M. H., and Willutski, U. (2003). Fifty years of psychotherapy process-outcome research: Continuity and change. In M. J. Lambert (Ed.), *Bergin and Garfield's handbook of psychotherapy and behaviour change* (5th ed.) (pp. 307–390). Chichester: Wiley.

Pedersen, C. B. and Mortensen, P. B. (2001). Evidence of a dose: Response relationship between urbanicity during upbringing and schizophrenia risk. *Archives of General Psychiatry*, *58*, 1039–1046.

Phelan, M., Slade, M., Thornicroft, G., Dunn, G., Holloway, F., Wykes, T., et al. (1995). The Camberwell Assessment of Need: The validity and reliability of an instrument to assess the needs of people with severe mental illness. *British Journal of Psychiatry*, *167*, 589–595.

Posner, A., Ng, M., Hammond, J., and Shepherd, G. (1996). *Working it out*. Brighton: Pavilion.

Pratt, J. H. (1908) Results obtained in the treatment of pulmonary tuberculosis. *British Medical Journal*, *2*, 1070–1071.

Pylkkanen, K. (1997). The Finnish National Schizophrenia Project: A strategy for psychotherapeutic treatment and balanced deinstitutionalization. In C. Mace and F. Margison (Eds.), *Psychotherapy of psychosis* (pp. 238–254). London: Gaskell.

Read, J. and Ross, C. (2003). Psychological trauma and psychosis: Diagnosed schizophrenics must be offered psychological therapies. *Journal of the American Academy of Psychoanalysis and Dynamic Psychiatry*, *31*, 247–268.

Repper, J. and Perkins, R. (2003). *Social inclusion and recovery*. London: Baillière Tindall.

Roberts, G. and Wolfson, P. (2004). The rediscovery of recovery: Open to all. *Advances in Psychiatric Treatment*, *10*, 37–49.

Royal College of Psychiatrists (RCP) (2004). *Rehabilitation and recovery now*. (College Rep. no. CR121). London: RCP.

Ryle, A. and Kerr, I. B. (2002). *Introducing cognitive analytic therapy: Principles and practice*. Chichester: Wiley.

van Os, J. (2004). Does the urban environment cause psychosis? *British Journal of Psychiatry*, *184*, 287–288.

Yalom, I. D. (1975). *The theory and practice of group psychotherapy* (2nd ed.). New York: Basic Books.

Zubin, J. and Spring, B. (1977). Vulnerability: A new view of schizophrenia. *Journal of Abnormal Psychology*, *86*, 103–126.

Chapter 3

The rehabilitation of psychoanalysis and the family in psychosis

Recovering from blaming

Brian V. Martindale

Introduction

Psychoanalysis and its derivatives are clinical and research endeavours attempting to do just what the word implies – make a psychological analysis of a particular problem whether it be that of an individual, a group, a family or other context. There is currently a revival of interest in the psychology of psychosis and in the talking therapies in psychosis including the involvement of relevant family members in the overall treatment. It seems appropriate therefore to consider the 'parent' of the talking cures – psychoanalysis – and its relationship and relevance to work with families where there is a member with a psychotic vulnerability.

Reductionism

A common human tendency in all fields of investigation is to make claims for the applicability to other situations of some findings, knowledge or understandings acquired in one particular situation. New findings are often overvalued and potential contributions from other sources devalued.

It takes time to clarify whether new findings and their wider application are fully justified, sometimes justified or rarely unjustified and even dangerous and erroneous. Psychiatry has been vulnerable to adopting the latest ideas or success story. The history of leucotomy, asylums, insulin therapy, the idealization of neuroleptics, the decades searching for 'the cause' of schizophrenia and the overvaluation of a variety of psychological explanations and approaches (currently cognitive approaches) are examples. In the USA, psychoanalysis dominated psychiatry at the expense of the growth of other disciplines, sometimes adopting a reductionist stance towards the aetiology of mental disturbance.

Just as explanations or a treatment method can be overvalued or its implementation overextended, so they can be undervalued, and restricted in use. Psychoanalysis and, in the context of this chapter, its contribution to understanding families in psychosis has swung between these extremes and is now currently excessively derided in some but certainly not all western psychiatric services.

Complexity and general system theory

The 'decade of the brain' (Bush, 1990) and its search for the exclusive biological 'cause' of major mental illness is passing, and perhaps western psychiatry is beginning to move out of its reductionist tendencies. There is recognition of different levels of explanation and understanding (Eisenberg, 2000; Robbins, 1993) and increasing acknowledgement of the complexity of the relationship between nature and nurture in much of mental illness, replacing arguments vying for the supremacy of one side as 'causal'. When used in a sophisticated manner, the stress–vulnerability interaction model of psychosis (Zubin and Spring, 1977) can be an excellent expression of that complexity. There is recognition of the serious limitations of simplistic evidence based approaches (perhaps more relevant to the physical illness model: Mace et al., 2001).

There is increasing interest in the less reductionistic Scandinavian ways of understanding and treating psychosis. Scandinavians have some quite mature models of psychosis and of its therapy that integrate multiple vantage points including psychodynamic and systemic understandings of individuals and families in psychosis with biological and genetic vulnerabilities (Alanen, 1997; Cullberg, 2006; Seikkula et al., 2006). The clinical outcomes are impressive (Cullberg et al., 2006; Seikkula et al., 2006).

Psychoanalysis, psychosis and the family

Psychoanalytic investigations and theorizing about families with a psychotic member perhaps began in the 1930s with Harry Stack Sullivan concluding that schizophrenia was the result of painful early relationships (Sullivan, 1931). David Levy (1931) wrote about the overprotective mother and Hartwell (1996) and other psychoanalytic investigators of this era described their family findings.

Robbins (1993) gives an excellent critique of the 1950s and 1960s publications. He summarizes the writings of Lidz et al. (1957) on 'skewed' families in which one parent is dominating: in male patients with schizophrenia, Lidz found it more usual that the mother was dominating and the father passive and the reverse in female patients with schizophrenia. Their investigations led to conclusions that the child's role was often to maintain the equilibrium by alliance with the dominant parent. Robbins (1993) reports a number of investigators who found 'a family complicity to deny basic problems and assert a false harmony'. These and later non-psychoanalytic investigators such as Bateson et al. (1956) added to the clinical descriptions of subtle threats to the 'schizophrenic' member if he or she used his mind to individuate from these situations. Indeed, in the double bind the most powerfully destructive factor is the unspoken injunction that the contradictions of the double bind are to be denied and not talked about.

In the 1960s, the detailed clinical descriptions of Searles (1965) elaborated on these powerful binding family systems in which the schizophrenic member was caught up. Robbins' own detailed family case studies find similar features. He emphasizes the importance of being aware that the findings of these investigators and teams resulted from prolonged clinical work with families, sometimes over years and the need to compare this with brief and simple statistical evaluation of families made from other vantage points.

The early investigators of the family constellation in psychosis often made errors: first, they tended to describe their findings as causal (in a reductionistic manner) rather than contributory, second, they looked at small numbers from select groups and tended to generalize their findings to all cases of schizophrenia and third, they sometimes described the phenomena they found in a language that came across as somewhat condemning especially of the mothers of schizophrenic patients.

The powerful and compelling psychoanalytic case descriptions of family patterns in psychosis were complemented by the findings from other groups such as that of Goldstein (1987) and Tienari et al. (1994) that stable (enduring) measurements of family communication disturbance was associated with far higher risks of later schizophrenia, other psychoses and other disturbances.

In counteracting the competing reductionist claims of psychoanalytic and other psychological investigators on the one hand and biological investigators on the other, one of the most important investigations is that of Tienari et al. (1994). They managed to conduct one of the very few statistical prospective studies that combined investigations of both nature and nurture in psychosis. They compared the long-term outcome of adopted away children known to have a mother with a schizophrenic illness with those adopted away but whose mother did not have such a disturbance, confirming increased vulnerability of those with a biological mother with psychosis but measuring the mental health of adopting parents gave evidence for the protective factor of those with good mental health. The increased vulnerability to psychosis was confined to those who had *a combination* of two features: those with biological mothers with psychosis and those adopted into families where the parents had adverse mental health features.

The work of Tienari and his colleagues therefore offers a rapprochement between the fiercely held reductionist views of both psychogenesis and biogenesis, and assists in pointing to the likelihood of a constitutional vulnerability to psychosis precipitated by adverse emotional and environmental circumstances. That rapprochement has certainly not happened. The accruing evidence that the family environment had some role in increasing vulnerability to psychosis has met a very great resistance, active opposition and resentment both within the psychiatric field and outside.

Unfortunately not only has the emotional reaction been about the possible tone of the reporting of original findings and any intended or unintended finger pointing, but also there has been widespread denial of the very findings to such an extent that many guidelines have statements such as that of an American Expert Consensus Guideline Series (1999) for schizophrenia. The guide for patients and families states that 'Many of the recommendations are based on a recent survey of over 100 experts on schizophrenia who were asked about the best ways to treat this illness'. It states categorically 'We do know that schizophrenia is not caused by bad parenting, trauma, abuse, or personal weakness' (Expert Consensus Guideline Series, 1999, p. 2). While one would have to agree that the word causal could not be acceptable in the reductionist sense, these kinds of statements are of a gross reductionist nature themselves and rather whitewash the issues. It is interesting that the funding for the guide was supported by five leading drug companies.

There is evidence that some psychoanalytic investigators and those who took up their ideas had some difficulty retaining their investigatory neutrality. Perhaps from sympathy based on their work with individual patients some clinicians perhaps did report family findings in a way that lost a neutral scientific approach and adopted a critical tone towards family members as if their psychology was not the result of unconscious processes that needed as much understanding as the individual patient with psychosis. A more sociological commentary on the era is made by Hartwell (1996). Alanen (1997) is of the general view that these early family studies have been excessively misinterpreted as blaming. Interestingly the criticism of the *psychoanalysts* is as if the latter were making statements about conscious intention of family members and as if the analysts were not referring to their area of expertise – the unconscious.

Robbins, as a contemporary psychoanalyst and commentator on the history of psychoanalysis and the family, is also well worth reading for his detailed case histories in which those family members with a psychotic member who were able to engage in a therapeutic process found their lives becoming enriched as they become aware of serious previously unacknowledged problems.

Expressed emotion and psychoanalytic ideas

The psychodynamic model of psychosis contributes to understanding of empirical findings of interpersonal processes reported in psychosis. In spite of the continuing controversy over the role of family in determining vulnerability to psychosis, it is established from much replicated empirical research that living where there is 'high expressed emotion' in relatives carries a much greater risk of psychotic *relapse* (Leff and Vaughn, 1985). Expressed emotion is a euphemism for 'excessively' expressed criticism and 'over-involvement' of family members.

When therapy leads to containment of such factors the relapse rate is considerably reduced. The psychoanalyst Migone (1995) has made important attempts to bridge the empirical atheoretical concept of expressed emotion in terms of the psychoanalytic theory of three phases of projective identification as espoused for example by Ogden (1979). In this theory, first unwanted or threatening mental contents such as feelings of inadequacy or guilt or fears of criticism from other relatives are projected (as a result they may criticize the patient or become excessively involved in order to compensate for these unwelcome feelings). Second, the projecting relative(s) places 'interpersonal pressure' (through expressed emotion) so that the other (e.g., the person vulnerable to psychosis) fits the projection that he or she is worthy of criticism (e.g., he is lazy). The latter cannot contain the projections and over time either decompensates and/or projects back into the relatives arousing further feelings in a negative circular fashion that cannot again be contained in the relatives.

Unfortunately these theories, which are based on careful observations, are themselves vulnerable to the possibility of blaming family members by inexperienced professionals rather than understanding. It is important to be clear that it is *unconscious mechanisms* by which consciously unacceptable feelings or thoughts are handled that are being inferred in the psychodynamic model. By their nature, they cannot necessarily be immediately accepted into consciousness even through empathic interpretation. The case of Mikko given later in this chapter is a clinical example of the kind of processes in expressed emotion that Migone (1995) is referring to.

Blame and guilt

Currently, there is a great sensitivity to any hint of blaming families with a psychotic member. This is of course right and proper and is intended to not arouse or exacerbate any unhelpful guilt in family members. However, my view is that this fear of blaming may, in part at least, account for the rarity (Burbach and Stanbridge, 2006) with which families are actually engaged in psychosocial approaches even though there are many forms of family engagement that are highly effective in a variety of ways (Pilling et al., 2002). The fear of being blamed is rarely even discussed with families.

Reparative guilt, punitive guilt and projected guilt

Reparative guilt

Not all guilt is unhelpful. Reparative guilt in a family context in psychosis is where a person senses that they may have done some harm in thought or deed that may have contributed. In reparative guilt, there is motivation to find a way of assisting the person with psychosis and it would be a major error to offer immediate reassurance to what is in fact healthy suffering. The professional should fully investigate what is making the person feel uncomfortable and to support that person's discomfort in the interest of both the person feeling the discomfort and in the interest of the patient. Professionals should not independently make judgements as to the cause or exacerbating factors in a psychosis without listening very carefully, probably over time to all parties. The case of Alicia described below illustrates the importance of attending carefully to reparative guilt.

Punitive guilt

Punitive guilt is where, at a conscious or unconscious level, the person is either punishing themselves or anticipating retribution for whatever it is they think they are doing wrong. This 'tooth for a tooth' response is very different from the reparative guilt described above. If the guilt is unconscious, a sensitive observer may just notice the consequence of the punitive guilt, perhaps a family member being particularly hard or depriving towards themselves. Depression is a common manifestation, for example feeling one does not deserve to live, let alone to have any pleasure.

Projected guilt

If the guilt is too unbearable it may be projected onto another person inside or outside the family (as Migone (1995) indicates). Another person is deemed responsible and is then criticized and attacked. In psychodynamic terms, this is psychotic guilt: psychotic because a new reality is created, it is no longer the sufferer who feels guilty; it is the other.

Guilt and its many different forms, its developmental aspects, its vicissitudes and its dynamic links with other affects is a vastly complex subject that has received extensive investigation in psychoanalysis (e.g., Grinberg, 1992). Singh (2000) provides an easy to read introduction. It is important clinically to differentiate these different forms of guilt. Theoretical considerations may help understand the virulence of the attacks on psychoanalysis which for the most part has attempted to do no more than describe the findings of its investigations. With the aid of psychoanalytic theory the question can be asked whether it may be too disturbing for some professionals, lay groups and family members to contemplate whether the very idea about a possible role of some family emotional and communication difficulties contributes to the vulnerability of certain family members to psychosis and/or the immediate stresses. This question does not mitigate the regrettable reductionist and sometimes blaming stance that may have been taken by some professionals.

Contemporary psychoanalytic work with families: towards a rapprochement

The rest of this chapter will consist of bringing three examples of clinical work with families in order to illustrate, in very simplistic form, the variety of clinical and psychological issues and phenomena that emerge when one offers families a setting to bring themselves. This setting does not have any set agenda other than an opportunity to join in understanding that particular family as far as possible and to see if those findings seem relevant to the family in their current difficulties in the hope that a better resolution may emerge.

Case study: an example of reparative guilt

Alicia was a 26-year-old South American gym instructor who was admitted to a psychiatric hospital in her home country for her own safety after becoming overactive and grandiose with brief suicidal moments. She was discharged on a neuroleptic in a more settled state of mind after three weeks. However, she soon stopped the medication and met and soon became engaged to Manuel, immediately relapsing in a similar way, for example, preoccupations with unrealistically grandiose aspirations for her pupils' gymnastic achievements. At times she believed herself to be the mother of Jesus and God's wife.

Following her marriage she became depressed for a prolonged period with dissatisfaction focused endlessly on her husband being 'the wrong person for her'. The depression did not respond to antidepressants, mood stabilizers and supportive counselling. She could work only occasionally and because of the lack of improvement and the negative focus on her husband, the couple elected, after two years of marriage, for a trial separation without benefit.

At this late point, three years after Alicia was first admitted, couple meetings were offered by an analytically trained member of staff. It transpired that Manuel had also been depressed from the start of the marriage as a result of Alicia's depression and its critical content with its focus on his 'inadequacy'. However Manuel, although possessing many qualities, lacked assertiveness to limit what he regarded as an abusive repertoire as he feared he would do irreparable damage by asserting himself. This fear had its roots in his own family background. It is important to emphasize that Alicia made it clear in these interviews that she felt distinctly uncomfortable and concerned about what Manuel had been going through from the way she was treating him.

From the beginning of these meetings, Alicia spoke to the analyst with minimal prompting of the close relationship with her identical twin sister until just before the breakdown, when they amicably elected to develop more separate social lives. Being identical twins had meant that from earliest days, no effort was required for Alicia to be in the limelight providing the twin sister was present. Alicia had developed a fixed phantasy (close to a belief) of marrying a super handsome film star (thereby effortless retaining that special centre of attention place simply by association with the film star/twin). Alicia also volunteered that Laura, although her *identical* twin, was just that more able than Alicia at singing and dancing at school. Being identical twins this difference stood out to others and her parents and had been too painful to come to terms with. Alicia tended to disrupt Laura in these activities, drawing attention to herself.

These and other matters emerged readily once the couple were given a regular time to meet the analyst who drew attention to the difficulty for Manuel in being allocated the role of 'the not good enough partner'. He wondered aloud with them that it was in fact Alicia who had broken down on several occasions and elicited that Alicia had indeed been secretly worried about the consequence of having had a breakdown for *her* marital eligibility. At this point Alicia 'rightly' complained rather contemptuously that Manuel just soaked up 'all her rubbish' implying awareness that she was dumping on him and was being disparaging of his tendency to 'take it'. At this crucial point, Manuel started to get help and attention for asserting himself to Alicia, who also cared a great deal for Manuel. Alicia had to face the fact that she had to make an effort for the marriage to work and mourn her wish that all would be well by simply being alongside a handsome man (God's wife). She clearly appreciated Manuel more than her denigrating would suggest and this more open appreciation helped her make more effort to attend to her guilt about her misuse of him including her relegation of him to the sidelines.

It emerged that this misuse of Manuel was a repetition of Alicia's way of coping with childhood wounds to her self-image, symbolized by Laura's greater ability than Alicia at singing, leading to Alicia making cruel attacks on Laura's greater ability. In the adult situation, Alicia found it difficult to tolerate Manuel's strength in not having had a breakdown in spite of her endless assaults on him.

The marriage improved very considerably indeed as a result of a combination of Manuel standing up to Alicia's denigration and Alicia taking increasing responsibility for containing the denigration and making a more active effort to appreciate Manuel and his contribution to the relationship. The couple went on to have a family. Over the years Alicia has had just one brief hypomanic relapse evoked by an employment issue that re-awoke rivalry with her sister and there have been no further significant depressive episodes.

Comment

This case illustrates many points of which I will mention two for the purposes of this chapter. Alicia (and Manuel) in the first two years of treatment had received 'psychoeducation' about psychosis. This education focused on the importance of medication in the face of stress and vulnerability. Neither the stress nor vulnerability were examined in ways that were at all personalised to their particular situation. So Alicia and Manuel had never had a previous chance to 'tell their story' in their own way. The professionals did not seem interested in being *educated* themselves as to what were the important and unique stresses for Alicia in her life and Manuel was certainly hardly listened to at all.

In relation to the theme of reparative guilt, in this case it was the very individual and specific aspects of stress and vulnerability. The details illustrate the dangers of generalizing from particular individuals or families to others in psychosis. Given an opportunity, Alicia readily talked about her life and required no prompting to convey her clear and quite conscious awareness of her guilty discomfort about her episodic cruelty to Laura throughout her life. She was aware that Manuel was now on the receiving end of something similar. Alicia was also revealing that within herself she was unable to 'assert herself' or stand up to this cruel aspect of herself. They were both aware that there was something 'not right' in the way they were interacting and wanted help for these factors. On the one hand Alicia wanted help to stand up to something 'not nice' in herself but this was competing with her wish for the problem to be located in Manuel (in Laura in her childhood). Manuel was already seeking help at work for lack of assertiveness and this problem (as well as his resilience to the denigration) was a source of both Manuel's attractiveness to Alicia (it suited the projection) and of her resentment of him.

The existence and potential availability from the beginning of reparative guilt in Alicia combined with Manuel's awareness of needing help with assertiveness were crucial to the success of the therapy. In this case, the therapeutic work utilizing the guilt for constructive purposes lasted just six months in this public sector context therapy though making clear that further help was potentially available from the analyst was important until the robustness of the improvement was clarified with time.

Case study: an example of expressed emotion and 'psychotic guilt'

In the previous example, 'responsibility' was projected by Alicia into Manuel (in the form of 'not being good enough') after she had two breakdowns that had affected her own self-esteem. This projection was accompanied by her awareness (insight) of the ongoing cruelty by doing this and close to conscious awareness of this being a continuity of an aspect of the way she related over many years with her twin sister.

In other cases in families, the projection of guilt and responsibility may be much more forceful, shifting to create a new reality to protect more completely the 'projector' from too painful or unacceptable feelings. Here is an example.

Mikko was from one of the Baltic States and had been labelled schizophrenic five years before he came into a service. One of his original complaints was that *his mouthwash had been replaced by street drugs* (Mikko did not use street drugs). Mikko's mother relentlessly complained of the inadequacy of Mikko's treatment before moving the family to another city. However, the dissatisfaction with Mikko's treatment was even more intense there. Mikko's attendance was thin and erratic, but his mother frequently appeared and became hated by staff because of her intrusive insistence that Mikko had inadequately treated schizophrenia. The staff began insisting that his main problems were of a personality disorder (wanting to believe that their psychosis service was not appropriate for him!).

In spite of mother's prominence, there had been no family meetings during the previous five years. Tensions were high at the time when an analyst offered to meet the family and it was noteworthy that from then on father, mother and Mikko came regularly. As the family engaged in fortnightly meetings, the family were gradually able to reveal longstanding problems and that the high degree of criticism and dissatisfaction previously directed towards the service gradually showed another dimension as the family patterns of interaction gradually came to be better known.

It transpired that Mikko had originally broken down soon after mother took 'early retirement' from a demanding career. From that time she was at home all day with Mikko. From this knowledge and her experience so far, the analyst had begun to understand the original presenting concrete 'psychotic' complaint of his mouthwash being replaced with street drugs; perhaps readers may also make some sense of this after reading the following account of one of these family meeting which took place a year after regular family meetings started.

A family meeting illustrating projected guilt

The session began with quite a 'good' atmosphere, the family giving examples of how Mikko was engaging more with the outside world. Mother seemed to be making a conscious effort to hold in her usual very intrusive impatient demands for more from Mikko – a welcome outcome of a lot of hard work on all sides over the months.

Mother: Mikko has received a present for some voluntary work he has done with children. Mikko – you should follow this work up.

Analyst: (*a few exchanges later and based on non-verbal cues*) Mikko, am I correct that you seemed perturbed by the idea of something that you have done being recognized and valued – and as mother suggests – pursued?

Mikko: (*without hesitation*) Yes, I would immediately be under pressure to pursue something that was *not really 'me'!!*

Mother: (*clearly not acknowledging what Mikko had said at all*) Mikko would like working with children – everyone does. I enjoyed it so much.

Mikko: (*neutrally*) That was not my impression mother.

(*The atmosphere immediately changed.*)

Mother: (*getting indignant*) Don't try that on – you know it was only in the latter years I did not enjoy work. *You* need to find work that is enjoyable.

Mikko: Mother: I was simply voicing *my* experience that you had not enjoyed your work.

Mother: (*getting very uptight indeed and now accusing Mikko*) Don't you start – you are trying to manipulate me.

Comment

In terms of unbearable guilt, this was the point at which a familiar pattern of pressure was applied by mother. Mikko had explained why he could not pursue mother's ideas. Mother was unable to bear thinking what Mikko was saying. He was commenting on how he would experience her identity intruding into him and his difficulty in finding an identity of his own. Because it would elicit too much guilt, it was just too difficult for mother to consider her effect on Mikko. She therefore put increasing pressure on Mikko to reflect on what *he was doing to her*. Up to this point, the analyst felt Mikko had indeed been trying to do no more than convey *his* experience of mother and to enlarge on his own wariness of work. There was nothing malevolent detectable but the word manipulate in the last exchange got under Mikko's skin and he now tried to shift the focus onto mother (being much more robust than he was a year previously).

Mikko: (*feeling accused*) Why is everything my fault? What about Saturday?

(*Mikko retaliates with counter-accusation*)

You [mother] simply lost it. You went completely wild blaming me.

Mother: What are you talking about – nothing happened.

(*Analyst comment: in the session she seemed genuinely bewildered and to have no idea what Mikko was talking about.*)

Father: I don't think I was there on Saturday.

Mikko: Mother you were in a rage accusing me of being responsible for *everything(!)* that goes wrong.

Mother: (*now recalling but again unable to consider her effect on others*) But I went out of the house after that and when I came back it was 'forgotten' it was nothing – it was water off a duck's back.

Mikko: For me it was not 'nothing'. Your outburst disturbed me a lot. You went berserk – and I had done nothing. I was simply telling you that Larissa [a therapist that Mikko was seeing individually] had said something about a positive change in me recently. You said what a load of rubbish and you got into a fury saying my sessions were a waste of time.

Mother then got even more defensive and attacking. The idea that this other woman could help Mikko change was perhaps very challenging to mother, who now must have felt very uncomfortable at her attack on helpful clinic staff being exposed. The analyst felt very perturbed and helpless at the speed with which the family attacks on one another escalated. The analyst had developed a good understanding and empathy for mother, who was herself orphaned when she was young and no one had recognized the load she was carrying.

Father: (*now joining in the attack on Mikko, recalling that he had been there on Saturday*) Why are you bringing this up – nothing has been said since Saturday? You are deliberately manipulating the situation *trying to blame us* – well we are not going to take it.

And so it escalated.

Comment

In contrast to the work with Alicia and Manuel, any attempt of the analyst to reflect on the process was felt like an accusation towards them and it was very difficult to say anything except to refer to exactly that (i.e., that whenever he said anything it felt to the parents like another accusation).

The reader will be painfully aware of the pressure from the parents for Mikko to be the sole source of the problem in spite of – or because of – the course of the session and what was happening in the session and what emerged as having happened at the weekend. Neither parent was able to acknowledge any part in the problems and therefore could not contribute to an improvement in the home situation in contrast to Alicia and Manuel. In fact the more evidence that came to the surface of their difficulties the more forceful the pressure on Mikko to be the sole source of responsibility.

It reminded the analyst of earlier sessions in which mother had tried to bring up aspects of her own depressed feelings that had not been heard about before, only for her husband to insist in a chastising way to her outside of the session that they were attending for Mikko and not for her! Father found it very difficult to offer emotional support to either Mikko or his wife (although physically present, his emotional absence from Mikko and his wife was painful to experience).

Although this case required much longer term work than that of Alicia and the material presented is very disturbing, it is worth noting the de-escalation that had happened over the course of year compared with the team who had been unable to tolerate the projections of guilt (mother had wanted Mikko to be diagnosed as having a pure biological disorder that someone else should be fully responsible for resolving). The team were trying to literally get rid of the problem mother was posing them (changing the diagnosis to one that their team did not deal with). The analyst did not get caught up in counter-accusations and made it relatively safe to allow the family to gradually bring the home problems into the open it transpired that episodes of verbal violence were longstanding.) It was important that the setting *allowed* the family to be very critical at times of the family work without retaliation and excessive defensiveness. In time, father was consistently clear that Mikko was functioning far better than he had been in the previous years and some of the above excerpts demonstrate Mikko having more of a mind of his own in the face of pressure to swallow mother's impatient demands.

Case study: an example of shame

The last two cases involved families where issues of guilt and the question of its tolerability was central. In the early history of psychoanalysis and the family, psychoanalysts tried to extrapolate from their findings with particular families to create a more general theory of particular family constellations in 'causing psychosis'. The evaluation of these theories perhaps does not support the generalizations, but in the process something central to psychoanalytic approaches has been lost which is contributing to a making sense of the *particular* psychological circumstances in a collaborative manner whilst acknowledging that psychoanalysis cannot investigate other contributory factors such as biology and genetics. In the rehabilitation of the psychotherapies and psychoses, the psychoanalytic approach has a great deal to contribute to clarifying the psychology of particular families and individuals.

I will end with a further example of how psychoanalytic approaches, with their emphasis on listening and learning and finding out, can contribute to what is unique to a particular family. In this case the main affective burden turned out not to be so much connected with guilt but more to do with shame.

A woman, in initial denial of her pregnancy, was admitted in a seriously suicidal psychotic state. The ward team caringly waited for three months to no avail for neuroleptics to work. She remained suicidal, with pre-occupations taking a psychotic form about an *alien*. A psychodynamically experienced professional was consulted and recommended calling a family meeting involving the patient where it became clear that shame about the circumstances of the conception of the pregnancy was the key unbearable and unspeakable dynamic for the whole family (and the staff). The shame had immense implications as to for whether the family could tolerate the (alien) baby in their midst which would be the first grandchild, or whether 'excommunication' was the only bearable solution.

All of these issues had been potentially available within the psychotic ideation of the patient but had not been utilized. However, once a regular safe setting was created for the patient and family for the very painful problem of shame to be contained, increasingly managed, good progress was made and the psychosis (the psychotic solution of eliminating the shame inducing baby/alien) quickly remitted.

Comment

This case illustrates again the potential importance of attending to the form and content of the psychosis to help identify unbearable affects contributing to the current stress and onset of psychosis. A search for the personal meaning of the psychosis in the minds of the ward team would have easily found clues likely to be relevant to the precipitating stresses of the psychosis. The recurrent reference to the alien in her suicidal or murderous impulses turned out to have layers of relevance not only for the pregnant patient but for the whole family too and for the future well-being of the baby.

In this example, the unbearable shame seemed to be the fulcrum of the problem. With regard to vulnerability, the continuing family work made it clear that there had been longstanding issues of shame and embarrassment in this family that the 'alien' impacted upon. The family were from a traditional Bangladeshi background and there were powerful emotive intergenerational and cross-cultural issues since their arrival in the UK. Being the oldest child, the daughter now pregnant with their first grandchild had been the 'pioneer' of these issues.

The case illustrates the danger of *not* taking a dynamic approach to identify the most potent dynamics and the dangers of not clinically engaging with those dynamics in a flexible way according to an assessment of the overall circumstances. In this case, family work started on the ward and later moved to the family home.

Concluding summary

The interest in psychoanalytic therapeutic work with families rose to prominence in the 1950s and 1960s but fell away for a number of reasons of which the pressure for a more purely biological explanation for schizophrenia was possibly central. It is possible that this pressure was partially fuelled by the very findings of psychoanalytic, and other investigators of family contributions to psychosis, was emotionally unacceptable for consideration. It was certainly unhelpful that these findings not only were sometimes presented in an over-reductionist manner as being causal but also were sometimes over-interpreted by others as blaming of families.

The case material presented here is intended to show a different perspective. The withholding of interest and sustained concern to understand the particular issues for a family where there is psychosis can be very damaging. It can lead to a prolongation of unnecessary suffering through lengthening of the psychosis by the persistence of potent dynamic factors that are not recognized or even looked for. This leads to a loss of opportunities for recovery and a more rewarding life for the whole family.

It is likely that families are nowadays suffering far more from neglect than from being blamed and there is a marked lack of sophistication in understanding the different psychodynamics of guilt and a tendency to regard guilt as necessarily counterproductive. Psychoeducation is at risk of being misused as a tool by which clinicians impose something very non-specific on a family and used to support the avoidance of involvement in a careful listening and getting to know the very specific unique strengths and vulnerabilities of each family.

In the three families described in this chapter, a great deal of suffering was perpetuated from the lack of provision of analytically orientated family work (and its cousin systemic family therapy) rather than its provision.

Psychoanalytic clinicians need to apologize for any harm they have wittingly or unwittingly caused families in the past, but need to have the courage to find a way back to involving themselves with families. To find this way back, they must be wary of attributing blame by being able to empathize with and understand, as far as possible, all family members, not just those members with psychiatric psychosis, and they need to be wary of generalizing from some families where there is psychosis to all cases.

What will certainly not be helpful to families, research and the development of clinical approaches is to respond to pressure to be silenced from describing what is found.

Note

All cases in this chapter are fictitious but based on everyday experience of work in a first-episode psychosis service.

References

Alanen, Y. (1997). *Schizophrenia: Its origins and need-adapted treatment.* London: Karnac.

Bateson, G., Jackson, D. D., Haley, J., and Weakland, J. (1956). Toward a theory of schizophrenia. *Behavioral Science, 1,* 251–264.

Burbach, F. and Stanbridge, R. (2006). Somerset's family interventions in psychosis service: An update. *Journal of Family Therapy, 28,* 39–57.

Bush, G. W. (1990). Proclamation on the Decade of the Brain, Presidential Proclamation 6158. *Office of the Federal Register:* http://www.loc.gov/loc/brain/

Cullberg, J. (2006). *Psychoses: An integrative perspective.* London: Routledge.

Cullberg, J., Mattson, M., Levander, S., Holmqvist, R., Tomsmark, L., Elingors, C., et al. (2006). Treatment costs and clinical outcome for first episode schizophrenia patients: A three-year follow-up of the Swedish 'Parachute Project' and two comparison groups. *Acta Psychiatrica Scandinavica, 114,* 274–281.

Eisenberg, L. (2000). Is psychiatry more mindful or brainier than it was a decade ago? *British Journal of Psychiatry, 176,* 1–5.

Expert Consensus Guideline Series (1999). The treatment of schizophrenia. *Journal of Clinical Psychiatry, 60,* s8–80, p. 2.

Goldstein, M. J. (1987). The UCLA high risk project. *Schizophrenia Bulletin, 13,* 505–514.

Grinberg. L. (1992). *Guilt and depression.* London: Karnac.

Hartwell, C. E. (1996). The schizophrenogenic mother concept in American psychiatry. *Psychiatry, 59,* 274–297.

Leff, J. and Vaughn, C. (1985). *Expressed emotion in families: Its significance for mental illness.* New York: Guilford.

Levy, D. M. (1931). Maternal overprotection and rejection. *Archives of Neurology and Psychiatry, 25,* 886–889.

Lidz, T., Cornelison, A., Fleck, S., and Terry, D. (1957). The interfamilial environment of the schizophrenic patient. I: The father. *Psychiatry, 20,* 329–342.

Mace, C., Moorey, S., and Roberts, B. (2001). *Evidence in the psychological therapies: A critical guide for practitioners.* Hove: Routledge.

Migone, P. (1995). Expressed emotion and projective identification: A bridge between psychiatric and psychoanalytic concepts? *Contemporary Psychoanalysis, 31,* 617–640.

Ogden, T. (1979). On projective identification. *International Journal of Psychoanalysis, 60,* 357–373.

Pilling, S., Bebbington, P., Kuipers, E., Garety, P., Geddes, J., Orbach, G., et al. (2002). Psychological treatments in schizophrenia. I: Meta-analysis of family intervention and cognitive behavioural therapy. *Psychological Medicine, 32,* 763–782.

Robbins, M. (1993). *Experiences of schizophrenia: An integration of the personal, scientific and therapeutic.* New York: Guilford.

Searles, H. F. (1965). *Collected papers on schizophrenia and related subjects.* New York: International Universities Press.

Seikkula, J., Aaltonen, J., Alakare, B., Haarakangas, K., Keränen, J., and Lehtinen, K. (2006). 5 years experiences of first-episode non-affective psychosis in Open Dialogue Approach: Treatment principles, follow-up outcomes and two case analyses. *Psychotherapy Research, 16,* 214–228.

Singh, K. (2000). *Guilt*. Duxford, UK: Icon.

Sullivan, H. S. (1931). Environmental factors in the aetiology and course under treatment of schizophrenia. *Medical Journal and Record, 133*, 19–22.

Tienari, P., Wynne, L. C., Moring, J., Lahti, I., Naarala, M., Sorri, A., et al. (1994). The Finnish adoptive family study of schizophrenia: Implications for family research. *British Journal of Psychiatry, 164* (Suppl. 23), 20–26.

Zubin, J. and Spring, B. (1977). Vulnerability: A new view of schizophrenia. *Journal of Abnormal Psychology, 86*, 103–126.

Chapter 4

Neuropsychological deficit and psychodynamic defence models of schizophrenia

Towards an integrated psychotherapeutic model

Andrew J. Lewis

Introduction

In recent psychiatric literature on schizophrenia the contribution of psychoanalytic ideas tends to be discounted on the basis of two claims: the first is that psychoanalytic treatments of schizophrenia have been shown to be ineffective and the second repeats Karl Popper's original critique that psychodynamic explanations are a priori unscientific because they are unfalsifiable (Bentall, 2006; McGorry, 2004). As Glen Gabbard notes, such statements follow the recent fashion in psychiatry which assumes that the success of the neurosciences renders psychodynamic contributions both redundant and outdated (Gabbard, 1994; Gabbard et al., 2002). While it is disappointing to read statements which ignore important theoretical debates, such summary dismissal also indicates a missed opportunity to consider the experience of many therapists and patients who have found some benefit in a psychoanalytic approach (Cullberg and Johannessen, 2004; Gottdiener and Haslam, 2003).

Psychoanalytic theory and practice is not an inert museum piece. At its best, psychoanalytic theory responds to developments in other sciences, changes in clinical presentations and the shifting social demands inherent in providing public mental health services. Psychoanalytic theories of affect and motivation, for example, are being integrated with developmental and social psychology, drawing on direct observation of young children and experimental studies (Westen, 1998). So too, some psychoanalytic theorists are proposing models of psychopathology which consider the roles of genetic factors in their interplay with developmental and psychosocial factors (Fonagy, 2001b; Plomin and Rutter, 1998; Rutter, 2000, 2005). The broader implications of such findings are that mental health sciences in general have renounced the dream of achieving scientific purity by being based exclusively on genetics and the neurosciences and have begun to develop complex and multi-causal models which synthesize the biological and psychosocial causal factors of psychopathology. Such models therefore require the synthesis of research findings that investigate phenomena at different levels of analysis and using divergent methods. A growing number of psychoanalytically oriented researchers realize that these more integrated and sophisticated models offer opportunities for the confirmation, modification and falsification of psychodynamic propositions in a way that has not previously been possible (Emde and Fonagy, 1997; Fonagy, 2001b; Gabbard et al., 2002).

Nevertheless, discoveries in biological psychiatry are not easily translated into clinical applications – be they pharmacological or psychotherapeutic (Fenton, 2000). The clinical application of these findings requires a focus on the individual patient, the uniqueness of the therapeutic relationship and the level of psychological meaning which any illness state produces, whereas the epistemological framework of biological sciences seeks generalized aetiological mechanism of psychopathology. Integration of these disciplines can begin only from an understanding that different epistemologies and thus methodologies apply to these different levels of analysis – biological, cognitive-psychological and behavioural. A complete research programme for the mental health sciences integrates these idiographic and nomothetic approaches. As Eric Kandel has noted, the traditional psychoanalytic methodology, based on the study of case histories, has exhausted its usefulness. In his view, psychoanalysis now needs to adopt a new intellectual framework integrating the latest findings in cognitive and neurosciences (Kandel, 1999). The future of the mental health sciences consists of developing the pharmacological and psychotherapeutic applications of gene, brain, cognitive, affective and social studies in their complementary role of treating what we now know to be complex mental illnesses (Kandel, 1998).

This is particularly true when considering how psychoanalysis might renew its understanding of schizophrenia while still retaining the key clinical insights it has accumulated. This chapter will examine one aspect of the neuropsychology of schizophrenia, namely deficits in theory of mind. First, the work of Chris Frith is used to introduce the idea that aspects of schizophrenia can be understood neuropsychologically as a deficit in theory of mind (Frith, 1992). This can be contrasted with the psychodynamic theories which are based on psychotic symptom formation resulting from specific defences against conflicting motivations. The chapter will put the argument that what psychodynamic theory typically describes as psychotic symptoms in schizophrenic patients, such as delusion and hallucination, may be a defensive distortion in the cognitive productions which are attempts to explain or respond to deficits in theory of mind processing. While the neuropsychological deficit model is aimed at a level of analysis consistent with the neurosciences, the defence model is an abstraction of the ensuing cognitive and affective processes and lends itself more readily to psychotherapeutic application. Therefore, the integration of both deficit and defence models may provide a better basis upon which to conceptualize the psychotherapy of schizophrenia by delimiting specific therapeutic strategies for deficits and others for defences. The chapter will conclude by discussing what aspects of the psychotherapy of schizophrenia might benefit from such a framework.

Neuropsychological deficits of 'theory of mind' in schizophrenia

Psychoanalysis, and indeed many of the current psychosocial interventions involved as a component of treatment for schizophrenia, would benefit from the integration of a theory of how neuropsychological deficits underpin the key features of psychotic symptoms. First, some definitional clarity is required with respect to the use of diagnostic terms. Psychoanalysts often loosely refer to psychosis and 'psychotics', and more specifically to psychotic defence mechanisms in cases that would not meet the criteria for a set of symptoms consistent with such a psychiatric diagnosis. In the present discussion the term 'schizophrenia' will be used to refer to a specific clinical condition which is a subset of the psychotic disorders whereas the term 'psychosis' will be used to describe symptoms that consist of impairment in reality testing. Psychotic symptoms form one characteristic of schizophrenia but are also associated with other disorders and can be artificially induced without implying the full syndrome of schizophrenia. Indeed, as a diagnostic entity, 'schizophrenia' may lack construct validity. Both clinical and genetic investigations suggest that the term may cover several different disorders with different aetiologies and mechanisms (Bentall et al., 1988a, 1988b; Elkin, 2004). Nancy Andreasen analysed data from her own symptom scales which suggested that the symptoms of schizophrenia tend to fall into three clusters: psychotic (delusion and hallucinations), negative (flattened affect, alogia, avolition, anhedonia) and disorganized (thought disorder, incongruent affect and bizarre behaviour) (Andreasen et al., 1995a; Andreasen et al., 1995b). Notwithstanding this important critique, this chapter will use the terms 'schizophrenia' and 'psychotic symptom' according to the more or less traditional psychiatric definition.

A growing body of research considers schizophrenia to be a disorder of social cognition – a term which can be defined as the capacity to mentally represent self and other as a guide to social interaction. Social cognition includes processes such as 'theory of mind' abilities, social perception, and attributional style. Impairment in social cognition may be an effect of information overload during the acute phase of schizophrenia (Drury et al., 1998) or may reflect a broader impairment in social functioning. Addington and colleagues found that deficits in social functioning are present throughout the course of schizophrenia and may persist despite antipsychotic treatment (Addington and Addington, 2000). Davidson and colleagues suggested that deficits in social functioning are present even before the onset of schizophrenia (Davidson et al., 1999). Some studies have suggested that this neurocognitive deficit in social functioning has a genetic origin. For example, one study found the same social deficits in children of a biological parent who has schizophrenia suggesting that social deficits may be related to what these researchers call a broader schizophrenic genotype (Hans et al., 2000). Although in some cases social functioning tends to remain stable in severity of impairment, or may even worsen in subsequent phases of the illness, there is considerable evidence that this is not necessarily the case and the social functioning of some patients does improve over time (Harding et al., 1987).

Chris Frith (1992) proposed a more specific hypothesis that schizophrenia is essentially a dysfunction of meta-cognition or mentalization, that is, the ability to represent or think about one's own thoughts. Drawing on the original observations of Bleuler, Frith made a comparison of aspects of schizophrenia such as social withdrawal and dysfunction to similar social deficits in autism – both can be conceptualized as deficits in the development of a theory of mind. The term 'theory of mind' (ToM) was originally used in the context of research on primate cognition and introduced by Premack and Woodruff (1978). It refers to what has turned out to be a uniquely human ability to understand human actions as based on the underlying mental states of their agent (Povinelli and Vonk, 2003). The definition of the term also includes the attribution of mental states, such as beliefs or desires, to explain one's own and other people's current, past and predicted behaviour.

ToM provides a framework within which to understand how the self is linked to other mental representations. For example, Frith noted that normal cognitive functioning permits awareness of perceptions (I know, 'it is raining') to be represented as beliefs attributed to others (John believes, 'it is raining') (Frith, 1994). Through the attribution of analogous mental states from the self to another, one might then infer the reason for certain behaviours (John is carrying an umbrella today because he believes it will rain). Beliefs about others' states of mind are formed in conjunction with a stable understanding of the self as having ownership of received perceptions, self-generated cognitions, and affects.

Impairment in ToM provides a useful theoretical model through which to understand the impairment of the ability to represent beliefs and intentions, particularly in the psychotic symptoms of schizophrenia. According to Frith (1992, 1994) anomalies can occur at three different levels of the perception of self and other. These consist of, first, disorders of willed action in which apathy or bizarre behaviours might result from the self's inability to perceive its own intentions or will, second, disorders of self-monitoring whereby there is a reduced awareness that thoughts and actions are generated by the self, and third, deficits in other monitoring which impairs the capacity to read others' thoughts, intentions, desires and behaviours. Bentall applied the argument to hallucinations saying that the ability to perceive if an event is real or imagined relies upon interpreting and integrating a number of sources of information in their relation to the agent who receives and processes the perceptions, that is, the self. Therefore, hallucinations may well result from a failure to locate the perceiver as the recipient of the perception, i.e., a failure in meta-cognitive ability to locate the self in the representations it receives and processes (Bentall et al., 1991).

Such a theory can be applied more broadly to features of other common psychotic symptoms. The loss of the self as 'owner' of thoughts is apparent in thought insertion or thought broadcasting. The impaired capacity for the correct perception of another is apparent in delusions of alien control and persecution. So too delusions of persecution, jealousy or erotomania can be understood as a failure to monitor or accurately understand another's intention or desire towards the self. Melancholic delusion appears to imply a misattribution of the value of the self by the self. This very brief overview at least shows that psychotic symptoms can be understood as a deficit in the capacity to relate thoughts, actions, or perceptions to subjective intentions, particularly in terms of understanding the self as the agent of mental events.

Of particular interest is research into the association of certain symptoms of schizophrenia with the ToM deficit. For example, Langdon and colleagues compared the pragmatic language skills and formal thought disorder of patients with schizophrenia to unaffected controls and found that poor appreciation of irony and poor mind-reading were associated with high ratings of thought disorder (Langdon et al., 2002). A further study found that people diagnosed with disorganized schizophrenia performed the most poorly on ToM tasks (Greig et al., 2004). This study suggested that ToM performance was also correlated with higher levels of thought disorder, cognitive disorganization and verbal memory. ToM impairment has also been studied in the relatives of patients with schizophrenia by comparing performance on a traditional false belief task and also a hinting task for a group of patients with schizophrenia, their first degree relatives and unaffected controls. Significant associations were found between schizophrenia risk, and failure on the hinting task which was designed to test a subject's ability to infer a speaker's real intentions when 'dropping a hint' in indirect speech. In this study first degree relatives scored intermediate values between patients and controls in the hinting task but the association between schizophrenia risk and failure on the false-belief tasks did not reach significance (Janssen et al., 2003).

Although, as previously discussed, this area of research was originally inspired by seeing a parallel between the social deficits in schizophrenia and those manifested in autism, two important distinctions have been noted which are likely to have important clinical implications. A study by Langdon et al. (2006) compared patients with schizophrenia to unaffected controls in their ability to discern the correct expression of affect corresponding to an emotionally laden cartoon strip. In addition to replicating findings suggesting impaired ToM abilities when measured by a subject's capacity to attribute false beliefs, they also found general difficulties in patients with schizophrenia attributing the correct emotions to the depicted social exchanges. They therefore proposed that schizophrenia is a generalized deficit in empathic perspective taking which is responsible for the inability to understand not only others' beliefs and perceptions but also emotions. In contrast, autism is a more specific deficit in social understanding, particularly beliefs and intentions, but the processing of the relation between simple events and basic emotions is not impaired (Langdon et al., 2006). The other major difference between autism and schizophrenia is developmental. As Frith (1992) originally pointed out, deficits in ToM in schizophrenia consist of a breakdown in more or less intact ToM, whereas in autism ToM is assumed to be impaired from birth. Therefore, it would appear that an understanding of the development of ToM is also relevant to understanding both its breakdown in schizophrenia and how one might integrate this developmental understanding into a mode of psychotherapy in order to repair ToM impairments, which will be discussed in the final section of the chapter.

There is already a substantial body of evidence to support the view that ToM is impaired in people with schizophrenia. The bulk of evidence is based on neuropsychological studies, but there have also been important neuroimaging studies. Frith and Frith (1999) have provided a discussion of the general neuroanatomy of ToM abilities. A subsequent neuroimaging study compared the performance of schizophrenic patients to controls when performing a socio-emotional task requiring metal state attribution and found lower activity in the left inferior frontal gyrus, a region of the brain believed to be involved in ToM function (Russell et al., 2000). While deficits in ToM capacities are clearly associated with schizophrenia, it is only one of several deficits which contribute to the susceptability and course of schizophrenia. As several recent reviews have emphasized, greater precision in understading the specific role of ToM deficits amoungst other deficits in social cogniton in schizophrenia awaits further research. In a review of some 30 studies on ToM in schizophrenia, for example, it was unclear how researchers ought to best measure ToM in schizophrenia and thus studies did not use standard measures (Harrington et al., 2005). Before drawing conclusions regarding the implications of this research for clinical practice, more data is required regarding the fluctuation of ToM over the course of schizophrenia, and how it affects patients' use of language, and social behaviour (Brune, 2005).

Psychoanalytic theories of the defensive function of psychotic symptoms

Although this research is still in its early stages, there is broad agreement that ToM deficits provide a useful conceptualization of an underlying social deficit in schizophrenia. While broadly speaking the research supports Frith's hypothesis, the theory does not provide a complete account for all aspects of psychotic symptom formation, most particularly delusional symptoms. Max Coltheart and Robyn Langdon extended the deficit theory and proposed that a single neurocognitive deficit is insufficient to explain the generation of some psychotic symptoms such as multi-thematic delusional beliefs (Langdon and Coltheart, 2000). They argued that an additional deficit in the capacity to evaluate belief formation is also required, what psychoanalysts refer to as 'reality testing'. Both deficits need to operate in tandem in order to generate more complex forms of delusional belief. The first factor accounts for the perceptual aberrations which generate the content of a delusion while the second factor accounts for why a delusion is first adopted and then maintained despite the lack of evidence to support it (McKay et al., 2005).

Capgras delusion offers a good test of the deficit theory. In this delusion a person forms the belief that their spouse or lover is an impostor who looks identical to the real partner. According to a deficit theory such as Langdon and Coltheart's model, such a delusion would result from a deficit in the capacity to link an affective response to facial recognition, i.e., the other person looks like my spouse but doesn't feel like him or her. In addition, those who adopt and maintain such a belief lack an ability to reject unsubstantiated beliefs. However, McKay argued that Capgras delusion could also be understood as a belief formation that is influenced by an attempt to satisfy unacknowledged motivations (McKay et al., 2005). In this case the motivation would be based on ambivalent feelings towards the partner. McKay's argument suggested that in addition to the neurocognitive deficits producing perceptual aberrations, defensive operations also distort information. Defensive operations process information in an unconscious manner in order to satisfy conflicting motivations. Impaired reality testing, the second factor, would enable beliefs formed on the basis of such erroneous information and the distortion derived from defensive modification of unpalatable motives to go unchallenged. Therefore, at least in some cases, the first factor in a two-factor model may be less the result of a neurocognitive deficit than a psychological defence. As McKay et al. (2005) noted, it may also be the case that the first factor arises out of a multitude of sources, both deficits and defences, because each interacts with the other.

The argument hinges on building a coherent theory of how internal motivations contribute to mechanisms that distort information concerning one's self and one's place in the world. As McKay et al. (2005) noted, psychoanalytic theories of motivation are only a subset of a broader set of theories of motivation. However, McKay does not elaborate more recent developments within psychoanalysis which recognize the theory of motivation as one of the key areas in need of theoretical renewal. Under the growing influence of attachment systems theory, many analysts have moved beyond Freud's articulation of drive theory and any requirement to posit underlying infantile, libidinal strivings in all human motivations. Motivation is not explicable by the pleasure inherent in the reduction of drive tensions but better attributable to the need to maintain a sense of security and self-worth, the need to seek proximity to attachment figures and the need for adjustment to social and developmental demands (Bowlby, 1988; Fonagy, 2001a). Therefore, motivations can be seen in a relational context, as meeting social demands and satisfying current needs, while drawing on what Bowlby (1988) called internal working models of social interaction based on past experiences in close relationships.

One of the hallmarks of psychoanalytic theory is its theory of defences which operate not only in psychopathology but are a component of everyday life. The notion of defence is integral to the psychoanalytic concept of the self. Very briefly, the self defends against incompatible ideas or affects in defence of its own integrity. This is threatened when certain ideas encroach which are incompatible or dangerous to a person's sense of himself or herself. Incompatible ideas may be motivated by desires which escape conscious awareness. While all defence involves a level of self-deception, not all defences require a distortion of reality.

Supreme Court Judge Daniel Paul Schreber's autobiographical account of his multi-thematic, paranoid and hypochondriac delusions provides the *locus classicus* of psychoanalytic theories of psychosis (Freud, 1958 [1911]). His psychotic break occurred after he had the idea that it would be pleasurable to be a woman submitting to intercourse. One of the key points that Freud emphasized in his discussion of the Schreber case is that the manifestations of psychotic symptoms are attempts to restore a gap which had opened in the relation of the self to the world. This gap has opened because an incompatible idea has been expelled in a radical form of defence. The precipitant to a psychotic break is therefore a vulnerability within the self which is later triggered by certain social demands and this initiates the process of psychotic symptom formation. Freud recognized very early in his work that the defensive operations which produce psychotic symptoms are of a quite different order of magnitude than those which repress ideas internally (i.e., into the unconscious) and therefore produce psychoneurotic symptoms such as conversion symptoms which have an unconscious meaning. Freud considered that psychotic defence was a radical form of defence based essentially on the mechanism of projection which attempts to modify the external world by projecting incompatible ideas into the external world, i.e., onto others. The defensive function of projection is to defend against self-generated ideas by denying that those ideas even belong to one's self. Projection therefore makes the world the bearer of all that is defended against, which may result in either withdrawal from a menacing world or greeting it with aggression. Therefore, implicit in Freud's account of psychotic symptom formation is a significant dysfunction and fragmentation of the self for the purpose of defence.

Leaving aside the argument over the accuracy of such a view, there are several key points to retain from Freud's initial account of the process of psychotic symptom formation. The impairment in social functioning means that therapeutic relations with patients with psychotic symptoms are of a different order to other patients. The therapeutic relation preferred by Freud assumes a relatively normal capacity for social cognition and intact reality testing whereas psychotic symptoms arise precisely in the context of an impairment in such cognitions. In short, we arrive at a reason why Freud considered that psychoanalysis has no clinical application when the patient does not manifest a transference neurosis. One can readily agree with those critics who suggest that Freud has little to directly offer for the psychological treatment of schizophrenia, indeed Freud says this himself. However, it is clear that the development of ideas of psychotic defence and symptom formation can be used to create a substantially different theory and clinical technique to be applied to psychotic symptoms. This is a position that has permeated most schools of psychoanalysis for many decades and yet is never considered in negative appraisals of the outcomes of so-called 'psychodynamic therapy'. The second point is that Freud's notion of defensive projection, like Frith's theory, considers the production of psychotic symptoms to result from a breakdown in the boundaries which contain thoughts, emotions and motivations as belonging to oneself. In this respect, although it may be stretching the point, one could also say that Freud's defence model is also based on a difficulty in mentalization. The difference is that in Freud's case impairment in mentalization is motivated and serves the function of defending the self while in Frith's model the problem is a neurocognitive abnormality not requiring explanation at a psychological level. Finally, it is apparent that Freud's view of defence implies that not only can defence motivate distorted perceptual information which may lead to psychotic symptoms such as delusion, but also psychotic defence impairs the capacity for reality testing which thereby maintains the delusional belief. These different theories of the relation of defence and deficit models of psychotic symptom formation are summarized in Table 4.1.

Therapeutic implications of the integration of defence and deficit models

To conclude, it is possible to briefly outline some of the therapeutic implications of the integration of deficit and defence models of schizophrenia

Table 4.1 Defence and deficit theories of the formation of delusional symptoms

Theory	Domain	
	First factor *Social cognition (i.e., ToM)*	*Second factor* *Belief evaluation/Reality*
Frith	Deficit	Nil
Langdon and Coltheart	Deficit	Deficit
McKay	Defence	Deficit
Freud	Defence	Defence

proposed by McKay et al. (2005) using a psychodynamic framework. There are four broad principles which can be elaborated:

1   The therapeutic relationship can be used as a means of understanding and processing mental states and thereby enhancing ToM capacities in a stable and secure setting.
2   The reflection on developmental and life history in the therapy should be restricted to addressing the motivation factors underlying defensive functions only when clearly indicated. However, developmental and life histories cannot be used as a means of explaining neuropsychological deficits in ToM capacities.
3   Practical social skills training can be focused on deficits in social-cognition abilities and integrated with techniques to help the patient understand the meaning of their illness and its optimal management.
4   Therapeutic intervention needs to actively address self-representations and the role of the self in meta-cognition in addition to reparative and palliative interventions following the acute phase of illness. This technique may also have a role in preventative interventions with populations at high risk of developing schizophrenia.

Using the therapeutic relation in the treatment of schizophrenia

Psychotherapeutic outcome research suggests that the therapeutic relationship may be the major contributor to positive therapeutic outcomes. Although this is a matter of considerable debate within the outcome literature on psychological treatments of schizophrenia, controlled trials have often struggled to show a significant effect of experimental therapies compared with supportive therapy or effective standard case management (Jackson et al., 2005; Turkington and McKenna, 2003). Although this is usually interpreted as a negative finding, it suggests that the role of social contact, the therapeutic relationship and forms of implicit social learning from professional contact may be the more active ingredients of therapy. Addington and Gleeson (2005) suggested that CBT, for example, ought to target directly the patient's social needs and that the therapy ought to emphasize the 'interpersonal context' and 'social consequences of relationships, including the therapeutic relationship'. A mentalization approach provides a more explicit focus on these aspects as well as a theory of why they might contribute to therapeutic efficacy.

Freud's often noted pessimism that psychoanalysis was an effective treatment of 'cases of paranoid and dementia praecox' was in part derived from the inadequate regression-fixation model of developmental psychopathology which suggested that the most severe forms of mental illness where a result of the earliest of libidinal fixations in development (Freud, 1958 [1911]). Freud's model of analytic technique was based on the role of free association which aims to relax the function of reality testing in order to reduce the ego's censorship of unconscious thinking. The regressive consequences were quickly discovered and a therapeutic technique was developed which made use of the experiential impact of regression within the analytic setting. However, one aspect of technique in the therapy of psychosis emphasized by analysts as diverse in their theories as Donald Winnicott, André Green and Jacques Lacan is that free association is to be used only when there is sufficient stability of ego function to allow regression to be beneficial, i.e., within the treatment of neuroses only (Green, 1998; Lacan, 2006 [1959]; Winnicott, 1975 [1954]). Since free association is designed to promote regression to earlier developmental stages, it is not a technique to apply in cases of schizophrenia (and so too the more severe personality disorders) where its use is more likely to result in what Balint (1992) termed malignant regression. Instead, in contemporary practice a conversational dialogue is encouraged with the therapist working actively to maintain mental closeness and prevent fragmentation, derailment and incoherence in speech. So too, in the treatment of schizophrenia a high degree of modulation of affect is called for in order to make sessions a safe and productive experience. Psychotic content is never directly challenged or contradicted. Instead the therapist works with the patient to try to understand from where such thoughts or perceptions might arise. Therefore, the treatment is highly collaborative, aims at promoting reflection on mental processes, and emphasizes the alliance between therapist and patient in seeking these common goals. Mentalization, that is the capacity to think about thinking, cannot be achieved in an adversarial atmosphere.

Understanding developmental and family dynamics in the therapy of defences

Psychoanalytic theory typically considers delusions to be productions which serve a restorative or adaptive function for the patient, even if they might contribute to what appears to be a social dysfunction. Therefore, the treatment approaches tend to favour constructive elaboration and examination of these productions, rather than a crude attempt to eradicate such symptoms on the grounds of an appeal to their evident unreality (evident, that is, to the therapist). The specific content of such productions, and in particular delusions and hallucinations, is considered to arise in the context of a patient's unique life history, a view which is not incompatible with the idea that the symptoms are formed because of underlying neurocognitive deficits in social cognition.

A psychodynamic treatment of schizophrenia based on mentalizing principles would include attempts to understand the content of psychotic symptoms within a framework of the patient's current social world, developmental history and family dynamics. Links between the content of delusions and hallucinations and a patient's personal history and developmental context may provide a narrative framework but ought not to be conceptualized as the sole cause of psychotic symptoms. Following McKay's model, psychotherapies directed towards some delusional symptoms, for instance, are more likely to be effective if they target the underlying motivation for the aberrant belief formation, rather than attempting to convince a patient that their belief is a delusion through recourse to some objective refutation (McKay et al., 2005). To some extent this would require the development of a formulation that entails aspects of developmental history and family dynamics which, following the psychodynamic tradition, informs the therapist's interventions but would not be communicated directly to the patient. This might be done effectively only on the basis of careful history taking, extended reflection of the patient's material and careful hypothesis testing within the context of a strong treatment alliance.

However, a common error in the application of psychodynamic ideas to the treatment of schizophrenia is to assume that developmental aspects offer an explanatory framework that provides a causal explanation to the patient for the neuropsychological deficits from which they suffer. Evidence from ToM studies would suggest that this approach is misguided in many if not most cases. One can draw from this research a clear demarcation between the deficit and defence model that is valuable clinically. The operationalization of these concepts clinically draws on the distinction between causes and meaning, i.e., deficits in ToM in schizophrenia are likely to have a strong biological basis and can be described using a physical causal model, whereas defences produce effects of meaning; they are a lived experience of the self and its relations with others. The specific form of psychotic symptoms, the content of delusions and hallucinations, may well have links to a patient's life history, development and family dynamics. Working through these aspects of a patient's symptoms can have beneficial results because it provides a meaningful framework and may be restorative of a personal narrative which includes, but is not overwhelmed by, the experience of psychotic symptoms. In this case, working through would consist of trying to help a patient gain some understanding of how their unique life events, family interactions, developmental pathways and family or developmental life stage interacts and influences the onset, content or response to psychotic symptoms. As we shall discuss, personal meaning, a palatable explanatory framework for their mental state experiences, and narrative continuity are critical to the patient's restoration of a functional sense of self.

In essence, the demarcation between deficits and defences reduces the likelihood of damaging modes of practice that result from the failure of integration in the mental health sciences. First, the likelihood of the iatrogenic effect of destroying a patient's sense of agency by declaring they suffer from a mental disease state that has nothing to do with them. Second, the equally damaging use of speculative and largely unfounded reconstructions of failures in early development or in the 'care-giving environment' which the therapist suggests to the patient are the cause of their schizophrenia.

Skills training to address social cognition deficits

Given the clear social deficiencies present in schizophrenia and the possibility that, at least in some cases there will be a progressive deterioration over the course of the illness, the direct targeting of ToM abilities would appear to be well within the domain of therapeutic treatments. It also follows that treatments such as the psychodynamic approach, which emphasizes the therapeutic relationship, would predominately address the misinterpretations of self and other implied in psychotic symptom formation, within the therapeutic relationship.

However, a more didactic and explicit focus on enhancing a patient's social cognition capacity needs to be considered. On the one hand, given the clear developmental and relational context in which ToM emerges, a discrete and simple ToM training model may be of little effect and even be somewhat alienating. Brune (2005) in his review of the ToM literature asserted that 'future studies may also address whether patients could benefit from cognitive training in this domain' (Brune, 2005, p. 21). There is somehow an assumption that ToM is acquired by some kind of social-learning process and therefore one could somehow 'train' it into patients when it is found to be defective. This is a problematic idea given that we know that ToM is not simply a cognitive skill and even less a learnt behaviour. Acquiring ToM is more likely to be achieved within the context of a specific social relation where aspects of the social interaction can be used for didactic purposes. On the other hand, it follows that if deficits in ToM have a neurocognitive basis, then therapies need to actively and explicitly address these deficits. This will involve a more directed and skill focused approach than is traditionally used in psychodynamic approaches. Whether such a training approach can be integrated with a psychodynamic or cognitive approach or would be better delivered as a separate adjunct therapy in selected cases can be determined only empirically.

Self-representations in the therapy of schizophrenia

Both cognitive and psychodynamic therapies for psychosis have specifically targeted the impact upon the self. For instance Jackson et al. (1996) used notions derived from constructivism which suggests that people construct their personal representation of the world, which creates representational models that serve as a framework for the attribution of meaning to personal events. Jackson et al.'s (1996) CBT model is focused on the protection of the self and the resumption of lifespan development following an initial psychotic episode. The means by which the developmental process is integrated into the therapy is limited in this cognitive-behavioural approach because the focus is more on the impact on the self of schizophrenia, rather than targeting a vulnerability in the self-schema. Indeed, researchers of differing orientations have considered the self to be a key target of therapeutic intervention (Frith, 2005; Morrison et al., 2004). However, the deficit/defence model provides a more robust view of the role of the self in both the vulnerability to psychotic symptoms and the role of the self in the formation of these symptoms.

For example, by way of comparison with autism, ToM research suggests that patients with schizophrenia suffer from an inability to understand themselves by accurately assimilating the perspective another has of them and this deficit crosses not only cognitive abilities but the processing of emotional states. One can infer that impairment in the critical feedback mechanism of self development would be an accumulating impoverishment in the representational schema of the self and other. Although clearly exacerbated by the onset and severity of psychotic symptomatology, some degree of ToM deficits typically predate onset as well as persisting beyond the resolution of a specific psychotic episode. This suggests that the psychotherapeutic targeting of ToM, broken down into self, other and self-other representations, could well be a key strategy in both preventative interventions for groups at high risk of their first episode of psychosis as well as having an important role in the prevention of relapse following initial psychotic episodes.

The use of a mentalizing framework aims to recreate within a therapeutic setting a situation where the boundaries of self can be recognized, intentionality of thought correctly attributed and the mental processes of others can be interpreted. This provides an experience of the patient's self as real via the therapist. Based on this theory, one can suppose that therapeutic gains are made at the point where this recognition can be clearly perceived by the patient. Unlike prior psychodynamic models, each of the goals which follow from this theory can be defined and measured within a programme of research. One would predict that a patient's recovery from illness and decline in psychotic symptoms would improve alongside improved capacities for mentalization.

Given the preliminary nature of research into ToM deficits in patients with schizophrenia, carefully targeted psychotherapeutic techniques must be framed in a tentative manner. The conceptual integration of deficit and defence models described in this chapter may well provide an enhanced framework within which to consider new therapeutic models and to reconfigure psychodynamic therapies in a manner guided by this research. In theory, it appears that orienting interventions around different strategies for addressing deficits in social cognition as distinct from defensive processes appears to be a reasonable approach. Many of the clinical applications discussed here can be integrated with the current variety of psychosocial interventions used as interventions for schizophrenic patients since all need to be guided by a coherent theory of the therapeutic aspects of their intervention. Furthermore, it is unlikely that any single psychological therapy will meet all of the needs of the diversity of patient suffering from schizophrenia. Whether enhanced efficacy for the psychosocial treatment of schizophrenia can be derived from the integration of deficit and defence models will need to await the further development, implementation and testing of such therapies in a clinical setting.

Acknowledgements

I would like to thank Dr Megan Galbally, Dr Louise Hayes and Mandy Commons for their assistance in the preparation of this chapter.

References

Addington, J. and Addington, D. (2000). Neurocognitive and social functioning in schizophrenia: A 2.5 year follow-up study. *Schizophrenia Research, 44*, 47–56.

Addington, J. and Gleeson, J. (2005). Implementing cognitive-behavioural therapy for first-episode psychosis. *British Journal of Psychiatry, 187* (Suppl. 48), s72–s76.

Andreasen, N. C., Arndt, S., Miller, D., Flaum, M., and Nopoulos, P. (1995a). Correlational studies of the Scale for the Assessment of Negative Symptoms and the Scale for the Assessment of Positive Symptoms: An overview and update. *Psychopathology, 28*, 7–17.

Andreasen, N. C., Arndt, S., Alliger, R., Miller, D., and Flaum, M. (1995b). Symptoms of schizophrenia: Methods, meanings, and mechanisms. *Archives of General Psychiatry, 52*, 341–351.

Balint, M. (1992). *The basic fault: Therapeutic aspects of regression.* Evanston, IL: Northwestern University Press.

Bentall, R. (2006). Madness explained: Why we must reject the Kraepelinian paradigm and replace it with a 'complaint-orientated' approach to understanding mental illness. *Medical Hypotheses, 66*, 220–233.

Bentall, R. P., Jackson, H. F., and Pilgrim, D. (1988a). Abandoning the concept of 'schizophrenia': Some implications of validity arguments for psychological research into psychotic phenomena. *British Journal of Clinical Psychology, 27*, 303–324.

Bentall, R. P., Jackson, H. F., and Pilgrim, D. (1988b). The concept of schizophrenia is dead: Long live the concept of schizophrenia? *British Journal of Clinical Psychology, 27*, 329–331.

Bentall, R., Baker, G. A., and Havers, S. (1991). Reality monitoring and psychotic hallucinations. *British Journal of Clinical Psychology, 30*, 213–222.

Bowlby, J. (1988). *A secure base: Clinical applications of attachment theory.* London: Routledge.

Brune, M. (2005). 'Theory of mind' in schizophrenia: A review of the literature. *Schizophrenia Bulletin, 31*, 21–42.

Cullberg, J. and Johannessen J. O. (2004). The dynamics of acute psychosis and the role of dynamic psychotherapy. In J. F. M. Gleeson and P. D. McGorry (Eds.), *Psychological interventions in early psychosis: A treatment handbook* (pp. 81–98). Chichester: Wiley.

Davidson, M., Reichenberg, A., Rabinowitz, J., Weiser, M., Kaplan, Z., and Mark, M. (1999). Behavioral and intellectual markers for schizophrenia in apparently healthy male adolescents. *American Journal of Psychiatry, 156*, 1328–1335.

Drury, V. M., Robinson, E. J., and Birchwood, M. (1998). 'Theory of mind' skills during an acute episode of psychosis and following recovery. *Psychological Medicine, 28*, 1101–1112.

Elkin, A., Kalidindi, S., and McGuffin, P. (2004). Have schizophrenia genes been found? *Current Opinion in Psychiatry, 17*, 107–113.

Emde, R. N. and Fonagy, P. (1997). An emerging culture for psychoanalytic research? *International Journal of Psychoanalysis, 78*, 643–651.

Fenton, W. S. (2000). Evolving perspectives on individual psychotherapy for schizophrenia. *Schizophrenia Bulletin, 26*, 47–72.

Fonagy, P. (2001a). *Attachment theory and psychoanalysis*. New York: Other Press.

Fonagy, P. (2001b). The human genome and the representational world: The role of early mother-infant interaction in creating an interpersonal interpretive mechanism. *Bulletin of the Menninger Clinic, 65*, 427–448.

Freud, S. (1958 [1911]). Psycho-analytical notes on an autobiographical account of a case of paranoia (dementia paranoides). In J. Strachey (Ed.), *The standard edition of the complete psychological works of Sigmund Freud* (Vol. 12, pp. 3–80). London: Hogarth Press.

Frith, C. (1992). *The cognitive neuropsychology of schizophrenia*. Hove: Lawrence Erlbaum.

Frith, C. (1994). Theory of mind in schizophrenia. In J. C. Cutting (Ed.), *The neuropsychology of schizophrenia* (pp. 147–161). Hillsdale, NJ: Lawrence Erlbaum.

Frith, C. (2005). The self in action: Lessons from delusions of control. *Consciousness and Cognition, 14*, 752–770.

Frith, C. and Frith, U. (1999). Interacting minds: A biological basis. *Science, 286*, 1692–1695.

Gabbard, G. O. (1994). Mind and brain in psychiatric treatment. *Bulletin of the Menninger Clinic, 58*, 427–446.

Gabbard, G. O., Gunderson, J. G., and Fonagy, P. (2002). The place of psychoanalytic treatments within psychiatry. *Archives of General Psychiatry, 59*, 505–510.

Gottdiener, W. H. and Haslam, N. (2003). A critique of the methods and conclusions in the patient outcome research team (PORT) report on psychological treatments for schizophrenia. *Journal of the American Academy of Psychoanalysis and Dynamic Psychiatry, 31*, 191–208.

Green, A. (1998). The primordial mind and the work of the negative. *International Journal of Psychoanalysis, 79*, 649–665.

Greig, T. C., Bryson, G. J., and Bell, M. D. (2004). Theory of mind performance in schizophrenia: Diagnostic, symptom, and neuropsychological correlates. *Journal of Nervous and Mental Disorders, 192*, 12–18.

Hans, S. L., Auerbach, J. G., Asarnow, J. R., Styr, B., and Marcus, J. (2000). Social adjustment of adolescents at risk for schizophrenia: The Jerusalem infant development study. *Journal of the American Academy of Child and Adolescent Psychiatry, 39*, 1406–1414.

Harding, C. M., Brooks, G. W., Asolaga, T. S., and Breier, A. (1987). The Vermont longitudinal study of persons with severe mental illness. *American Journal of Psychiatry, 144*, 718–726.

Harrington, L., Siegert, R. J., and McClure, J. (2005). Theory of mind in schizophrenia: A critical review. *Cognitive Neuropsychiatry, 10*, 249–286.

Jackson, H. J., McGorry, P., Edwards, J., and Hulbert, C. (1996). Cognitively-oriented psychotherapy for early psychosis. In P. Cotton and H. J. Jackson (Eds.), *Early intervention and prevention in mental health* (pp. 131–154). Melbourne: Australian Psychological Society (an APS Imprint Book).

Jackson, H., McGorry, P., Edwards, J., Hulbert, C., Henry, L., Harrigan, S., et al. (2005). A controlled trial of cognitively oriented psychotherapy for early psychosis (COPE) with four-year follow-up readmission data. *Psychological Medicine, 35*, 1295–1306.

Janssen, I., Krabbendam, L., Jolles, J., and van Os, J. (2003). Alterations in theory of mind in patients with schizophrenia and non-psychotic relatives. *Acta Psychiatrica Scandinavica, 108*, 110–117.

Kandel, E. R. (1998). A new intellectual framework for psychiatry. *American Journal of Psychiatry, 155*, 457–469.

Kandel, E. R. (1999). Biology and the future of psychoanalysis: A new intellectual framework for psychiatry revisited. *American Journal of Psychiatry, 156*, 505–524.

Lacan, J. (2006 [1959]). On a question prior to any possible treatment of psychosis. In *Ecrits* (pp. 445–488). New York: Norton.

Langdon, R. and Coltheart, M. (2000). The cognitive neuropsychology of delusions. *Mind and Language, 15*, 184–218.

Langdon, R., Coltheart, M., Ward, P. B., and Catts, S. V. (2002). Disturbed communication in schizophrenia: The role of poor pragmatics and poor mind-reading. *Psychological Medicine, 32*, 1273–1284.

Langdon, R., Coltheart, M., and Ward, P. B. (2006). Empathetic perspective-taking is impaired in schizophrenia: Evidence from a study of emotion attribution and theory of mind. *Cognitive Neuropsychiatry, 11*, 133–155.

McGorry, P. D. (2004). An overview of the background and scope for psychological interventions in early psychosis. In J. F. M. Gleeson and P. D. McGorry (Eds.), *Psychological interventions in early psychosis: A treatment handbook* (pp. 1–21). Chichester: Wiley.

McKay, R., Langdon, R., and Coltheart, M. (2005). 'Sleights of mind': Delusions, defences, and self-deception. *Cognitive Neuropsychiatry, 10*, 305–326.

Morrison, A. P., French, P., Walford, L., Lewis, S. W., Kilcommons, A., Green, J., et al. (2004). Cognitive therapy for the prevention of psychosis in people at ultra-high risk: Randomised controlled trial. *British Journal of Psychiatry, 185*, 291–297.

Plomin, R. and Rutter, M. (1998). Child development, molecular genetics, and what to do with genes once they are found. *Child Development, 69*, 1223–1242.

Povinelli, D. J. and Vonk, J. (2003). Chimpanzee minds: Suspiciously human. *Trends in Cognitive Science, 7*, 157–160.

Premack, D. and Woodruff, G. (1978). Does the chimpanzee have a theory of mind? *Behavioral and Brain Sciences, 5*, 515–526.

Russell, T. A., Rubia, K., Bullmore, E. T., Soni, W., Suckling, J., Brammer, M. J., et al. (2000). Exploring the social brain in schizophrenia: Left prefrontal underactivation during mental state attribution. *American Journal of Psychiatry, 157*, 2040–2042.

Rutter, M. (2000). Psychosocial influences: Critiques, findings, and research needs. *Developmental Psychopathology*, *12*, 375–405.

Rutter, M. (2005). How the environment affects mental health. *British Journal of Psychiatry*, *186*, 4–6.

Turkington, D. and McKenna, P. (2003). Is cognitive-behavioural therapy a worthwhile treatment for psychosis? *British Journal of Psychiatry*, *182*, 477–479.

Westen, D. (1998). The scientific legacy of Sigmund Freud: Toward a psychodynamically informed psychological science. *Psychological Bulletin*, *124*, 333–371.

Winnicott, D. W. (1975 [1954]). Metapsychological and clinical aspects of regression within the psycho-analytical set-up. In *Through paediatrics to psychoanalysis* (pp. 278–294). London: Karnac.

Integration of psychotherapy: an international perspective

Introduction to Section 2

Eóin Killackey

One of the common and valid complaints about most of the literature concerning interventions for schizophrenia is that it is produced by those working in developed western settings. This is supported by the fact that 80 per cent of the 5000 randomized controlled trials in the database of the Cochrane Schizophrenia Group are from western countries (Gaebel and Weinman, 2006). Usually, where this information is about diagnosis or techniques in treatment there may be a token sentence such as 'local cultural practices may need to be taken into account', or 'presentation may vary dependent on culture'.

In this section of the book we have attempted to address this imbalance which typically pervades the literature. Four chapters are included here which focus upon different aspects of treatment for schizophrenia, psychoses, or for those at risk of these illnesses.

In Chapter 5, Tor K. Larsen describes Norwegian efforts to integrate biological and psychological interventions and outlines how this goal has been translated into treatment guidelines in Norway and specific programmes.

In Chapter 6, Traceyanne Herewini writes about the way in which Maaori concepts are joined by western concepts of treatment in New Zealand. While many formerly colonized countries make statements about respecting indigenous cultures, New Zealand does this more so than many others. This chapter is not only a fascinating insight into the complexities of this, but also a spur to action for how other countries may start to think about addressing the mental health needs of their indigenous peoples.

In Chapter 7, Lisa J. Phillips and colleagues survey the way in which three centres around the world are approaching psychological interventions for those at risk of developing psychosis. Studies from this area show that psychological interventions have an important role in this developing area (Killackey and Yung, 2007).

Finally, in Chapter 8, Ishita Sanyal writes about the challenges facing those in India who are attempting to integrate psychosocial recovery into the approaches of treatment for mental illness. This is interesting because India is a culture which is rapidly changing due to economic development. This chapter explains that much of this development has bypassed mental health treatment, but centres like Turning Point are finding ways to utilize technology to assist recovery.

In all the different parts of the world there are common and unique challenges to the implementation and integration of treatments for schizophrenia. For example we had also hoped to include a chapter from Cambodia in this section, describing the challenges of reconstructing a mental health system from nothing, but were unable to find someone with the time to write it. We were informed that there were only twelve psychiatrists in Cambodia. It is to be hoped that the importance of inclusion in order to develop a real picture of treating psychotic illnesses in different parts of the world is highlighted by this section.

References

Gaebel, W. and Weinman, S. (2006). Call for a European guidelines institute: Author's reply. *British Journal of Psychiatry*, *188*, 193.

Killackey, E. and Yung, A. R. (2007). Effectiveness of early intervention in psychosis. *Current Opinion in Psychiatry*, *20*, 121–125.

Chapter 5

Biological and psychological treatments for psychosis

An overdue alliance?

Tor K. Larsen

Introduction

From a theoretical point of view biological, social and psychological treatment procedures ought to be integrated into the treatment of patients with first-episode psychosis. In twenty-first century clinical psychiatry, a biological bias seems to be the reality. In countries such as the United States, Denmark or Italy, for example, homelessness (especially in large cities) poses a significant problem in schizophrenia (Folsom et al., 2005). To a substantial degree, homeless people are a symbol of a country's lack of ability and willingness to provide proper treatment for mentally ill people. Some studies indicate that as many as 30 per cent have untreated psychotic disorders (Folsom and Jeste, 2002). Lack of rehabilitation resources and long-term psychosocial treatment is clearly a problem when too much focus is put on biological therapy. In Norway, the prevalence of homeless and untreated psychiatric patients is low. This is due to the combination of large resources and involuntary treatment being used in cases where the patients are continuously psychotic, and lack insight into their own illness (Norwegian Board of Health, 2006). Long-term rehabilitation is paid for by public funding. It is regarded as a basic human right to have housing, financial support and active treatment, even if you have a severe mental disorder with lack of insight and no understanding for the requirement of treatment.

The fact that we do not know the causes for psychosis (schizophrenia) and that the prognosis is very heterogeneous gives us strong arguments against all kinds of reductionism, be it either biological or psychosocial. Even with the use of new treatment methods such as second generation antipsychotic drugs or cognitive therapy, a substantial proportion of the patients remain psychotic when followed up (Larsen et al., 2006a; Marshall et al., 2005). Poor compliance with medication is a significant problem even in the controlled studies that compare modern drugs. In the Clinical Antipsychotic Trials of Intervention Effectiveness (CATIE) study as many as 74 per cent of patients with schizophrenia changed antipsychotics within 18 months (Lieberman et al., 2005).

Though Parkinson-like side effects are rare with the new types of antipsychotics, we now have to deal with both weight gain and metabolic disturbances. Since the mid 1990s, a large number of evidence-based guidelines have been made regarding the effective treatment of schizophrenia. In a review, Gaebel et al. (2005) identified 27 international guidelines from 21 different countries. They differed in methodological quality, and the authors pointed out lack of financial resources as being a major obstacle towards their use in clinical practice.

This chapter will start with a critical discussion of the PORT study (Lehman and Steinwachs, 1998; Lehman et al., 2004). This is one of the most commonly cited guidelines for the treatment of schizophrenia. It defines a standard for evidence-based medicine and is frequently referred to in clinical practice. It has also been in focus in the special issue of the *Journal of American Academy of Psychoanalysis and Dynamic Psychiatry* in which 'the ISPS task force on psychological treatment of schizophrenia' presented its work in 2003 (Silver and Larsen, 2003). The next step will be to present the treatment model that was established as a part of the early Treatment and Intervention in PSychosis (TIPS) programme in Norway and Denmark, and focus on the integration of biological and psychological treatment much valued in the Scandinavian countries. The basis for treatment of schizophrenia solely in Norway, specifically in relation to political and organizational focus will also be discussed.

Norway is a wealthy country with relatively few inhabitants (approximately 5 million). It has both the economic ability and political will to offer all people presenting with first-episode psychosis biological, psychological and social treatment. The official Norwegian guidelines for the treatment of schizophrenia lay out the framework for clinical practice. Here, psychological therapy is described as one possible treatment. In addition, the Norwegian health authorities have recently given SEPREP (Centre for Psychotherapy and Psychosocial Rehabilitation of Psychoses) the responsibility for educating a large number of clinicians in the treatment of schizophrenia, which will be presented in detail here. Some prototypic case histories which exemplify the use of integrated treatment in Norway will be discussed.

The PORT study

The Patients Outcome Research Team (PORT) was initiated by the Department of Health and Human Services in the United States. The PORT programme compiles the scientific literature on the efficacy of treatments for various medical conditions such as heart disease, diabetes, cataracts, arthritis and asthma (Lehman and Steinwachs, 2003). In 1992 the Schizophrenia PORT programme received funding, and in 1998, Anthony Lehman together with his colleagues published the first report; updated recommendations were published in 2004 (Lehman and Steinwachs, 1998; Lehman et al., 2004).

These recommendations describe in detail how antipsychotics should be used including dosages, type, duration and side effects. Furthermore, PORT gives recommendations regarding psychotherapy and rehabilitation, and makes some remarks regarding the aetiology of schizophrenia. It must be stated however that these recommendations can hardly be read as being solely supported by evidence-based research. In recommendation 26, PORT states that no family therapy should be used that is 'based on the premise that family dysfunction is the aetiology of the patient's schizophrenic disorder' (Lehman et al., 2004, p. 8). At the same time, though, PORT states clearly that the aetiology of schizophrenia is still unknown. So how is it possible to categorically exclude one aetiological path – for example a traumatic childhood? One explanation is that PORT wishes to give a warning against approaches that assume that the family environment is causing schizophrenia. Historically this seems to make sense. But a recommendation such as this probably implies a biological bias that cannot be justified by referring to evidence-based research alone. In some cases massive trauma within the family, such as incest and other types of abuse, cannot be ruled out as the major cause of psychosis (Bak et al., 2005).

Some research clearly supports the notion that the family environment plays an important role in protecting vulnerable children from developing schizophrenia. Conversely, a malfunctioning family seems to pose a risk for the development of psychosis (Tienari and Wynne, 1994). Since we clearly do not know the causes of schizophrenia, it is not possible to rule out any aetiological causes. The ISPS task force emphasized that the clinician must retain an open mind regarding aetiology and 'stay in the clinical position of not knowing to ensure the most constructive ethical treatments for our patients' (Larsen et al., 2003, p. 212). This is not easy. In everyday life there will be pressure from families, patients, pharmaceutical companies and colleagues to choose a side: do you believe in biological or social causes? As mentioned above, we do not know the causes of schizophrenia, as professionals we need to accept that, and act accordingly.

PORT presented two recommendations related to psychological treatments: recommendations 22 and 23. Recommendation 23 is in line with the idea of need-adapted treatment and does not raise much controversy. It reads as follows:

Recommendation 23
Individual and group therapies employing well-specified combinations of support, education, and behavioral and cognitive skills training approaches designed to address the specific deficits of persons with schizophrenia should be offered over time to improve functioning and enhance other targeted problems, such as medication noncompliance.

Recommendation 22, however, was more problematic;

Recommendation 22
Individual and group psychotherapies adhering to a psychodynamic model (defined as therapies that use interpretation of unconscious material and focus on transference and regression) should not be used in the treatment of persons with schizophrenia.

For this recommendation PORT gave the following rationale:

> The scientific data on this issue is quite limited. However, there is no evidence in support of the superiority of psychoanalytic therapy over other forms of therapy, and there is a consensus that psychotherapy that promotes regression and psychotic transference can be harmful to persons with schizophrenia. This risk, combined with the high cost and lack of evidence of any benefit, argues strongly against the use of psychoanalytic therapy, even in combination with effective pharmacotherapy.
>
> (Lehman and Steinwachs, 1998, pp. 7–8)

This recommendation was based upon evidence at level C; that is to say based primarily on expert opinion with minimal research-based evidence, but significant clinical experience. Obviously the selection of 'experts' is crucial for these kinds of recommendations. It was remarkable that recommendation 22 was negatively formulated: 'you should not'. Remarkable, since many clinicians would say that in some cases, a more psychodynamic focus might be adequate, and necessary. The tradition of need-adapted treatment (e.g., as developed in Finland by Yrjø Alanen, 1997) would keep the possibility for insight-oriented explorative psychotherapy open, at least for some unique patients. One patient we treated in the TIPS study experienced no effect from antipsychotic medication, and stayed psychotic over a long period of time. She possessed good insight, and had experienced severe sexual trauma in her childhood. She responded to insight-oriented psychotherapy with sessions twice a week following rules that were tailored for use in psychotherapeutic settings. Free associations were used, she received little 'advice' from the psychotherapists, and the focus was on conflict instead of deficit processes. The PORT recommendation 22, though, seemed to rule out such therapy, and we believe that this probably expresses a biological bias from the authors of the recommendations. Recommendation 22 was removed from the updated version of the guidelines, but the commentary attached to the new guidelines suggested that the underlying assumptions remained.

The TIPS study

The early Treatment and Intervention in PSychosis is a study in the early detection of psychosis. We have succeeded in reducing the duration of untreated psychosis (DUP) to 4.5 weeks in the early detection sector (Melle et al., 2004). TIPS is a quasi-experimental study with early detection in one sector (in Rogaland County, Norway) and detection as usual in two control sites (Ullevaal sector, Oslo, Norway and Roskilde, Denmark). From 1997 to 2000, 301 patients between the ages of 15 and 65 were included in the study. In order to examine the effect of the reduction of DUP on the outcome, we developed identical treatment-modules for all sectors. The modules consisted of medication that was based on a specific algorithm, and began with the newest antipsychotics. For non-responders to either the new or the traditional antipsychotics, treatment with clozapine is recommended. All families were offered participation in multi-family groups (McFarlane et al., 2003). These groups consisted of four or five families and patients, which met twice a month over a period of two years. Psychiatric nurses and social workers were educated according to McFarlane's manual. The multi-family group's focus on psychoeducation regards the families as a support for the patients, and uses problem-solving discussions in the sessions. In accordance with the TIPS protocol, supportive psychotherapy is offered to all patients. The duration should be at least two years for schizophrenia, and at least two sessions per week should be scheduled. No description of the specific content of the psychotherapy is given; it should, however, be both need-adapted and related to each case's motivation and abilities.

At baseline level we saw a clear correlation between early detection and fewer symptoms (Melle et al., 2004), and less suicidal ideation (Melle et al., 2006). The one year follow-up revealed that the patients who were detected early had a better outcome in relation to negative symptoms (Larsen et al., 2006a). Regarding utilization of the treatment package that was offered during the first year, we found that approximately 50 per cent of the families participated in the multi-family groups, the average duration of psychotherapy was 44 weeks, with the average duration of taking antipsychotics being 39.9 weeks.

Treatment of schizophrenia in Norway

Norwegian guidelines for the treatment of schizophrenia

In 2000, the Norwegian Board of Health published *Schizophrenia: Clinical guidelines for assessment and treatment* in collaboration with the Norwegian Psychiatric Association (Norwegian Board of Health, 2000). Similar to the PORT recommendations, the Norwegian guidelines are a mixture of evidence-based knowledge and expert opinion. In the introduction the editor writes that the content represents a 'Norwegian majority-consensus within the field of psychiatry'. The guidelines emphasize the importance of early detection and contact with the families, i.e., the family should be contacted by phone within 24 hours after hospitalization, and one-to-one contact should be established within three days. The guidelines underline the fact that antipsychotic medication is the most effective treatment for schizophrenia, but at the same time make it clear that 20–40 per cent can be expected to either have a moderate or no positive response to treatment. It is recommended that one should try to have one to two weeks with no medication when commencing treatment, in order to make early assessment more valid and thorough. It is emphasized that systematic assessment is important both initially and during follow-up.

The guidelines also state that for 'people with schizophrenia a good relationship with a primary therapist is often required for a long period of time'. 'It is important that a stable relationship with a therapist is established and that confidence is developed through a personal commitment from the side of the therapist'. Furthermore 'biological, psychological and social factors should be integrated in the treatment programme'. Regarding individual psychotherapeutic interventions, although they mention that only few systematic studies have been carried out, they do refer to two approaches: Hogarty's Personal Therapy (PT) (Hogarty et al., 1997) and Alanen's need-adapted model (Alanen, 1997). PT is said to 'focus on better adaptation and reduction of relapses during the first two years of illness'. Alanen's model is described as consisting of a combination of individual psychotherapy, family work and antipsychotic medication.

The Norwegian guidelines have been cited both by family support groups and mental health workers in discussions regarding financial issues and the patient's rights. It seems that the guidelines support individual psychotherapy for schizophrenia in cases where antipsychotic medication is either ineffective, or only partially effective. These signals from the Norwegian Board of Health are important because it is expensive to offer all first-episode schizophrenia cases a need-adapted treatment that includes psychotherapy, if appropriate. In the TIPS study we found that 87 per cent received more than 26 weeks of psychotherapy during the initial follow-up phase, and 59 per cent participated for 52 weeks. These figures clearly show that when first-episode psychosis patients are offered need-adapted psychotherapy they will, to a large degree, participate.

SEPREP

SEPREP (Centre for Psychotherapy and Psychosocial Rehabilitation of Psychoses: SEPREP, 2005) is one of the organizations that ensured the quality of the Norwegian schizophrenia guidelines that focus on psychotherapeutic aspects. SEPREP is responsible for educating psychiatric health personnel in the so-called 'National Strategy for Quality Improvement in Health and Social Services' organized by the Norwegian National Directorate for Health and Social Affairs. The initiative began in 1999 and is to continue until 2008. The education programme consists of 80 hours of theoretical lectures, 80 hours of group supervision, and 40 hours of group literature studies. It is a two-year education with 25 per cent of the programme relating to theoretical discussions regarding psychosis (criteria for diagnosis etc.), 50 per cent to the integrated treatment and 25 per cent to network-building. A total of 3201 health professionals have either completed, or are still participating (SEPREP, 2005). This is a huge task in a country such as Norway that has just 5 million inhabitants. A majority of the participants are nurses or psychiatric nurses, some are social workers, and both psychologists and psychiatrists are represented. The programme is primarily aimed at training case managers as most of the patients will also have a general practitioner (GP), psychiatrist or psychologist as their main therapist.

Individual Plan (IP)

In 2002, the National Directorate for Health and Social Affairs in Norway introduced the so-called Individual Plan (IP) for the treatment and rehabilitation of patients who are in need of 'long-lasting and co-ordinated health or social services'. In January 2005, the IP was legislated as being a right for all patients. The IP should be developed in cooperation with the patient and should contain the following elements: an assessment of the need for psychiatric health care, a description of the treatment's goal, and a list of which elements of psychiatric care that are appropriate. The IP should also describe how the goals can be achieved and how collaboration should be carried out with the various agencies in the health care system. A very important side of the IP is that the patient possesses this right, and the development of an IP is something that they can (and should) both demand and require that is carried out. If the different agencies such as the County Office for Housing or Social Services do not cooperate in accordance with the IP, the County Board of Health will enforce their compliance.

Case examples

These cases are drawn from our experiences either with first-episode psychosis or hypopsychosis in the TIPS study, or from the early detection of hypopsychosis project in Rogaland.[1] All descriptions are anonymous; we have changed the socio-demographics details in order to ensure that the patients are not identified. The cases are, however, prototypic, and have all been presented and discussed in the early detection teams related to these projects during the spring of 2006.

Case study: good outcome despite a long DUP

Per was 25 years of age and had been going to the outpatient clinic for approximately one and a half years when the Detection Team (DT) first saw him. Per had been hearing voices for almost one year, but this had not been explored in the supportive psychotherapy that he received from the outpatient clinic. In the therapy, he had complained about being socially isolated. He was afraid of developing a serious mental disorder, since his sister suffered from chronic schizophrenia. The voices were hostile and would not allow him to tell anyone about them. He had suffered severe trauma in his childhood, and the therapist (a psychiatric nurse) at the outpatient clinic had focused on this. The therapist had assumed that the patient suffered mainly from either a post-traumatic stress disorder, or from a dissociative disorder of some kind. The therapist contacted the DT because they felt that the patient acted strangely and could possibly be psychotic. He fulfilled the criteria for schizoaffective disorder and commenced treatment with antipsychotic medication. To our surprise he responded extremely well to this treatment, the voices disappeared, and his tendency to social isolation vanished. When we interviewed him at a five-year follow up in the TIPS study, he was still doing well, had a job, and a new relationship with a woman. He had continued with the antipsychotic medication and said that the voices returned only when he tried to reduce the dose.

Comment

We expected Per to be a non or slow-responder to treatment; he had both a long duration of untreated psychosis (DUP) and severe trauma in his history. On the other hand, he probably had both a genetic predisposition and a good premorbid functioning. From this case we learned that it is extremely important to use systematic assessment tools, as patients with hostile voices might never talk openly about hallucination simply because they are not permitted to. Even though patients with severe trauma often need and will benefit from psychotherapy, we should neither forget that trauma does not prevent psychosis, nor that antipsychotic medication is the most effective treatment. Therefore, all patients with psychosis must be offered this.

Case study: drug abuse and schizophrenia

Kari was 18 years old and suffered from both severe drug abuse and schizophrenia when we saw her initially. She had been discharged from the psychiatric ward several times during the last two years because of her drug abuse, which was mainly cannabis and ecstasy. She came from a very supportive family who were tired of having to take care of her every time she was discharged from the hospital. A thorough assessment with the TIPS model (Positive and Negative Syndrome Scale (PANSS) and Structured Clinical Interview for DSM Disorders (SCID)) made it clear that she had continuous psychotic experiences that were not related to her intake of drugs. When she took drugs (especially psychostimulants such as ecstasy or amphetamines), she developed a more anxiety ridden state. In the case notes we discovered considerable confusion regarding her diagnosis. Several psychiatrists had concluded that she suffered 'only' from drug abuse and discharged her as a consequence of her drug taking. The family were exhausted because they saw that she was clearly psychotic when she came home, and they were not too pleased with the treatment. Our first intervention was to have a session with the patient, the family and the main therapist in which we both discussed the diagnosis (drug abuse and schizophrenia) and formulated an Individual Plan (IP) as prescribed by the National Directorate for Health and Social Affairs (see discussion above). In the following five years we had two or three such meetings annually. We made it clear that we had no doubt that Kari suffered from a severe psychosis (schizophrenia) and that it was the responsibility of the psychiatric services to offer treatment, even if she did abuse drugs. Kari did not want to talk much about the psychotic symptoms and she denied that she was ill. However, she understood that she could not manage to survive without some support. She realized that she had changed from being socially active and participating in sports, to having no hobbies and few friends. She also managed to express her basic feeling related to the psychotic symptoms as being anxiety. Regarding the antipsychotic medication, she saw little meaning in taking it, but her behaviour was clearly less bizarre when she was on depot medication. She participated in social skills courses according to Lieberman's model and, surprisingly, described hearing more hostile voices as an early warning sign of a relapse of the psychosis. At the same time she denied that she was having any hallucinations. The family participated in multi-family groups, which focused on psychoeducation and problem solving. Meetings were held twice a week for two years and the five families still meet regularly. The parents expressed gratitude for finally being taken seriously and regarded as a support, rather than a burden. At the five-year follow-up the patient was no longer actively psychotic, but she suffered from prominent negative symptoms, especially social inactivity. She participated in some rehabilitation services and had just moved to a group of apartments staffed by psychiatric nurses during the day. She still abused drugs, but much more seldom and in lower doses.

Comment

It is quite common that patients with schizophrenia also suffer from drug abuse. In an article from the TIPS group we found that in a first-episode sample of psychosis, 23 per cent abused drugs and 16 per cent alcohol (Larsen et al., 2006b). It is difficult to treat these patients, and a systematic assessment focusing on the relationship between periods with psychosis and drug abuse is important. Negative countertransference processes often bring colleagues into positions in which these patients are rejected and even punished. Treatment helps, but often in order to stabilize rather than to heal.

Case study: hypopsychosis?

Nina was referred to the early Treatment of PrePsychosis (TOPP) clinic by her mother. Her mother had read one of the advertisements regarding the TIPS study in which it is stated that 'it is important to seek help as early as possible' (see Figure 5.1).

When her mother called the Detection Team, she said that she felt it was provocative that we 'advertised for patients in the local press, when everybody knew that there are long waiting lists for psychiatric treatment.' She was very pleased when we could offer a session for assessment on the same day. With Nina we soon carried out a Structured Interview for Prodomal Symptoms (SIPS) interview (Miller et al., 2003), because it was clear from the PANSS (Positive and Negative Syndrome Scale ratings: Kay et al., 1987) that she did not fulfil the criteria for psychosis. In the SIPS interview she told us that she at times experienced 'almost hearing

Figure 5.1 Advertisement from the TIPS study.
It reads: 'Are you hearing voices? . . . To feel controlled by voices from the outside can often be a sign of severe psychiatric illness and should be treated as soon as possible. TIPS offer advice and help for people who have psychiatric problems for the first time, or feel that psychiatric symptoms already present, have been worsening.'

voices'. She said that she had heard short comments three to four times a week during the last month, and believed them momentarily to be a voice. When she considered the matter, she believed that her 'mind was playing tricks on her'. She emphasized that she never acted upon what the voices said or believed the voices were real. She also told us that she had developed a recent interest in religious ideas, and this was something that she had never had before. She went on to express having a strange feeling of not being herself any more, but could neither describe this in more detail, nor give any examples that allowed us to understand her experience. In addition, she said that she felt disconnected from people, and did not socialize as much as she used to. She was afraid of 'turning crazy' since her grandfather had been ill with schizophrenia and had been hospitalized for many years. Nina fulfilled the criteria for 'attenuated positive symptoms' according to the SIPS, which we term hypopsychosis (Larsen, 2004). She was offered weekly supportive psychotherapy, which she participated in for 18 months. The focus of the therapy was to discuss and offer normal explanations for her strange experiences. She needed to conceptualize her symptoms within a non-psychiatric framework. After some months the pseudo voices disappeared and she started to be more socially active. Nina also stated that she started to feel more 'like her old self'. During the treatment she did not receive any medication and developed a close relationship with her therapist, who was a psychologist with special experience in work with hypopsychotic patients. At two years follow-up she was managing well and did not need further psychotherapy. She was still interested in religion, but in a more positive manner. She had more friends, but still felt a little 'disconnected' socially. The psychologist assumed that there was still a risk that she would develop psychosis and offered more psychotherapy, but Nina declined. We are going to complete a five-year follow-up, and hope that she will remain well and contact us if she develops new symptoms that border on psychosis.

Comment

Primary prevention of psychosis is a controversial task. With new assessment methods it is probably possible to identify people who are at high risk of conversion to psychosis. It is important to justify treatment that is based on the symptoms that the patients report, rather than the possibility of the development of psychosis. No treatment should be given simply because patients have relatives who are worried, and no antipsychotic medication should be used as routine treatment. In some cases psychosis might be prevented, but care is needed on conceptual, psychotherapeutical and ethical levels.

Conclusions and future directions

First-episode psychosis is a potentially severe experience for people who may develop it. Treatment is, however, more effective than lay people tend to believe. In the early phases of treatment it is important to convey hope. Treatment can be effective, but obtaining the patient's compliance and cooperation is a sizeable problem. Globally, there is an unacceptably high percentage of patients who do not receive the therapy that we know is effective. In this chapter we have discussed and presented the treatment algorithm followed in the TIPS project in Norway and Denmark, and we have described in detail how the treatment is organized in Norway. Our experiences clearly show us that biological, psychological and rehabilitation treatment modules can and must be combined. If patients are offered a combination of individual psychotherapy, family work and antipsychotic medication they will, to a large degree, accept the treatment. It ought to be the right of every patient in the world who has a first-episode psychosis to be guaranteed a similar package, just as every patient who suffers a cardiac arrest has the right to receive acute treatment. In psychiatry we are far away from that, but we can start by integrating the different perspectives in the treatment of psychosis, and then hope that our attitude will inspire other treatment services.

Note

1 Hypopsychosis equals attenuated positive symptoms according to SIPS criteria. It is a concept similar to the 'at risk mental state' developed in the EPPIC model. See Chapter 7 for more details.

References

Alanen, Y. O. (1997). Vulnerability to schizophrenia and psychotherapeutic treatment of schizophrenic patients: Towards an integrated view. *Psychiatry*, *60*, 142–157.

Bak, M., Krabbendam, L., Janssen, I., de Graaf, R., Vollebergh, W., and van, O. J. (2005). Early trauma may increase the risk for psychotic experiences by impacting on emotional response and perception of control. *Acta Psychiatrica Scandinavica*, *112*, 360–366.

Folsom, D. and Jeste, D. V. (2002). Schizophrenia in homeless persons: A systematic review of the literature. *Acta Psychiatrica Scandinavica*, *105*, 404–413.

Folsom, D. P., Hawthorne, W., Lindamer, L., Gilmer, T., Bailey, A., Golshan, S., et al. (2005). Prevalence and risk factors for homelessness and utilization of mental health services among 10,340 patients with serious mental illness in a large public mental health system. *American Journal of Psychiatry*, *162*, 370–376.

Gaebel, W., Weinmann, S., Sartorius, N., Rutz, W., and McIntyre, J. S. (2005). Schizophrenia practice guidelines: International survey and comparison. *British Journal of Psychiatry*, *187*, 248–255.

Hogarty, G. E., Kornblith, S. J., Greenwald, D., DiBarry, A. L., Cooley, S., Ulrich,

R. F., et al. (1997). Three-year trials of personal therapy among schizophrenic patients living with or independent of family. I: Description of study and effects on relapse rates. *American Journal of Psychiatry, 154,* 1504–1513.

Kay, S. R., Fiszbein, A., and Opler, L. A. (1987). The Positive and Negative Syndrome Scale (PANSS) for schizophrenia. *Schizophrenia Bulletin, 13,* 261–276.

Larsen, T. K. (2004). The use of concepts in relation to early intervention in psychosis: A critical discussion. In C. McDonald, K. Schulze, R. Murray, and P. Wright (Eds.), *Schizophrenia: Challenging the orthodox* (pp. 91–98). London: Taylor and Francis.

Larsen, T. K., Bechdolf, A., and Birchwood, M. (2003). The concept of schizophrenia and phase-specific treatment: Cognitive-behavioral treatment in pre-psychosis and in nonresponders. *Journal of the American Academy of Psychoanalysis and Dynamic Psychiatry, 31,* 209–228.

Larsen, T. K., Melle, I., Auestad, B., Friis, S., Haahr, U., Johannessen, J. O., et al. (2006a). Early detection of first-episode psychosis: The effect on 1-year outcome. *Schizophrenia Bulletin, 32,* 758–764.

Larsen, T. K., Melle, I., Austad, B., Friis, S., Haahr, U., Johannessen, J. O., et al. (2006b). Substance abuse in first-episode non-affective psychosis. *Schizophrenia Research, 88,* 55–62.

Lehman, A. F. and Steinwachs, D. M. (1998). Translating research into practice: The Schizophrenia Patient Outcomes Research Team (PORT) treatment recommendations. *Schizophrenia Bulletin, 24,* 1–10.

Lehman, A. F. and Steinwachs, D. M. (2003). Evidence-based psychosocial treatment practices in schizophrenia: Lessons from the patient outcomes research team (PORT) project. *Journal of the American Academy of Psychoanalysis and Dynamic Psychiatry, 31,* 141–154.

Lehman, A. F., Kreyenbuhl, J., Buchanan, R. W., Dickerson, F. B., Dixon, L. B., Goldberg, R., et al. (2004). The Schizophrenia Patient Outcomes Research Team (PORT): Updated treatment recommendations 2003. *Schizophrenia Bulletin, 30,* 193–217.

Lieberman, J. A., Stroup, T. S., Mcevoy, J. P., Swartz, M. S., Rosenheck, R. A., Perkins, D. O., et al. (2005). Effectiveness of antipsychotic drugs in patients with chronic schizophrenia. *New England Journal of Medicine, 353,* 1209–1223.

McFarlane, W. R., Dixon, L., Lukens, E., and Lucksted, A. (2003). Family psychoeducation and schizophrenia: A review of the literature. *Journal of Marital and Family Therapy, 29,* 223–245.

Marshall, M., Lewis, S., Lockwood, A., Drake, R., Jones, P., and Croudace, T. (2005). Association between duration of untreated psychosis and outcome in cohorts of first-episode patients: A systematic review. *Archives of General Psychiatry, 62,* 975–983.

Melle, I., Johannesen, J. O., Friis, S., Haahr, U., Joa, I., Simonsen, E., et al. (2006). Early detection of the first episode of schizophrenia and suicidal behavior. *American Journal of Psychiatry, 163,* 800–804.

Melle, I., Larsen, T. K., Haahr, U., Friis, S., Johannessen, J. O., Opjordsmoen, S., et al. (2004). Reducing the duration of untreated first-episode psychosis: Effects on clinical presentation. *Archives of General Psychiatry, 61,* 143–150.

Miller, T. J., McGlashan, T. H., Rosen, J. L., Cadenhead, K., Cannon, T., Ventura, J., et al. (2003). Prodromal assessment with the structured interview for prodromal syndromes and the scale of prodromal symptoms: predictive validity, interrater reliability, and training to reliability. *Schizophrenia Bulletin, 29,* 703–715.

Norwegian Board of Health (2000) *Schizophrenia: Clinical guidelines for assessment and treatment.* Oslo: Norwegian Board of Health and Norwegian Psychiatric Association. Available at http://sintef.no/

Norwegian Board of Health (2006). *Use of involuntary treatment in psychiatric health care* (Norwegian). Oslo: Statens helsetilsyn (Norwegian Board of Health). Available at http://sintef.no/

SEPREP (2005). *Yearly report.* Available at http://www.seprep.no/

Silver, A. L. and Larsen, T. K. (2003). FRONTLINE: The schizophrenic person and the benefits of the psychotherapies – seeking a PORT in the storm. *Journal of the American Academy of Psychoanalysis and Dynamic Psychiatry, 31,* 1–10.

Tienari, P. J. and Wynne, L. C. (1994). Adoption studies of schizophrenia. *Annals of Medicine, 26,* 233–237.

Chapter 6

New Zealand Maaori conceptual models utilized within early intervention services

Traceyanne Herewini

Ti hei Mauri Ora,
Behold I sneeze the breath of life,
Whakamoemiti, whakawhetai ki a Io Matua Kore te kaihanga o ngaa mea katoa.
Prayers and thanksgiving to Io Matua Kore the creator of all things.
Ngaa poroporaki ki te hunga kua wehea haere ra.
We pay respects and homage to the deceased, farewell.
Apiti hono tatai hono raatou ki a raatou e Apiti hono
Let they be united in the spiritual world
tatai hono taatou te hunga ora
Therefore let us the descendants greet and acknowledge
Kia ora taatou katoa
Each other in unity.

Whakatauaki
Proverb
Hutia i te rito o te harakeke, kei hia te komako e ko
If you cut the heart of the flax bush, from where the bell bird sings
Ki mai ki ahau e aha te mea nui o teenei aao
If you ask me what is the greatest thing of this world
Maaku e ki atu – He tangata, he tangata, he tangata.
I reply it is people, it is people, it is people.

A proverb is a pithy, traditional message that provides an image (Collins, 1991). Working with Maaori (indigenous people of New Zealand) is often like taking the scenic route (Barlow, 1991; Ryan, 1999). The journey of healing and recovery can be challenging, interesting and often take longer to arrive at the destination. However, the most important thing is people, in this case the clients we serve.

Pepeha
My cultural identity
Ko Ohautieke, Rangitumau ngaa maaunga
Ohautieke and Rangitumau are my mountains
Ko Towai me Ruamahanga ngaa awa
Towai and Ruamahanga are my rivers
Ko Karangahape me Ngaa tau e waru ngaa marae
Karangahape and Ngaa tau e waru are my meeting place
Ko Kaitangata me Ngaati Hamua ngaa hapu
Kaitangata and Ngaati Hamua are my subtribes
Ko Ngaati Kahu ki Whangaroa, Rangitane me Ngaati Kahungunu ngaa iwi
Ngaati Kahu ki Whangaroa, Rangitane and Ngaati Kahungunu are
my tribes
Ko Mataatua, Ngatokimatawharoa, Kurahaupo, Takitimu ngaa waka
Mataatua, Ngatokimatawharoa, Kurahaupo and Takitimu are my
canoes
Ko Traceyanne Herewini ahau.
I am Traceyanne Herewini.

Background

As a Maaori person of Aotearoa (New Zealand) it is appropriate to acknowledge the Creator, the deceased and the living and then introduce myself as a form of establishing, extending a relationship and connectedness with you, the reader. I acknowledge and identify proudly with my diverse cultural heritage of Maaori, English, Irish, Scottish and Scandinavian. In addition my training as a primary teacher, previous work as a Maaori clinician and currently as a cultural worker allows me to stand proudly and competently in both the Maaori and psychiatry worlds in Aotearoa (New Zealand). These factors allow me to function as a knowledge holder who has learnt from respected knowledge holders, while I continue to add to my worthiness through the pursuit of qualifications. I am an example that it is acceptable to maintain healthy tensions around different bodies of knowledge, be it clinical, cultural or both. It has been a challenging process to write for myself, my ancestors and my people. At times it has been a journey of responsibility, burden, shame, procrastination, tears, learning, love, laughter and achievement. I acknowledge all of these processes that have allowed this chapter to evolve, have a voice for this moment and time.

Introduction

This chapter aims to address the gap of information about psychotherapeutic and psychosocial treatments for schizophrenia and psychoses in Aotearoa (New Zealand). The intention of this chapter is, first, to provide information about the various models utilized in New Zealand. Second, and more importantly, to educate people outside of Aotearoa about indigenous Maaori approaches to behaviours and symptoms when they are integrated into care with and for Maaori. Third, six Maaori models of health will be discussed and illustrated through theory and case study. This chapter provides a snapshot of the work that I and other cultural workers do on a daily basis, when integrating cultural and psychological interventions into 'real' settings. Furthermore these shared experiences demonstrate integration of clinical and cultural perspectives or medical intervention and spiritual realignment that may or may not blend together. The intention of blending clinical and cultural perspectives are to gain best outcomes for *tangata whaiora* (people striving for wellness, clients or patients), their *whaanau* (family), *hapuu* (subtribe) and *iwi* (tribes). These relationships highlight the importance of individuation and community, moreover relationships are paramount. It is my hope that this chapter will provide the reader with a historical and practical context of New Zealand culture and encourage colleagues and students to learn, question, consider, reflect upon and creatively integrate psychotherapeutic thinking and practice with other cultures and paradigms that exist within their treatment settings.

History

New Zealand has a colourful and interesting history. This is illustrated through founding documents, policies and initiatives in health policies, service delivery and societal changes (see Table 6.1).

Making sense of my cultural heritage and the Treaty of Waitangi has been both painful and challenging. I have experienced racism, negativity and doubt arising from both European and Maaori biases. I see the Treaty from both perspectives and believe the Treaty is for all people. The Treaty remains relevant now and in the future. One of the significant themes in the Treaty is the protection of Maaori health while respecting Maaori cultural practices. When this theme is applied to mental illness, this has not always been the case as will be seen.

Health system history

Eighteenth century

The New Zealand health system is based upon the eighteenth-century English system. Institutions and asylums were a priority and reflected western ideals (Olssen and Stenson, 1989). Thus no consideration was given to Maaori ideals and health care at this time.

Table 6.1 Summary of history

1835	The 'Declaration of Independence' was the first written statement about Maaori before colonization (Way, 1996). Each *iwi* (tribe) was a separate state and would recognize their own and other *iwi* lores and laws (Way, 1996).
1840	The 'Treaty of Waitangi' countered the Declaration and removed the possibility of being a Maaori-led state (Durie, 1998; Orange, 1997). Two versions of the Treaty exist, one in Maaori and the other in English. Herein lies some tension with translation, intention of language and word meanings.

- The *Kawanatanga* (governorship, sovereignty) principle allows the British crown the right to govern and make laws.
- The *Rangatiratanga* (full chieftainship and self management) principle gives the right to organize as an *iwi*, control the resources of that *iwi* and autonomy.
- The *Oritetanga* (equality) principle states that all New Zealanders are equal before the law.
- The principle of cooperation means that Treaty partners are obliged to collaborate on major issues of common concern.
- The principle of redress mean the government is responsible for providing effective processes for the resolution of grievances.
- The fourth article refers to Maaori custom, beliefs, religious freedom, and faith and rituals being honoured (Henare, 1990; Palmer, 1992).
- Protection ensures the government is proactive in health promotion, Maaori enjoy at least the same level of health as non-Maaori while protecting Maaori cultural values and practices (Williams, 2002).
- Participation ensures Maaori involvement at all levels of sector planning, development and delivery of health and disability services relevant to Maaori (Williams, 2002).
- Partnership refers to the government working together with *whaanau, hapuu, iwi* and Maaori communities to develop strategies for Maaori health gain and appropriate health and disability services. This backdrop provides a platform of complexities when delivering health for all people in Aotearoa.

1907	The Tohunga Suppression Act saw Maaori practices outlawed and was aimed at replacing traditional healers with 'modern' medicine. This halted development and mechanisms within *wananga* (higher level learning centres). Although Maaori culture did not die, *tohunga* (experts) were not allowed to assemble, nor claim they possessed special powers, nor able to foretell future events. Strong leaders were quietened through this Act and their practices went underground (Durie, 2001; Te Pumanawa Hauora, 1996). This Act was repealed in 1962; however the negative and psychological impact had already been set. In the 1980s Maaori culture was not fashionable nor something to be proud of. Maaori have struggled and continued to evolve within the law and society of the times.

Nineteenth and twentieth centuries

Asylums, otherwise known as 'loony bins', were located on the outskirts of settlements. Many patients were considered incurable and needed life-time care. Changes to community care through deinstitutionalization and psychoactive drugs saw a new era develop between 1950 and 1990 (School of Maaori Studies, 2005). Rehabilitation and care outside institutions became a possibility.

Health reforms in 1970

Inefficient systems developed with poor lines of accountability. The public demanded access and a monopoly developed.

Between 1983 and 1993

Area Health Board model was implemented and public health services were fully government funded.

Reforms 1994–1997

The 'Quasi market' model was promoted, i.e., the purchaser/provider split. Health funded authorities were abolished and district health boards (DHBs) were established (School of Maaori Studies, 2005).

Strategies

Until 1994 there was no dedicated mental health strategy in Aotearoa. Since this time, some of the most pertinent documents for Maaori in Aotearoa include *Looking forward* by the Ministry of Health (MOH, 1994) and *Moving forward* strategy (MOH, 1997). These documents were very broad and the subsequent *Blueprint for mental health services* by the Mental Health Commission (MHC, 1998) was used to redress these shortfalls. Next saw the development of the *Kia tuu kia puawai* (Stand and blossom) strategy (Health Funding Authority, 1998). Significantly, the *Early intervention in psychosis: Guidance note* (MOH, 1999) was published in a collaboration with key professionals. This document is important for two reasons, first, for Maaori and Pacific Island people because it acknowledges their place in New Zealand society. Second, considerations for access and care in the delivery of services for Maaori and Pacifica people are also included. Later documents like *Te Puawaitanga* (Blossom) strategy (MOH, 2002a), and *Building on strengths* strategy (Williams, 2002) provided broad concepts and limited implementation. These shortfalls allowed *He korowai oranga* (Cloak of healing) strategy (MOH, 2002b) to be developed. Other important international documents and research from preliminary research conducted in Australia, Sweden and Birmingham (UK) that has been useful and provided a foundation for early intervention for psychosis in New Zealand Services (McGorry et al., 1996; Singh and Fisher, 2005) to develop and continue to evolve from.

Whilst these strategies have evolved in intention and theory, and have built on the strengths and weaknesses of the prior documents, there remains a shortfall in the consistent implementation and achievement of outcomes for Maaori. For these aspirations to be realized more funding, research, education and resources are required. The most relevant strategies that I use in my work are the *Blueprint for Mental Health Services*, the *Early intervention in psychosis: Guidance note*, *He korowai oranga* and research from Australia and Birmingham (UK).

The past

Timeline

1960s   Maaori care within *whaanau* (family) was strong. Urbanization impacted on one's cultural identity and connection to *hapuu* and *iwi*. Maaori did not access mental health services in large numbers.

1970–2000 Some benefit for Maaori health despite care coordination problems; access was difficult and confusing. Standards of care varied throughout Aotearoa (School of Maaori Studies, 2005).

Mid 1970s Maaori were lower users than non-Maaori of services. Patterns began to change.

Mid 1980s Two-thirds more Maaori were admitted than non-Maaori due to judicial and drug and alcohol issues. The shift in Maaori presentation is unclear (School of Maaori Studies, 2005).

Maaori mental health

Maaori mental health is the single most significant threat to Maaori health development and welfare and is identified by the Ministry of Health (2000) as a health priority. One in seven people in Aotearoa identify as Maaori. The median age of Maaori is 22 years and one in four Maaori people speak Maaori as a first language. About 36 per cent of Maaori are aged 14 years or younger; 19 per cent of Maaori are aged between 15 and 24 years. Currently, one in four children in Aotearoa is Maaori. In 2050 this will be one in three. Nearly 50 per cent of all Maaori language speakers are under 25 years of age (Statistics New Zealand, 2005; Te Puni Kokiri, 2000). These demographics indicate that the majority of the Maaori population are young, have some cultural identity, and live in urban areas (Noble, no date). History has shown the 'urban migration drift' by Maaori from the country to the city, primarily for work, has added to issues for Maaori. These trends confirm the impact on Maaori presentations with first-episode psychosis, at a higher rate than non-Maaori to legal services such as police and courts (Durie, 2001).

Often Maaori require admission and more readmissions to psychiatric inpatient units, usually under the Mental Health Act, and receive intramuscular medication and seclusion more than non-Maaori (MHC, 1998; Statistics New Zealand, 2005). Maaori are more likely to be seriously unwell before they seek help, be younger when diagnosed and have a diagnosis of schizophrenia or other psychotic disorders than non-Maaori (Durie, 2001; Te Puni Kokiri, 1998). Some possible explanations for these disparities could be historical and current influences, colonization, alienation, dispossession, loss of economic base, urbanization, deculturation and acculturative stress. Additionally the effects of other health determinants on mental well-being like housing, education and employment also have an effect (Durie, 2001).

There are multiple causes of psychosis, like substance abuse, extreme stress (Zubin and Spring, 1977), biological predisposition and mood disorder. It is difficult to interpret signs and symptoms of first-episode psychosis (Turner et al., 2002). In some cases cultural explanations can mask symptoms and illness from western psychiatry and vice versa (Turner et al., 2002). Without both cultural and clinical understanding it is possible to mistake a normal auditory experience with a hallucination or mistake tangential thinking for elusive thinking (Durie, 2001). In New Zealand it is important to learn about Maaori perspectives as Maaori have unique status as *tangata whenua* (indigenous people).

Professionals have a strong likelihood of encountering Maaori clients in their careers. This principle would also be true in other countries with more than one cultural group, particularly in countries which were formerly colonized. According to Ihimaera et al. (2004) signs, symptoms and treatment must be a 'cultural-clinical interface'. This means that cultural and clinical paradigms must meet and cross over when working with Maaori who are mentally unwell. Culturally, experiencing voices, seeing or smelling or sensing things that others cannot are neither unusual nor abnormal within the cultural context of deceased ancestors, relatives and friends (Durie, 2001). These concepts are not unique to Maaori. Often having these changed experiences is regarded as a gift or an opportunity for the individual to make sense of and or attempt to understand these changed experiences in order to integrate these experiences into their everyday reality. There are often subtle and obvious cultural indicators in defining wellness and unwellness. Some further contrasts between western psychiatric (W) and Maaori (M) views are as follows:

W Separation of physical, mental and spiritual dimensions
M Integration
W Emphasis on individuality
M Collective approach
W Reliance on medication
M Emphasis on spiritual matters
W Emphasis on privacy
M Emphasis on company

W Healthy nuclear family
M Healthy extended family
W Disease/disorder of the mind, schizophrenia
M Presence of entities, imbalance, transgression
W Negative connotations regarding visitations, hallucinations and spiritual activity
M Positive, respectful views regarding visitations, hallucinations and spiritual activity
W Those with mental illness seen as disabled, unwell and abnormal
M Those with mental illness seen as gifted and spiritually aware
W People respected for the jobs they hold
M People respected for *whakapapa* (genealogy), *tohunga* (expert), and skills in *te reo* (Maaori language)
W Training and education for jobs with status
M Power and skills given by God.

(Te Ngaru Learning Systems, 2002)

The six case studies will illustrate some of these differences.

The present: six Maaori models of health

My life experiences and training have brought me to a place and time where in my work I utilize a selection of Maaori models of health, including and not limited to the following:

- Te Whare Tapa Wha model (Four Cornerstones)
- Te Powhiri Poutama model (Maaori Welcome model)
- Te Wheke model (Octopus model)
- Rangi matrix (Sky model)
- Dynamics of whaanautanga
- Te Pae Maahutonga

I am fortunate to work with three Maaori staff within a large multidisciplinary team. Depending upon the situation and appropriateness a 'clinical' and 'cultural' interface are utilized with consent and involvement from *tangata whaiora* (the client or patient) and *whaanau*. My 'real world' setting requires outlining some Maaori values and concepts through six cultural health models as an illustration of how Maaori worldviews and western psychiatry can work together to provide the best outcomes for Maaori *tangata whaiora*.

I proceed with caution in my advocacy of information, education and training as there are many training institutes, courses and resources available to learn about indigenous cultures around the world, their similarities and differences, especially when working with people with mental health issues, whether this is in formulations, diagnoses, explanatory models, treatment and recovery. While this is useful to learn about the clinical and cultural interface within the Canadian, Australian and South African indigenous brothers and sisters, as a Maaori person I can only share my work and experiences. Therefore, my plea is that Maaori tools be implemented by Maaori for Maaori with Maaori who are trained in these tools and have the necessary skills to conduct these processes competently. The efficacy of a cultural assessment or a formulation using a Maaori model of health is dependent upon an individual's understanding and experiences. Increased knowledge can inform clinicians of the broader contexts in which cultural workers practise. Sometimes a non-Maaori clinician may not understand the subtle nuances, norms, body movements and terminology which leads to misunderstandings. As long as clinicians are open, utilize a collaborative approach, are willing to take their time, be flexible, seek advice, consultation and supervision then goodwill will be present. Tension arises around issues of what should non-Maaori clinicians do if there are no Maaori workers available? What should Maaori workers do within clinical constraints? The role of gender and best fit matching adds to these complexities.

While there are several Maaori models of health they all have common themes. These include a holistic approach, feature spirituality, place individuals in a collective context, relate to identity and cultural identity, and incorporate relationships with the environment whether tangible or intangible (Durie, 2001; Te Ngaru Learning Systems, 2002). Some of these models have been around for thousands of years orally and more are developed to fit with changing society and priorities.

Te Whare Tapa Wha model

Te Whare Tapa Wha model is based on the four cornerstones of holistic health (MHC, 1998). An interdependent relationship exists between these cornerstones and is vital for strength, balance, stability and harmony. This model was recommended as the foundation of Maaori cultural models and service delivery (MOC, 1999; Turner et al., 2002). Poor health occurs as either a manifestation of a breakdown in harmony within the wider environment or if there has been a transgression of *tapu* (sacred, forbidden, confidential, taboo, formal or enforced restrictions) often enforced for safety and typically within a particular context. Meanwhile, in contrast *noa* includes the context (freestyle, inexact or unrestricted). For example, not listening to wise advice given about safety and behaviour around water during certain times of the year, an individual may have a little accident or a serious injury – this is a breech of *tapu*. Yet at other times of the year, this same situation will be *noa*.

Four cornerstones

Taha tinana (physical health)

This is not only about reducing mortality and morbidity, but also emphasizes physical fitness and ability.

Taha whaanau (extended family)

Within an interdependent system of extended *whaanau, hapuu, iwi, whenua* (land), *moana* (sea), *te ao* (the world), *te taha whaanau* represents 'the capacity to belong, to care, and to share' (Durie, 1994). As well as the ability to care, *taha whaanau* also includes providing sustenance culturally, emotionally and physically.

Taha hinengaro (mental health)

Maaori do not separate thoughts and feelings or mind and body. The ability to be able to express one's appropriate affect is valued.

Taha wairua (spirituality)

Spirituality is essential for full health and healing. Health and healing are not dependent on denomination rather on faith and one's ability to understand the links between people and the environment.

Case study: Aroha

This case study is about 'Aroha' (not her real name), a 20-year-old Maaori female. Aroha had been with the service for 21 months before discharge. She currently lives at home with her Mum, Dad and four siblings in the city. Her diagnosis is psychosis and she is prescribed clozapine.

Taha tinana (physical health)

Aroha had a number of symptoms that in western psychiatry would have been classified as somatic delusions. She initially experienced 'rotting guts'. She also believed that she had a broken ankle for which she made several requests for X-rays. This was despite her being able to walk adequately and no obvious abnormality in her stomach. No amount of consoling or reasoning was helpful. Aroha had also drunk from a toilet bowl while in a police station cell after an arrest for fraud. She could not explain why she did this, and thought that maybe she had breeched a *tapu* (formal/

restricted) deed. Aroha has experienced sexual abuse and rape, worked as an under-age prostitute, and contracted a sexually transmitted disease prior to becoming unwell.

Taha whaanau (extended family)

Initially, her *whaanau* were chaotic and united in not trusting mental health services due to past negative interactions with the law and other agencies. There was also a family history of mental illness, cultural disconnection, transient living, gang and drug affiliations, selling and using illicit substances, parties, abuse and trauma. Aroha has a close bond with her immediate family; despite these huge challenges, they continue to love, support and attempt to understand her.

Taha hinengaro (mental health)

Aroha has experienced fish swimming in her body. It has been debated whether this belief is purely delusional, or representative of sperm due to her history of trauma, sexual abuse, and rape. A third option is that it may be a cultural sign because where she is from there are many *taniwha* (sea monsters, guardians) in her river.

Aroha has a past history of suicidality and self harm risk by hanging herself, and wanting to cut her neck and upper thighs to let the fish out, then she wanted to sew her skin back together.

Aroha also had paranoid thoughts, where an ex-boyfriend had taken her pregnant sister's engagement ring. Aroha believed he had a link to her sister and the baby. Aroha's sister confirmed she did not have an engagement ring, Aroha wanted to find him and burn his house down as he would not return the ring. She was unable to locate him as he lived in another part of the city and no one was willing to forward his address. At this time she had a brief admission into hospital.

Taha wairua (spirituality)

This cornerstone was significant. Aroha received three pure (cleansing ceremonies) within the inpatient and community settings. These included one *powhiri* (formal welcome) which included rituals of prayer, hands-on healing and talking. As well, three cleansing rituals were performed involving the sea before dawn to invoke cleansing, healing, restoration of transgressions, wrongdoings, and forgiveness in order to increase healing and to work in conjunction with medication and the clinical paradigm.

Summary

Aroha's clinical care has been transferred to a Maaori adult mental health service.

This has meant that she has been exposed to both western and Maaori approaches, service delivery and care thus far. The western paradigm provided a quicker and more effective pathway to address her mental health and social needs. The Maaori paradigm identified spiritual realignment needs and allowed learning to occur. Subjectively, and with an evaluation session after discharge with Aroha and her *whaanau*, they felt that having cultural input within the clinical setting allowed learning processes of both paradigms. Over time and with a lot of psychoeducation both of western and Maaori paradigms, trialling and learning, Aroha and her *whaanau* became more confident in their understanding of illness and wellness. This foundation work allowed Aroha to develop her sense of identity, rights, and confidence regarding whom she accesses, and for what purpose. Therefore, Aroha's contact with Maaori services builds on this foundation and encourages Aroha to increase her supports in the community from a wider network than what was thought possible. The use of Maaori healing ceremonies were useful in each unique situation and worked in a complementary fashion with western psychiatry. Aroha remains on medication and has closer relationships with her immediate and extended *whaanau*. She has increased cultural and self identity awareness. She is now in a committed relationship and is the proud mother of a healthy, bonny baby boy.

Reflection

This model is simple and clear, and provides a foundation for the work I do. It is apparent while individuation is important, in this case, it is Aroha, so is her collective community of *whaanau*, so too is my individual, professional relationship and the collective community I work with. It is also transparent that at times we individually and collectively came to our own formulations, be it clinical or cultural. In sum, it appeared this fluidity worked well in this case. The Te Whare Tapa Wha model is often used in education within nursing and doctors' training programmes in Aotearoa; because of the vast information available regarding this model it is consistently comprehensible from both a western and Maaori perspective. Due to its popularity this model has been researched and developed, and is the only Maaori model that is currently validated and awaiting publication (Kingi and Durie, 2000). This validation process will contribute to the growing body of knowledge and provides opportunities of reliability and future evolution.

Te Powhiri Poutama model

Te Powhiri (welcome) Poutama (staircase) (Te Ngaru Learning Systems) is a process that establishes relationships in a way that supports a Maaori world-view. Most Maaori have some familiarity with this process which often puts them at ease. It is often used when conducting an initial session. It is not imperative to start from the bottom step and work sequentially upwards; rather it depends on the specific situation at the time. Sometimes the middle steps may be out of sequence. However, as long as each step is conducted throughout the meeting, or treatment process, then this model will be productive for all involved.

Case study: Craig

'Craig' is a 15-year-old Maaori male who lives with his Mum, uncle and partner. His referral came to the community team via his GP after an impulsive attempt to run on the road as a deliberate self harm attempt. The Powhiri Poutama model was used at the initial and subsequent meetings. Initially, I met Craig in reception while offering to make him a drink and assist him in familiarizing with the environment. I asked him if he wished to start the meeting with a *karakia* (prayer). He declined this offer and was happy to discuss his cultural understanding and beliefs at the time, while waiting for his Mum to arrive. The initial meeting included greetings, introductions about the service, confidentiality, process, and the purpose of the meeting. Craig stated that he was happy to meet with us as he wanted to get on with his life and happy to consider any advice or treatment we may recommend at the end of the meeting. Thus, Craig

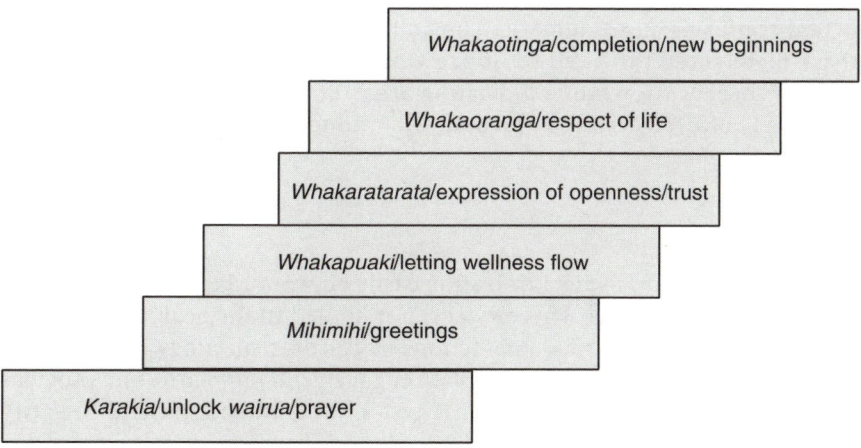

Figure 6.1 Te Powhiri Poutama model.

indicated his openness and trust of the process and us as workers. Shortly after this Craig was joined by his Mum and both expressed their love, respect and worry for one another and the value of life. Mum's genetic link (information generated via a genogram) indicates that five out of thirteen of her siblings had experienced psychosis over and above cultural norms of giftedness.

Craig comes from a complex, small *whaanau* system and has experienced neglect, sexual abuse, rape, trauma, substance abuse, bullying and assault over a long period of time. He has some cultural understanding of *te reo* (language) and *tikanga* (customs), and is a little comfortable in both clinical and cultural worlds. Mum finds medical jargon and *whaanau* meetings overwhelming and has commented that my presence often makes these meetings less stressful and less difficult. That is to say the cultural process ensured engagement, familiarity and comfort on a different level.

Summary

From this first assessment Craig was placed in respite over the weekend and prescribed Risperidone as he experienced hearing voices, tangential thoughts, low mood, thoughts of suicide, feelings of hopelessness and helplessness. He also believed all Tongans were after him and people were watching him. On the follow-up review Craig was admitted as an informal patient after taking ten Risperidone tablets as a way to stop the voices. His admission lasted two months and he returned home on medication with a plan for psychological and occupational interventions. The cultural interaction has been a vital key to engagement and ongoing involvement. This key allowed other clinicians to meet and interact with the *whaanau* and collectively share concerns and successes which made the journey for all less confusing and traumatic. The cultural assessment and intervention phase highlighted the need to utilize western psychiatry as the initial and primary intervention while indicating areas of strengths, weaknesses and priorities culturally that can be built on in time. His journey is only at the beginning.

Reflection

This model is easy to use as I transition easily between Maaori/European and clinical/cultural tensions. This model is not limited to the health setting, and often underpins most formal interactions of welcome, meetings and farewells. For many Maaori this model assists with engagement, familiarity and provides a bridge for the tensions to be addressed and maintains spiritual integrity (Te Ngaru Learning Systems, 2002).

Te Wheke model

This model is based on the octopus (Pere, 1984, 1991). The eight tentacles include *wairuatanga* (spirituality), *taha tinana* (physical health), *hinengaro* (mental health), *whaanautanga* (extended family), *mana ake* (uniqueness), *mauri* (life-sustaining principles), *ha a koro ma a kui ma* (positive awareness of ancestors) and *whatumanawa* (open and healthy expression of emotion). Finally, *waiora* (total well-being for the individual and family) is represented by the eyes of the octopus.

Case study: Tia

'Tia' is a 16-year-old Maaori female who lives with her Mum, stepfather and two younger siblings in the city. Her initial referral was activated after withdrawing from both drugs and isolating herself in her bedroom for six days, and concern about a recent experience of rape and increased weight loss. This model illustrates the first six months of her journey within the mental health services.

Wairuatanga (spirituality)

Tia is not religious, and her belief systems are about survival and *whaanau*.

Taha tinana (physical health)

At the time of referral, she was dishevelled in her appearance, had head lice, increased sleep and would stay in her room. She saw splinters in her nails that no one else could see and laughed to herself while no one was around. There was also a delay in her response to verbal prompts, and her thoughts and actions were disorganized. Tia has a history of cigarette smoking, using marijuana and binge drinking. Due to concerns for her safety, and her inability to care for herself or make decisions hospitalization under the Mental Health Act was enforced.

Hinengaro (mental health)

Initially she heard background noises and later on admitted to hearing negative voices. She had thoughts of buying a million dollar home and attempted to organize a loan. In the last year she had not attended school, and did not participate in sports or socializing. Her childhood experiences included parental separation, which led to her supporting her Dad with his ongoing alcohol and drug dependence, and supporting Mum in her new relationship, and caring for her younger siblings. She disliked her stepfather. These experiences, combined with having limited friends, little success at school, and substance misuse and recent rape, have resulted in

Tia operating in a 'survival mode' in which she is unable to utilize a broad range of learning and knowledge.

Whaanautanga (extended family)

Initially, Tia believed her sister was her niece and also had increased difficulties with her Mum. There was limited support from her immediate family, two aunts and grandparents. Her parents' separation caused a lot of tension, discord and disconnection between these families many years ago, which remains to some degree. We have attempted to bridge these relationships in the unity of their love and care for Tia by many separate and combined meetings which have attempted to address this situation and to empower Tia. It is hoped that this modelling will provide a positive experience of reconnecting with her extended family and identity. Past relationships have generally been conflictual and emotional with Tia being the 'fix it' person.

Mana ake (uniqueness)

She has had little input around things Maaori and does not appear to connect, if at all, with her culture and identity. This could be said with Mum and Dad, not so for paternal grandparents.

Mauri (life-sustaining principles)

Due to Tia's life experiences her life principle and ethos is limited. It has been difficult to ask and challenge safely to increase her being and sense of self.

Ha a koro ma a kui ma (positive awareness of ancestors)

Other than Tia's grandparents she has a limited relationship with her heritage in a nurturing manner, if at all.

Whatumanawa (open and healthy expression of emotion)

Emotionally she has suppressed her feelings and at times withdrawn from those closest to her. Tia usually responds freely and her emotions are usually appropriate to the situation at an everyday functioning level. There is much work to be done due to past trauma, attachment issues, an enmeshed relationship with Mum, and problems with making sense of her world, cultural and self identity, and the journey of mental illness.

Waiora (total well-being for the individual and family)

Her health is shared with her Mum and grandparents. They are now all aware of mental illness, signs and symptoms, Tia's difficulties, and strengths. In addition, they understand her need to take medication, develop more of a sense of self, and expand her support networks so that she can live her life fully and independently.

Summary

Tia has psychosis and remains on antipsychotic medication, attends a computer course with high attendance and achievement, and has closer relationships with her Dad and his family. She appears to be making sense of her psychosis, stress and vulnerability. Furthermore Tia loves shopping, doing 'girlie' things and socializing. She is taking better care of herself and contemplates going to the gym one day, some day. Ultimately Tia is now far more aware of her body image, self care and worth. Tia, her *whaanau*, and the services hold out a lot of hope for her future.

Reflection

This model is overlooked by many due to the depth and complexity required in understanding. While this case study appears simplistic and identifies a lot of what is missing from a cultural perspective, there are layers upon layers that we addressed from this starting place.

Rangi matrix

The model in Figure 6.2 was formulated by Huata (Te Ngaru Learning Systems, 2002) who identified the five states. It is based on the *Rangi* (sky) imagery of the different states people can get in – be it 'head in the clouds', confused, heavy or immobilized.

Case study: Peta

'Peta' is a 17-year-old Maaori male who lives with his Mum, stepfather and four siblings in a chaotic and busy *whaanau* in a rural area. He is in a state of *poorangi* after experiencing low mood for a year, difficulties at school, peer disagreements, past abuse of all forms, and death of a Nana. More recently while attending a party he became intoxicated on marijuana and alcohol. He remembered being locked in a room, falling asleep and waking up with no, clothes on, wrapped in carpet. He is unable to recollect further details. His family are impoverished and have many underground and illegal activities occurring within the home. Because of his past experiences, which were compounded by the party experience, he wanted to be

STATE OF	ACTION	CREATES A	USE	REQUIRES	FOCUS ON
Pirangi/desire	Kapo Reflective gesture	Transitory desire		The heart	
Wairangi/mania	Piopio – possessive stance and being overcome	Hunger to satisfy	Family connections	Love	Isoteric
Haurangi/intoxicated	Hurori Staggering/ imbalance	An urge that needs attending to	Family connections	Assistance	
Porangi/depression	Keka Spasmodic attempts to be free	Panic to be free	Genealogy	Support	People
Wheturangi/ schizophrenia	Toitu Frozen immobility Catatonia Numbness	A vaccum	A vaccum	An awakening	Spiritual

Figure 6.2 Rangi matrix.

Source: This model was created in 1999; taught and cited in the Te Ngaru Learning Systems (2002).

free of these heavy and unusual experiences which were occurring daily. This was demonstrated by his request for time away from his family situation in order to spend weekends with his extended family. Combined with his suicidal ideation, thoughts of harming himself with a knife, and his belief that his family were going to be killed or that people were after him, Peta commenced antidepressant medication and agreed that he could not guarantee his safety; his thoughts were worrying, negative and would not stop. He thought he would benefit from daily contact from the Crisis Team during the weekend and weekly contact with our team. Respite options were discussed and initially declined. There was a lot of discussion with *whaanau* about depression from a Maaori perspective. Peta was able to identify his own plan which included the support of significant people. He was able to contact an elder by phone and request that he come and conduct a *karakia* (prayer) in the home. Extended *whaanau* set up a schedule to ensure Peta was not alone, and always had someone to talk to. A medication regimen was arranged and daily activities were also discussed. At this particular time the additional input of caring people and communities made the difference, in addition to the fusion of culture and clinical care.

Summary

Peta is now involved in a Maaori adult mental health service, on medication and enrolled in a mechanics course. He has increased access in his taha Maaori, social activities, peers, activities and interests. Both he and his *whaanau* have received psychoeducation, stress management and techniques to assist all in their healing. They all attend more *marae* (meeting place) and *whaanau* functions, which they find supportive and fun. They are able to access both clinical and cultural supports if and when they need to. Collectively they have reported the importance of both paradigms in his recovery which was useful and had meaning for them.

Reflection

This is not a well known model. In my experience is it the closest to the *Diagnostic and statistical manual of mental disorders* (DSM-IV) because the Maaori terms align with psychiatric terms (American Psychiatric Association, 1994). I have used this model simultaneously with one or more other models. Typically, the *tangata whaiora* and *whaanau* appreciate the imagery and agree to the senses, language and location in their bodies as validating.

Dynamics of whaanautanga

This model was originally formulated by Pa Henare Tate and developed further by Malcom Peri (Peri, 1999). This model reflects a Maaori paradigm of key principles of the individual. The components of this model include the importance of self, others, skills required to communicate, contribute and resolve conflict effectively. As well as including the individual's pride and prestige, their connection to land and spirituality within the extended family is also considered, so that they can collectively move forward positively and in a healthy manner.

Case study: Hera

'Hera' is a 20-year-old Maaori female who experienced psychosis after a period of depression after additional stresses. She has two young children and a new partner. She is facing redundancy and a court case with her employer, needing to find a new home, change childcare arrangements and is experiencing pressing financial difficulties. She has increased her alcohol use and her sleep and energy have decreased. Hera comes from a large Maaori *whaanau* and has access to a lot of support.

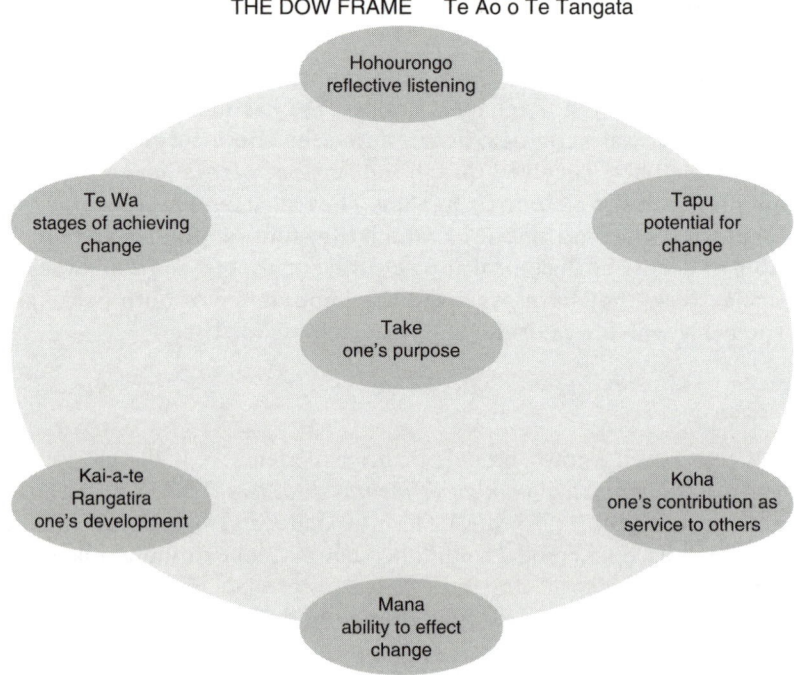

THE DOW FRAME   Te Ao o Te Tangata

Hohourongo
reflective listening

Te Wa
stages of achieving
change

Tapu
potential for
change

Take
one's purpose

Kai-a-te
Rangatira
one's development

Koha
one's contribution as
service to others

Mana
ability to effect
change

Figure 6.3 Dow frame.

Source: Peri (1999).

Take (one's purpose)

Initially Hera thought her purpose was to serve others and forgot or lost herself along the way. Hera identified that after her psychotic experience, her purpose was to focus on herself, by prioritizing her needs, solve problems, and form a plan with support from *whaanau*, and clinical staff. This was a new challenge that required a lot of commitment and energy; she used her psychotic experience and love of family as key motivators for a new future.

Tapu (potential for change)

There was a lot of potential for change. Many different techniques were used collaboratively, e.g., cognitive behaviour therapy (CBT), cultural discussions, psychoeducation, relationship counselling, legal advice, *whaanau* support with shifting home, childcare, and assistance with cooking and cleaning. Both *whaanau* and partner became more involved and supportive with guidance from Hera. Thus, more communication, relationship and values maintained and extended upon. In many ways it was a step at a time that allowed the progress to be implemented.

Koha (one's contribution as service to others)

Hera has the ability and historically contributed more fully to others than herself. She has a strong religious belief about service to others. It has been a process of prioritizing herself and finding a balance within the notion of contribution and service to self and others. Hera now celebrates having a stronger sense of self than others, and happily finds the art of balance a pleasure than a chore.

Mana (ability to effect change)

Hera was able to work through all issues in her plan to a significant extent within six months.

Kai-a-te Rangatira (one's development)

Hera realized that she mattered. She decided to put herself first and to work through her plan which allowed her to develop into someone almost unrecognizable to her former self. She became radiant, a more positive Mum and partner, enjoyed going to the gym, making new friends, spending more quality time with the extended family and new interests.

Te Wa (stages of achieving change)

Hera achieved change over time in accordance with her priorities.

Hohourongaa (reflective listening)

Reflective listening was required by all to ensure acknowledgement, discussion and progress could be made. This was not a natural or easy skill for Hera to display or master, especially when distressed. It was also important for professionals to model these skills in a relaxed and useful manner which allowed acknowledgement, safety and space for whatever issues to arise when they did.

Summary

Hera achieved her goals within one year, initiating an early discharge. She continues to make use of her additional supports, skills learnt, and makes positive gains with a full passion and love of life.

Reflection

Whaanautanga is very important for Maaori; it is the key to our worldview. This is a more complex model, and is difficult to use due to individual experiences and understandings. It is not a model that I would use frequently; however, some core elements are important and adaptable, and I use them on a daily basis.

Te Pae Maahutonga

This model (Durie, 2001) is based upon the Southern Cross star constellation. It is a navigational tool that also brings together elements of modern health promotion. The two pointer stars are *te mana whakahaere* (autonomy) and *ngaa manukura* (community leadership), and the four stars that form the cross include *mauriora* (cultural identity), *waiora* (physical environment), *toiora* (healthy lifestyles) and *te ora* (participation in society).

Case study: Whetu

'Whetu' is a 14-year-old Maaori male who spends his time between his separated parents in two different suburbs of Auckland. He has a diagnosis of psychosis and is ambivalent about medication. Whetu hears voices and when unwell he speaks in rap, he is very expressive, believes he is owed money from Tupac for his lyrics, and appears over-confident and provocative.

Whakahaere (autonomy)

He enjoys some sense of autonomy as he often gets to choose which parent he is with and for how long.

Ngaa manukura (community leadership)

He enjoys his role of community leadership via his *whaanau*, peers and gang affiliations. This is often both positive and negative depending upon which community he is interacting with. He does not identify strongly as Maaori and has no relationship with his extended family nor his ancestry at this stage. When unwell he will use Maaori words and concepts which confuse clinicians and can occur as ramblings or tangential ideas. At these times, he speaks some kernels of truth and often vital information transpires. The clinicians struggled with understanding this behaviour and often needed to discuss debate and confirm details. Cultural considerations became important and are often the focus or balance in these situations.

Waiora (physical environment)

His physical environment ensures that his physical needs are met despite a history of neglect, and physical abuse. He does not enjoy healthy lifestyle choices and often eats junk food, using alcohol, cigarettes and marijuana when he can, has poor sleep routines, and limited social skills. His participation in society is dependent upon his wellness.

Te ora (participation in society)

He currently does not play sports or attend school; in fact his socialization and meaningful occupation is limited. We have attempted to utilize course or school options or outings to little effect.

Summary

He continues to be involved with the mental health services. Currently his mental health difficulties have lessened due to less use of illicit substances, minimal access to alcohol, improved relationships with his parents and siblings and being more accepting of medication. Whetu now has a higher level of awareness about his health and he is attempting to address the issues often identified all at once, which can cause his case manager some stress and anxiety.

Reflection

The strength of this model is the focus on promotion of health. It provides a fresh perspective when working with an individual that is strengths based.

Conclusion

This chapter attempted a challenging task of providing an overview of founding documents, of the Declaration of Independence, Treaty of Waitangi and

Tohunga Suppression Act and the implications positively and negatively for Maaori and European people. Key strategies have been outlined that have contributed to Aotearoa's legacy in the mental health services. The aim of providing strategies and history was to provide a balanced dialogue for you to enquire about and participate in. Strategies which I would advocate include the *Blueprint* (MHC, 1998), the *Early intervention in psychosis: Guidance note* (MOH, 1999), 'He Korowai Oranga' and research from Australia and Birmingham, due to their flexibility and transferability to my work. While the policies, strategies and history appear tedious and lengthy it is important to have a fuller understanding of our history and context to see how we have progressed as individuals, communities, organizations, and a nation. The six Maaori models and case studies illustrate both the cultural and clinical interface often with multifaceted concepts through sharing these young people's stories. It is possible to weave the past, present and future together. I remain optimistic for the future, for our *rangatahi* (youth), *whaanau, hapuu, iwi,* staff and services. In my work, in conjunction with many individuals and communities we have achieved some outstanding results. Many go unsung and are not verbally acknowledged. However, for those of us involved we know the pain and the pleasure of the journey to wellness and continue to strive to make a positive difference. It is my hope that other indigenous workers and mental health professionals around the world travel the journey of integrating cultural and clinical paradigms, with individuals, families and communities to gain some extraordinary outcomes and results. Integration of clinical and cultural interface can be a process learning, training and assist healing that is certainly worth contributing to wellness.

> **Kia mau tonu ra ki ngaa kaupapa**
> Hold onto those values, traditions and concepts
> **Mai ano hoki**
> That have been gifted since the beginning of
> **Mana Atua, Mana Tangata, Wairua Maaori e.**
> Spiritual deity, total human well-being and Maori spirituality.

Ngaa Whakatauaki
Proverbs
Ruia te kaakano o te tumanako ki roto i te mara o te hinengaro
Plant the seed of hope in the garden of the mind

Kotahi te koohau o te ngira e kuhuna ai te miro maa,
There is but one eye of the needle through which the white,
Te miro pango, te miro whero. I muri, kia mau ki te aroha,
Black and red threads pass. After I am gone, hold fast to love,
Ki te ture me te whakapono
To the law and religion.

Glossary

Aotearoa New Zealand
Aroha Love
Ha a koro ma a kui ma Positive awareness of ancestors
Hapuu Subtribe
Haurangi Intoxicated
He korowai oranga Cloak of health
He puawaitanga A blossom
Hinengaro Mental health, the mind
Hohourongo Reflect, listening
Hurori Semblance of content
Iwi Tribe
Kai-te Rangatira One's development
Kapo Darkness
Karakia Prayer, incantation
Kawanatanga Governorship, sovereignty
Keka Spasmodic attempts
Kia tuu kia puawai Stand and blossom
Koha Contribution to serve others
Maaori Indigenous person of New Zealand
Mana Ability to affect change
Mana ake Uniqueness
Manawa Heart
Marae Meeting place
Mauri Life-sustaining principles
Mihimihi Greetings
Moana The sea
Ngaa manukura Community leadership
Noa Freestyle, inexact, unrestricted
Nu Tirene New Zealand
Oritetanga Equality
Piopio Possessive stance
Pirangi Desire
Poorangi Depression
Puku Stomach
Pure Cleansing ceremonies
Rangatiratanga Full chieftainship, self management
Rangi Sky
Roro Head
Take One's purpose
Tangata whaiora Someone striving for wellness, client, patient
Tangata whenua Indigenous people
Taniwha Sea monsters, guardians

Tapu Restrictions, potential for change
Te ao The world
Te Ngaru The wave
Te ora Participation in society
Te Pae Maahutonga Constellation
Te powhiri poutama Formal Maaori welcome model
Te reo Maaori language
Te Tiriti o Waitangi Treaty of Waitangi
Te Wa Time/stage achieve change
Te whare tapa wha The house of four cornerstones
Te wheke Octopus
Tikanga Maaori protocols, customs
Tinana Physical health, body
Tohunga Expert
Toito Frozen immobility
Waiora Total well-being, physical environment
Wairangi Mania
Wairua Spirituality
Wananga Higher level learning centres
Whaanau Family
Whaanautanga Extended family
Whakahaere Autonomy
Whakaoho Wake up
Whakaoranga Respect of life
Whakaotinga Completion, new beginnings
Whakapapa Genealogy
Whakapuaki Letting wellness flow
Whakaratarata Expression of openness, trust
Whatumanawa Open and healthy expression of emotions
Whenua The land
Wheturangi Schizophrenia

References

American Psychiatric Association (APA) (1994). *Diagnostic and statistical manual of mental disorders* (4th ed.). Washington, DC: APA.

Barlow, C. (1991). *Tikanga Whakaaro: Key concepts in Maaori culture*. Auckland: Oxford University Press.

Collins (1991). *Pocket dictionary and thesauraus*. Glasgow: HarperCollins.

Durie, M. H. (1994). Maaori psychiatric admissions patterns and policies. In J. Spicer, A. Trlin and J. Walton (Eds.), *Social dimensions of health and disease: New Zealand perspectives* (pp. 323–335). Palmerston North: Dumore.

Durie, M. H. (1998). *Te Mana, Te Kaawanatanga: The politics of Maaori self-determination*. Auckland: Oxford University Press.

Durie, M. H. (2001). *Mauri Ora: The dynamics of Maaori health*. Auckland: Oxford University Press.

Health Funding Authority (1998). *Kia tu kia puawai*. Wellington: Health Funding Authority.

Henare, M. (1990). *He Whakaputanga o te Rangatiratanga o Nu Tirene 1835: Te Tiriti o Waitangi 1840*. Aotearoa-New Zealand: Catholic Commission JPD.

Ihimaera, L. V., Maxwell-Crawford, K. M., and Tassell, N. A. (2004). *He Waka Arahi*. Palmerston North: Te Rau Matatini.

Kemara, R. (2005). Maorihealth graphics. Retrieved 1 December 2005 from http://www.maorihealth.govt.nz

Kingi, T. K. and Durie, M. (2000). 'Hua Oranga': A Maori measure of mental health outcome. In *Mental health outcomes research in Aotearoa*. Auckland: Health Research Council of New Zealand.

McGorry, P. D., Edwards, J., Mihalopoulos, C., Harrigan, S., and Jackson, J. (1996). EPPIC: An evolving system of early detection and optimal management. *Schizophrenia Bulletin, 22*, 305–326.

Mental Health Commission (MHC) (1998). *Blueprint for mental health services in New Zealand*. Wellington: MHC.

Mental Health Commission (MHC) (2004). *Delivery of cultural assessment for Maaori*. Wellington: MHC.

Ministry of Health (MOH) (1994). *Looking forward: Strategic directions for mental health services*. Wellington: MOH.

Ministry of Health (MOH) (1997). *Moving forward: the national mental health plan for more and better services*. Wellington: MOH.

Ministry of Health (MOH) (1999). *Early intervention in psychosis: Guidance note*. Wellington: Health Commission.

Ministry of Health (MOH) (2002a). *Te Puawaitanga Maaori mental health national strategic framework*. Wellington: MOH.

Ministry of Health (MOH) (2002b) *He korowai oranga: Maaori health strategy discussion document*. Wellington: MOH.

Noble, S. (no date) Best practice in community mental health service delivery. Unpublished paper. Wellington.

Olssen, E. and Stenson, M. (1989). *A century of change: New Zealand 1800–1900*. Auckland: Longman Paul.

Orange, C. (1997). *The Treaty of Waitangi*. Wellington: Bridget Williams Books.

Palmer, G. (1992). A Maaori constitutional revolution. In *New Zealand's constitution in crisis: Reforming our political system* (pp. 71–102). Dunedin: John McIndoe.

Pere, R. (1984). Te Oranga o te Whaanau the Health of the Family. In *Hui Whakaoranga Maaori health planning workshop*. Wellington: Department of Health.

Pere, R. T (1991). *Te Wheke: A celebration of Infinite Wisdom*. Gisbourne: Ao Ako Global Learning New Zealand Limited.

Peri, M. (1999). The Dynamics of Whakawhanaungatanga: Te ao o Te Tangata Workshop. Presentation to 'Children and Family Violence Effective Interventions Now Conference'. Northcote: Te Raki Pae Whanau Support & Counselling Centre.

Ryan, P. M. (1999). *The Reed pocket dictionary of modern Maaori*. Auckland: Reed.

School of Maaori Studies (2005). *Planning for Maaori health course material*. Palmerston North: Massey University.

Singh, S. P. and Fisher, H. L. (2005). How to intervene early for people with psychosis. *Advances in Psychiatric Treatment*, *11*, 71–78.

Statistics New Zealand (2005). *Census snapshot*. Wellington: New Zealand Government.

Te Ngaru Learning Systems (2002). Ariari o te Oranga: Dual diagnosis, co-morbidity, co-existing disorders. East Coast, New Zealand: Te Ngaru Learning Systems.

Te Pumanawa Hauora (1996). *A framework for purchasing traditional healing services*. Palmerston North: Massey University.

Te Puni Kokiri (1998). *Factsheets*. Retrieved 1 December 2005 from http://www.tpk.govt.nz/publications/factsheets.

Turner, M., Nightingale, S., Mulder, R. and Maginness, A. (2004). Evaluation of early intervention for psychosis services in New Zealand: what works? Wellington: Health Research Council of New Zealand.

Way, K. (1996). *Implementation of A+ bicultural policy and the implications of the Treaty of Waitangi: Institutional racism intervention for health service delivery*. Auckland: Auckland Healthcare Services.

Williams, N. (2002). *Building on strengths: A new approach to promoting mental health in New Zealand/Aotearoa*. Wellington: Ministry of Health.

Zubin, J. and Spring, B. (1977). Vulnerability: A new view of schizophrenia. *Journal of Abnormal Psychology*, *86*, 103–126.

Chapter 7

Development of psychotherapy in the pre-psychotic phase

Comparison of three approaches: Australia, Germany and UK

Lisa J. Phillips, Shona M. Francey, Steven B. Leicester, Andreas Bechdolf and Anthony P. Morrison

Introduction

Clinical research addressing the pre-psychotic or prodromal phase of illness has been conducted since the mid 1990s at a number of sites around the world. Initially the focus of this work was the development of valid and reliable criteria to identify individuals who were at heightened risk of psychosis. More recently, the emphasis has expanded to the development and evaluation of treatment to address the clinical needs of young people who meet high-risk criteria, with the aim of delaying or even preventing further deterioration and the onset of psychotic illness. This chapter describes the development of pre-psychosis treatment approaches in Melbourne, Australia, Cologne, Germany and Manchester, United Kingdom.

Development of criteria to identify young people at heightened risk of psychosis

There have been two pathways to the development of criteria for the identification of young people at heightened risk of developing a psychotic disorder: ultra high risk (UHR) criteria and the basic symptoms approach.

UHR criteria

The development of criteria to identify young people thought to be at 'ultra high risk' of developing a psychotic disorder has been described in detail elsewhere (Addington et al., 2006; Yung et al., 1998; Yung et al., 2003). Much of this work took place in Melbourne following the establishment of the Personal Assessment and Crisis Evaluation (PACE) Clinic in 1994. The development of the UHR criteria (also referred to as At Risk Mental State or ARMS criteria) drew upon earlier research that had sought to describe the prodromal phase of illness primarily through retrospective descriptions. According to this research, an extremely diverse array of symptoms and behaviours can be experienced during the prodromal phase (Yung and McGorry,

1996a). Many of these symptoms, such as sleep disturbance, depression, anxiety and social withdrawal, are non-specific to psychosis. Others such as low-level suspiciousness and brief hallucinations are more specific to psychotic disorders and it is these symptoms which have been used to develop the first two groups of UHR criteria formulated at PACE (see Table 7.1). These criteria have been operationalized according to two measures that were specifically developed to assist in identifying the UHR cohort: the Comprehensive Assessment of At Risk Mental States (CAARMS: Yung et al., 2005) and the Structured Interview for Prodromal Symptoms (SIPS: Miller et al., 2002) as well as according to well-established scales, such as the Positive and Negative Syndrome Scale (PANSS: Kay et al., 1987) and the Brief Psychiatric Rating Scale (BPRS: Overall and Gorham, 1962). The third UHR group, trait and state risk factors, is based on the fact that individuals with a family history of psychotic disorder or a schizotypal personality disorder have a higher risk of developing the disorder than individuals without such a family history (Gottesman and Shields, 1982). To increase the risk of transition to psychosis above that associated with family history alone, young people who meet

Table 7.1 UHR criteria

Group 1: Subthreshold psychotic symptoms
- Presence of at least one of the following: ideas of reference, odd beliefs or magical thinking, perceptual disturbance, paranoia and suspiciousness, odd behaviour and speech.
- Symptoms have occurred at least several times a week.
- Symptoms have occurred during the past twelve months.
- Symptoms have occurred for at least one week and no longer than five years.

Group 2: Brief limited intermittent psychotic symptoms (BLIPS: transient psychotic symptoms)
- Presence of at least one of the following: ideas of reference, odd beliefs or magical thinking, perceptual disturbance, paranoia and suspiciousness, odd behaviour and speech.
- Symptoms have occurred at least several times per week.
- The duration of each episode of symptoms is less than one week.
- Symptoms have resolved spontaneously.
- An episode of symptoms must have occurred during the last twelve months.

Group 3: Trait and state risk factors
- Schizotypal personality disorder in the identified individual or a first-degree relative with a psychotic disorder.
- Significant deterioration on mental state or functioning, maintained for at least one month.
- The deterioration in functioning occurred within the past twelve months.

Psychotic episode threshold
- Presence of at least one of the following: ideas of reference, odd beliefs or magical thinking, perceptual disturbance, paranoia and suspiciousness, odd behaviour and speech.
- Symptoms have occurred daily for at least one week.

these criteria must also have experienced a recent, significant deterioration in functioning (Table 7.1). Criteria were also developed to identify when the ARMS had crossed the threshold to psychosis (these criteria were based on the level of symptoms that would result in antipsychotic medication being prescribed: see Table 7.1). UHR individuals are also aged between 14 and 29 years and have not previously experienced a psychotic episode or been prescribed antipsychotic medication.

The twelve-month transition rate to psychotic disorder associated with these criteria has been reported to range from 22 to 54 per cent despite the provision of supportive psychotherapy and antidepressant or anxiolytic medication, where appropriate (Cadenhead, 2002; Larsen, 2002; Mason et al., 2004; Miller et al., 2002; Morrison et al., 2004b; Yung et al., 2003). These criteria have subsequently been adopted at many other sites, such as Outreach and Support in South London (OASIS: Broome et al., 2005), Early Detection and Intervention Evaluation in Manchester, England (EDIE: Morrison et al., 2004a), Psychological Assistance Service in Newcastle, Australia (PAS: Mason et al., 2004) and the Prevention through Risk Identification, Management and Education Clinic in North America and Canada (PRIME: McGlashan et al., 2003).

Basic symptoms approach

The other strategy for characterizing and identifying individuals during the pre-psychotic phase of illness stems from an important body of research that has mainly been conducted in Germany. This approach is based on the concept of two distinct periods of heightened risk known as the Early Initial Prodromal State (EIPS) and the Late Initial Prodromal State (LIPS) (Bechdolf et al., 2005b; Häfner et al., 2004; Klosterkötter et al., 2001; Ruhrmann et al., 2003). The LIPS resembles the UHR subthreshold psychotic symptoms and BLIPS groups as described above and in Table 7.1. The EIPS is defined by the presence of 'basic symptoms' – subjectively experienced abnormalities of cognition, perception, attention and movement (Gross, 1989; Huber and Gross, 1989; see also Table 7.2). The Early Recognition Instrument (ERI) has been developed specifically to assess the presence of EIPS (Maurer et al., 2000; Maurer et al., 2004). Basic symptoms are less obviously related to psychotic symptoms than subthreshold psychotic symptoms and cross-sectional studies have indicated that levels of symptoms, disability, neurophysiological and neuropsychological deficits of individuals who experience basic symptoms are lower than those of people fulfilling UHR/LIPS criteria (Bechdolf et al., 2005a; Brockhaus-Dumke et al., 2005; Pukrop et al., 2006). Therefore it has been hypothesized that basic symptoms may identify people in an earlier phase of the psychotic prodrome than UHR criteria (Bechdolf et al., 2005b; Häfner et al., 2004; Klosterkötter et al., 2001; Ruhrmann et al., 2003). In the Cologne Early Recognition (CER) study, 70 per cent of participants who met

Table 7.2 Criteria for the EIPS

EIPS criteria: meet criteria for at least one of the following groups

- *Group 1:* One or more of the following self-experienced cognitive thought and perception deficits (basic symptoms) in the last three months several times a week: thought interferences, thought perseveration, thought pressure, thought blockages, disturbances of receptive language, either heard or read, decreased ability to discriminate between ideas and perception, fantasy and true memories, unstable ideas of reference (subject-centrism), derealization, visual perception disturbances (blurred vision, transitory blindness, partial sight, hypersensitivity to light, etc.), acoustic perception disturbances (hypersensitivity to sounds or noise, acoasms, etc.).
- *Group 2:* Reduction in the Global Assessment of Functioning (GAF: DSM-IV) of at least thirty points (within the past year) and at least one of the following risk factors: first-degree relative with a lifetime diagnosis of schizophrenia or a schizophrenia spectrum disorder, pre- or perinatal complications.

Group 1 of the EIPS developed schizophrenia within an average of 5.4 years after initial assessment. The transition rate within the first twelve months was 19.2 per cent and another 17 per cent developed schizophrenia during the following twelve months (Klosterkötter et al., 2001). In a separate cohort of 147 individuals who met EIPS criteria, 17 per cent developed a psychotic episode psychosis within twelve months (Schultze-Lutter et al., 2004). Thus, prevention efforts in people in the EIPS may have an especially good chance to prevent the full-blown illness and to avoid serious problems that arise later during the initial prodrome. To date, the EIPS criteria have been adopted only at the Early Recognition and Intervention Centre for Mental Crises (FETZ) in Cologne, Germany.

Treatment approaches for young people in the pre-psychotic phase of illness

Ethical considerations

Ethical concerns associated with treatment of young people who meet ARMS criteria have been widely discussed in the literature (e.g., Corcoran et al., 2005; Haroun et al., 2006; McGlashan, 2001; McGorry, 2005; Warner, 2005). Pertinent issues generating ongoing debate include concerns about the potential stigma associated with being identified as being at risk of psychosis and what education should be provided to young people and their families about their 'at risk' status. Further ethical issues relate to concerns about the provision of treatment to individuals who, although they met UHR/EIPS criteria at the time of referral, were never going to develop full-blown psychosis, and thus were incorrectly considered to be at risk. Questions have also been raised about the length of treatment that should be provided to those considered to be at risk (in other words, how long is the period of risk). Recently developed guidelines for the treatment of young people who meet UHR/EIPS criteria suggest that if they meet criteria and are help-seeking, they should be offered regular monitoring of their mental state and psychological treatment that targets their presenting problems. This would include cognitive behavioural therapy (CBT) for anxiety, depression and relationship difficulties, psycho-education about early psychosis and family support and education all conducted within low-stigma settings (Haddock and Lewis, 2005). It is recognized that more research is required to enhance the identification of 'at risk' cohorts and to develop and evaluate appropriate treatment strategies.

Psychological treatment

Many previous studies have shown that a diverse range of symptoms and problematic behaviours can be experienced during the pre-psychotic or pro-dromal phase of illness (reviewed in Yung and McGorry, 1996b). Further, retrospective studies of patients with schizophrenia have reported that a significant degree of psychosocial decline occurs even before the onset of frank psychosis, which can create a ceiling for future recovery (Agerbo et al., 2003; Häfner et al., 1995; Yung and McGorry, 1996b). Previous research has shown that UHR individuals also experience a broad array of symptoms extending beyond the UHR criteria, with depression, anxiety, substance use problems and personality disorder traits commonly reported (Meyer et al., 2005; Svirkis et al., 2005). These symptoms are often associated with significant functional problems and high levels of distress and often prompt young people to seek treatment.

In light of the above, treatment for young people who meet UHR or EIPS criteria not only has focused on the range of symptoms that form the basis of those criteria, but also addresses the broader range of difficulties with which the young person might present. It has previously been argued that psychological treatment may be the most appropriate treatment approach – particularly during the earliest stages of the pre-psychotic period when the presenting symptoms are less specific and severe (Phillips et al., 2008). The range of symptoms experienced by UHR/EIPS individuals may be particularly amenable to CBT and an extensive evidence base exists for the treatment of mood and anxiety difficulties (Butler et al., 2006), drug-resistant psychotic symptoms and in psychotic relapse prevention (Valmaggia et al., 2005; Zimmermann et al., 2005) using this approach. Therefore it is likely to be appropriate for addressing subthreshold or brief intermittent psychotic symptoms and in assisting clients to develop effective strategies to protect against the impact of environmental stressors that may contribute to the emergence of psychosis. The collaborative and problem-oriented nature of CBT is also well accepted by clients (French and Morrison, 2004).

Pharmacological treatment

Pharmacological treatment, particularly antipsychotic medication, has also been suggested as appropriate to treat young people who are at heightened risk of developing psychosis. To date, such treatment has been applied only within the context of clinical trials and, although the results of these trials are encouraging (McGlashan et al., 2006; McGorry et al., 2002), current clinical guidelines suggest that such treatment should be limited to clinical trials at present (Haddock and Lewis, 2005). Side effects associated with antipsychotic medications have been well documented (Jayaram et al., 2006; Kane, 2004; Lieberman et al., 2005; Margolese et al., 2005) and there are concerns about the use of these medications in young people who, despite meeting UHR or EIPS criteria, do not subsequently develop psychosis. It also appears that the use of antipsychotic medication in this cohort is not as well accepted by the clients as the provision of psychologically oriented treatment (Phillips et al., 2008) and may in fact deter young people from seeking treatment. Other medications such as lithium and antidepressants have been proposed for use in the UHR/EIPS client group, but no studies using these medications have yet been published. The remainder of this chapter focuses on the development and evaluation of psychological treatment for young people at high risk of psychosis.

Description of three psychological treatment approaches for young people at high risk of psychosis

PACE Clinic, Melbourne, Australia

The treatment approach developed at the PACE Clinic is primarily cognitive behavioural and draws upon the techniques and strategies that have demonstrated efficacy in the treatment of people with both first-episode and established psychotic disorders (Drury et al., 1996; Kuipers et al., 1997; Lewis et al., 2001; Sensky et al., 2000). The aim of this treatment approach is to assist young people who are identified as being at heightened risk of psychosis to develop an understanding of their symptoms and to develop strategies to cope with those symptoms. Acquiring an understanding of the cognitive processes that influence thoughts and emotions is emphasized and the client is assisted in the development of more realistic and positive views of themselves. Cognitive models of psychosis propose that perceptual abnormalities and disturbances in information processing that form the core of psychosis develop from disrupted information processing. Cognitive biases, inaccurate appraisals and maladaptive core self-schema contribute further to the development of unusual beliefs (Garety and Hemsley, 1994; Garety et al., 2001).

The stress vulnerability model of psychosis (Drury et al., 2000; Fowler et al., 1995; Haddock et al., 1999; Jackson et al., 1998) has also informed the treatment approach developed at PACE. This model suggests that while biological factors may underpin the development of psychotic disorders, psychological and social factors contribute to their onset and maintenance (see Gleeson et al., Chapter 1 in this volume). An underlying assumption of the stress vulnerability model is that ambient/environmental stressors (such as relationship issues, substance use, lifestyle factors) are key precipitants to psychosis, implying that the implementation of appropriate coping strategies may ameliorate the influence of vulnerability (Boeker et al., 1989). As a result, strategies for managing stress and the enhancement of an individual's coping response are integral to the PACE treatment.

In addition to promoting stress management, the therapy was also designed to target the wide range of symptoms that can be experienced during the onset phase of a psychotic disorder – psychotic symptoms, neurotic symptoms, substance use problems, family and relationship difficulties, self-esteem issues and so forth. Four 'treatment modules' addressing different target symptoms were developed to respond flexibly to the range of experiences of young people attending the PACE Clinic: Stress management, Depression/ negative symptoms, Positive symptoms and Other comorbidity. Each of these modules is described in detail in Phillips and Francey (2004). The strategies incorporated in the modules draw upon previously validated cognitive-behavioural techniques (such as CBT approaches to addressing anxiety (Andrews et al., 2003; Wells, 1997), depression (Beck et al., 1979) and psychotic symptoms (Fowler et al., 1995) and applies them to the at-risk population.

The first step towards establishing the efficacy of the psychological treatment developed at PACE occurred within a randomized controlled trial conducted during the late 1990s (McGorry et al., 2002). In this study, 59 young people who met UHR criteria were randomized to 6 months of specific preventive intervention (SPI: CBT plus risperidone 1–2 mg/day) or needs-based intervention (NBI) alone. The needs-based intervention was provided to individuals in both treatment groups and incorporated case management (addressing practical issues such as crisis management and difficulties with housing, education or employment), and symptom monitoring. By the end of 6 months' treatment, significantly fewer individuals in the active treatment group had progressed to a first episode of psychosis (9.7 per cent versus 36 per cent); 6 months after treatment ended, more of the SPI group developed a psychotic episode but no one in the NBI group did. Therefore, the transition rate between the groups did not significantly differ at this follow-up stage (19 per cent versus 36 per cent). These results suggest that a combination of antipsychotic medication and CBT may delay but not necessarily prevent the onset of psychosis in symptomatic high-risk young people. Unfortunately the design of this study did not allow the relative contributions of the different components of SPI to be assessed independently.

A second randomized trial which will allow this comparison is currently being completed at PACE. The psychological treatment provided in this second study differed slightly from the first study in that it was offered for longer (12 months) and broadened the focus to incorporate a more comprehensive understanding of the developmental origins of the difficulties experienced by the participants and to allow a more extensive formulation to be developed.

EDIE, Manchester, UK

The cognitive-behavioural intervention developed at EDIE in Manchester is based on a cognitive model of the development and maintenance of psychosis developed by researchers working within that programme (French and Morrison, 2004; French et al., 2003; Morrison, 2001). The model is based on the assumption that it is the interpretation of and response to psychotic experiences that is problematic, rather than the experience itself, and that this is especially so in the early stages. It emphasizes cognitive and behavioural responses such as selective attention, safety behaviours aimed at preventing feared outcomes, and thought control strategies and the importance of beliefs about the self, world and others, as well as metacognitive beliefs in influencing the development of distressing psychotic experiences. The intervention that was developed based on this model does not specifically aim to reduce the experience of psychotic phenomena, but rather to reduce the distress associated with those experiences whilst also improving quality of life. Research has confirmed that many of these factors may be implicated in the development of psychosis, with participants meeting ARMS criteria scoring significantly higher than a matched control group (Morrison et al., 2006).

CBT at EDIE is based on the general structure and principles of cognitive therapy, such as including agenda setting and homework tasks, being time-limited, problem-orientated and involving collaborative empiricism and Socratic questioning (Beck, 1976). An idiosyncratic case formulation and a list of problem areas and goals for therapy are collaboratively developed with each patient in the first few sessions, enabling the intervention to be personalized for each client by guiding the selection of treatment strategies that are to be implemented. Patients often prioritize problem areas that do not appear directly related to psychotic experiences, such as relationship issues, anxiety and mood disorders, fears regarding the onset of madness and a lack of meaningful daily activity, so cognitive models of anxiety or mood disorders often inform the selection of intervention strategies. Common treatment strategies include consideration of the advantages and disadvantages of holding particular beliefs or having certain experiences, and, if appropriate, the generation of alternative explanations for distressing events. Metacognitive beliefs about thoughts and beliefs about hallucinatory phenomena are also often explored and behavioural experiments are implemented to test out problematic beliefs. Normalization of psychotic experiences is another very common aspect of treatment, which often helps to reduce distress immediately. These strategies are related back to the formulation, and the success of such approaches is used to inform any revisions of this case conceptualization. Therapy finishes with the development of a relapse prevention plan and a therapeutic blueprint, which identifies the strategies the patient has found helpful and assists in the consolidation of treatment gains. Treatment sessions follow a detailed manual containing assessment, formulation and change strategies, examples of interventions and model responses for the therapist (French and Morrison, 2004).

The EDIE CBT approach was compared with monthly mental state monitoring in a randomized controlled, parallel group trial (Morrison et al., 2004a). Both treatment conditions incorporated elements of case management; 58 participants were included in the study. CBT was provided for the first 6 months (up to 25 sessions) and all patients were monitored on a monthly basis for 12 months. The average number of sessions received was 12. CBT significantly reduced the likelihood: of progressing to psychosis as defined by the PANSS (Kay et al., 1987) over 12 months (6 per cent versus 22 per cent; odds ratio = 0.04; 95 per cent confidence interval 1 = 0.01–0.71; $p = 0.028$); of being prescribed antipsychotic medication (6 per cent versus 30 per cent; odds ratio = 0.06; 95 per cent confidence interval 1 = 0.01–0.57; $p = 0.014$); and, of meeting criteria for a DSM-IV (American Psychiatric Association (APA), 1994) diagnosis of a psychotic disorder (6 per cent versus 26 per cent; odds ratio = 0.04; 95 per cent confidence interval = 0.01–0.57; $p = 0.019$). CT also improved positive symptoms in the sample over the 12-month period ($F(1,48) = 4.09$, $p = 0.049$). There were no significant differences between groups on Global Assessment of Functioning or General Health Questionnaire scores at 12 months.

A three-year follow-up of this cohort (with a follow-up rate of 47 per cent) has now been completed (Morrison et al., 2007). Logistic regression analyses demonstrated that CT significantly reduced likelihood of being prescribed antipsychotic medication over a three-year period (14 per cent versus 35 per cent; odds ratio = 0.13; 95 per cent confidence interval = 0.02–0.76; $p = 0.024$), but it did not affect transition to psychosis defined using the PANSS (20 per cent versus 22 per cent; odds ratio = 0.38; 95 per cent confidence interval = 0.08–1.88; $p = 0.236$) or probable DSM-IV diagnosis at three years (20 per cent versus 30 per cent; odds ratio = 0.34; 95 per cent confidence interval = 0.08–1.48; $p = 0.152$). However, exploratory analyses revealed that CT significantly reduced the likelihood of making progression to psychosis as defined on the PANSS over 3 years (odds ratio = 0.03; 95 per cent confidence interval = 0.01–0.64; $p = 0.026$) after controlling for cognitive factors hypothesized to be mediators of treatment (dysfunctional attitudes and metacognitive beliefs). This suggests not only that CT may have a preventative effect over a longer term, but also that booster sessions may be indicated. Providing booster sessions may maximize the likelihood that any treatment gains are maintained, although further research is required to answer this issue.

Following the success of the EDIE trial, a clinical service for young people at risk of psychosis has been established in the Manchester area and is funded by the local health commission. Young people who meet UHR criteria are offered a range of choices regarding treatment options including individual cognitive therapy, monthly monitoring of their mental state and family intervention. In addition, a trial of CBT for the prevention of psychosis with a two-year follow-up period (EDIE-2) across five sites in the UK has been funded by the Medical Research Council and results of this trial will be reported in 2010. This trial has numerous methodological improvements in comparison to the first trial, including a primary outcome measure specifically designed for the population (CAARMS: Yung et al., 2005), the incorporation of booster sessions, a much larger sample (with a recruitment target of 320) and a health economics analysis.

FETZ, Cologne, Germany

The vulnerability stress coping model of schizophrenia (Nuechterlein and Dawson, 1984; Zubin and Spring, 1977) and the basic symptom concept (Huber and Gross, 1989; Süllwold and Herrlich, 1998), both underlie the framework of the FETZ intervention. A cognitive model of the EIPS has been developed drawing on recent cognitive models of psychosis (Fowler et al., 1995; Kingdon and Turkington, 1994) as well as upon evidence that cognitive, thought and perceptual disturbances precede negative affective states, social withdrawal and social decline in the onset of psychosis (Klosterkötter et al., 2001). According to this model biological, psychological, social stress and vulnerability factors all contribute to the overall risk of the development of psychotic experiences. Pre-psychotic symptoms trigger negative appraisals and assumptions associated with the basic symptoms that are experienced. This may then result in emotional disturbances, like depression or anxiety, social withdrawal and social decline, which jointly contribute to the development and maintenance of symptoms and distress (Larsen et al., 2003).

The aims of the intervention at FETZ are reduction of prodromal symptoms, prevention of social decline or stagnation, and prevention or delay of further progression to psychosis. The treatment draws upon cognitive therapy strategies that have been developed to treat individuals with established psychosis (Chadwick et al., 1996; Fowler et al., 1995; Kingdon and Turkington, 1994) as well as strategies for anxiety or depressive symptoms (APA Working Group, 1998, 2000). The intervention is delivered to clients for 12 months as an outpatient treatment. It consists of 30 sessions of individual therapy, 15 sessions of standardized group intervention, 12 sessions of cognitive training and 3 sessions of psychoeducational or multi-family intervention. The psychotherapist who implements individual therapy also covers case management issues.

The individual therapy component occurs first and begins with a period of building and establishing a collaborative, therapeutic relationship in which enabling the client to feel understood is of major importance. The therapist attempts to clarify the particular life circumstances, events, and experiences that form the background for the onset of the EIPS symptoms and shared goals of therapy are developed. These are often broader than basic symptoms and include anxiety, depression, family or occupational problems. Work on coping strategies follows directly from the assessment, and the goal is to manipulate any factors that contribute to the experience of symptoms. A range of cognitive and behavioural strategies, including attention switching, attention narrowing, reattribution, awareness training, de-arousing techniques, social engagement and disengagement are applied to reduce the occurrence or duration of such problems. Computerized cognitive training is provided as a tool to train cognitive thought and perception disorders directly. The aim of these strategies is to foster feelings of control and hope and to provide practical help in the early stages of therapy. A particular emphasis is paid to attributional styles that underpin the key problem areas that have been collaboratively identified. Clinical experience with the EIPS population suggests that individuals who experience thought form and perception difficulties are likely to link these experiences with early life trauma and with negative self-evaluations and beliefs. These attributions could precede further feelings of loss and demoralization as well as experiences of depression, social anxiety and social withdrawal. In these circumstances, standard cognitive therapy approaches are applied such as identifying automatic thoughts and dysfunctional assumptions, and exploring alternative appraisals. During the termination phase, the course of therapy is reviewed and a crisis plan is developed for the future. Further details about this treatment approach and case examples have been published elsewhere (Bechdolf et al., 2003; Larsen et al., 2003).

The group therapy offered at FETZ encourages participants to share their experiences. This often results in relief and reduced negative self-evaluations (see also Miller et al., Chapter 9, and Woodhead, Chapter 14 in this volume). Within the group, treatment is also offered addressing social anxiety, social withdrawal and depression. A short multi-family psychoeducation group has also been developed (see also Couchman, Chapter 15 in this volume). Information about the stress vulnerability model and the rationale for early intervention is provided. These groups also provide an opportunity for family members to share their experiences and to recognize that their relative is not alone in struggling with the problems they have experienced.

A randomized controlled, parallel group, multicentre trial is currently being conducted to evaluate the FETZ psychological intervention. The sites that are involved are the Early Recognition and Intervention Centres in Cologne,

Bonn, Düsseldorf and Munich (Bechdolf et al., 2005b; Ruhrmann et al., 2003). Participants are block randomized to receive either the CBT intervention described above (including individual, group and family components) or clinical management (CM) over a 12-month period (both treatment conditions incorporate elements of case management). Psychopathology assessments are conducted at intake, post treatment, at month 24 and (for a subgroup) at month 36 to determine if symptoms have improved or there has been deterioration and a psychotic episode has developed.

Preliminary comparisons of baseline and follow-up data suggest that global psychopathology and basic symptoms were reduced in the group who received CBT ($p = 0.009$; $p = 0.008$ respectively) (Bechdolf et al., 2005c). Additionally improvements were recorded in levels of depression and global functioning ($p = 0.009$; $p = 0.005$). The effect sizes for these comparisons were large ($d = 1.85$–3.80) (Cohen, 1988). The transition rate to psychosis in the CBT group was 5.3 per cent and in the control group was 14.8 per cent (Häfner et al., 2004). Further results should be available shortly.

Conclusions

A number of specialized services for young people identified as being at high risk for developing psychosis have demonstrated that psychological treatment is effective in addressing the diverse needs of this patient group and potentially reduces their risk of transition to psychosis. These approaches have generally been well received by patients and families, compared to anti-psychotic medications where acceptance, side effects and compliance have raised concern.

All of the psychological treatments that have been described are cognitively oriented with an emphasis on collaborative identification of problem areas and the development of strategies to better cope with sources of distress and mental health problems. They draw on the stress vulnerability model of the onset of psychosis and other mental health problems and the opportunities this model provides for the effective use of self-regulation to minimize stress and illness. As young people who are identified as being at heightened risk of psychosis often experience difficulties in a number of domains, not only positive psychotic symptoms, the therapy is often broad ranging with multiple targets. Case management is also often prominent in the treatment that is provided.

Further work is obviously required to better understand the onset of psychosis and to establish the validity of psychological treatment in preventing onset. The development of group-based interventions, family work and attention to vocational outcomes is also required.

References

Addington, J., Francey, S. M., and Morrison, A. P. (2006). *Working with people at high risk of developing psychosis: A treatment handbook*. Chichester: Wiley.

Agerbo, E., Byrne, M., Eaton, W. W., and Mortensen, P. B. (2003). Schizophrenia, marital status and employment: A forty year study. *Schizophrenia Research, 60* (Suppl. 1), 32.

American Psychiatric Association (APA) (1994). *Diagnostic and statistical manual of mental disorders* (4th edn). Washington, DC: APA.

Andrews, G., Crino, R., Hunt, C., Lampe, L., and Page, A. (2003). *The treatment of anxiety disorders*. Cambridge: Cambridge University Press.

APA Working Group (1998). American Psychiatric Association Practice Guidelines: Practice guideline for the treatment of patients with panic disorder. *American Journal of Psychiatry, 155* (Suppl. 5), 1–34.

APA Working Group (2000). American Psychiatric Association Practice Guidelines: Practice guideline for the treatment of patients with major depressive disorder (revision). *American Journal of Psychiatry, 157* (Suppl. 4), 1–45.

Bechdolf, A., Maier, S., Knost, B., Wagner, M., and Hambrecht, M. (2003). Psychological intervention in the early prodromal state: A case report. *Nervenarzt, 5*, 436–439.

Bechdolf, A., Pukrop, R., Köhn, D., Tschinkel, S., Schultze-Lutter, F., Ruhrmann, S., et al. (2005a). Subjective quality of life in subjects at risk for first episode psychosis: A comparison with first episode schizophrenia patients and healthy controls. *Schizophrenia Research, 79*, 137–141.

Bechdolf, A., Ruhrmann, S., Wagner, M., Kuhn, K. U., Janssen, B., Bottlender, R., et al. (2005b). Interventions in the initial prodromal states of psychosis in Germany: Concept and recruitment. *British Journal of Psychiatry* (Suppl.), *48*, 45–48.

Bechdolf, A., Veith, V., Schwarzer, D., Schorrmann, M., Stamm, E., Janssen, B., et al. (2005c). Cognitive-behavioural therapy in the pre-psychotic phase: An exploratory pilot study. *Psychiatry Research, 136*, 251–255.

Beck, A. T. (1976). *Cognitive therapy and the emotional disorders*. New York: International Universities Press.

Beck, A. T., Rush, A. J., Shaw, B. F., and Emery, G. (1979). *Cognitive therapy of depression*. New York: Guilford.

Boeker, W., Brenner, H. D., and Wuergler, S. (1989). Vulnerability linked deficiencies, psychopathology and coping behaviour of schizophrenics and their relatives. *British Journal of Psychiatry, 155* (Suppl. 5), 128–135.

Brockhaus-Dumke, A., Ruhrmann, S., Tendolkar, I., Pukrop, R., and Klosterkötter, J. (2005). Impaired mismatch negativity (MMN) generation in prodromal and schizophrenia patients. *Schizophrenia Research, 73*, 297–310.

Broome, M. R., Woolley, J. B., Johns, L. C., Valmaggia, L. R., Tabraham, P., Gafoor, R., et al. (2005). Outreach and support in south London (OASIS): Implementation of a clinical service for prodromal psychosis and the at risk mental state. *European Psychiatry, 20*, 372–378.

Butler, A. C., Chapman, J. E., Forman, E. M., and Beck, A. T. (2006). The empirical status of cognitive-behavioral therapy: A review of meta-analyses. *Clinical Psychology Review, 26*, 17–31.

Cadenhead, K. (2002). Vulnerability markers in the schizophrenia spectrum: Implications for phenomenology, genetics and the identification of the schizophrenia prodrome. *Psychiatric Clinics of North America, 25*, 837–853.

Chadwick, P., Birchwood, M., and Trower, P. (1996). *Cognitive therapy for delusions, voices and paranoia.* Chichester: Wiley.

Cohen, J. (1988). *Statistical power analysis for the behavioural sciences* (2nd ed.). Hillsdale, NJ: Lawrence Erlbaum.

Corcoran, C., Malaspina, D., and Hercher, L. (2005). Prodromal interventions for schizophrenia vulnerability: The risks of being 'at risk'. *Schizophrenia Research, 73*, 173–184.

Drury, V., Birchwood, M., Cochrane, R., and MacMillan, F. (1996). Cognitive therapy and recovery from acute psychosis: A controlled trial. I: Impact on psychotic symptoms. *British Journal of Psychiatry, 169*, 593–601.

Drury, V., Birchwood, M., and Cochrane, R. (2000). Cognitive therapy and recovery from acute psychosis: A controlled trial. 3: Five-year follow-up. *British Journal of Psychiatry, 177*, 8–14.

Fowler, D., Garety, P., and Kuipers, E. (1995). *Cognitive behaviour therapy for psychosis: Theory and practice.* Chichester: Wiley.

French, P. and Morrison, A. P. (2004). *Early detection and cognitive therapy for people at high risk of developing psychosis: A treatment approach.* New York: Wiley.

French, P., Morrison, A. P., Walford, L., Knight, A., and Bentall, R. P. (2003). Cognitive therapy for preventing transition to psychosis in high risk individuals: A case series. *Behavioural and Cognitive Psychotherapy, 31*, 53–67.

Garety, P. A. and Hemsley, D. R. (1994). *Delusions: Investigations into the psychology of delusional reasoning.* Oxford: Oxford University Press.

Garety, P., Kuipers, E., Fowler, D., Freeman, D., and Bebbington, P. E. (2001). A cognitive model of the positive symptoms of psychosis. *Psycholological Medicine, 31*, 189–195.

Gottesman, I. I. and Shields, J. (1982). *Schizophrenia: The epigenetic puzzle.* Cambridge: Cambridge University Press.

Gross, G. (1989). The 'basic' symptoms of schizophrenia. *British Journal of Psychiatry, 155* (Suppl. 7), 21–25.

Haddock, G. and Lewis, S. (2005). Psychological interventions in early psychosis. *Schizophrenia Bulletin, 31*, 697–704.

Haddock, G., Tarrier, N., Morrison, A. P., Hopkins, R., Drake, R., and Lewis, S. (1999). A pilot study evaluating the effectiveness of individual inpatient cognitive-behavioural therapy in early psychosis. *Social Psychiatry and Psychiatric Epidemiology, 34*, 254–258.

Häfner, H., Riecher-Rössler, A., Maurer, K., Fatkenheuer, B., and Loffler, W. (1992). First onset and early symptomatology of schizophrenia: A chapter of epidemiological and neurobiological research into age and sex differences. *European Archives of Psychiatry and Clinical Neuroscience, 242*, 109–118.

Häfner, H., Nowotny, B., Loffler, W., an der Heiden, W., and Maurer, K. (1995). When and how does schizophrenia produce social deficits? *European Archives of Psychiatry and Clinical Neuroscience, 246*, 17–28.

Häfner, H., Maurer, K., Ruhrmann, S., Bechdolf, A., Klosterkötter, J., Wagner, M., et al. (2004). Are early detection and secondary prevention feasible? Facts and visions. *European Archives of Psychiatry and Clinical Neuroscience, 254*, 117–128.

Haroun, N., Dunn, L., Haroun, A., and Cadenhead, K. S. (2006). Risk and protection in prodromal schizophrenia: Ethical implications for clinical practice and future research. *Schizophrenia Bulletin*, *32*, 166–178.

Huber, G. and Gross, G. (1989). The concept of basic symptoms in schizophrenic and schizoaffective psychoses. *Recent Progress in Medicine*, *80*, 646–652.

International Early Psychosis Association Writing Group (2005). International clinical practice guidelines for early psychosis. *British Journal of Psychiatry*, *187* (Suppl. 48), s120–s124.

Jackson, H. J., McGorry, P. D., Edwards, J., Hulbert, C., Henry, L., Francey, S., et al. (1998). Cognitively-oriented psychotherapy for early psychosis (COPE): Preliminary results. *British Journal of Psychiatry*, *172* (Suppl. 33), 93–100.

Jayaram, M. B., Hosalli, P., and Stroup, S. (2006). Risperidone versus olanzapine for schizophrenia. *Cochrane Database of Systematic Reviews*, *2*, CD005237, 2006.

Kane, J. M. (2004). Tardive dyskinesia rates with atypical antipsychotics in adults: Prevalence and incidence. *Journal of Clinical Psychiatry*, *65* (Suppl. 9), 16–20.

Kay, S. R., Fiszbein, A., and Opler, L. A. (1987). The positive and negative syndrome scale (PANSS) for schizophrenia. *Schizophrenia Bulletin*, *13*, 261–269.

Kingdon, D. and Turkington, D. (1994). *Cognitive-behavioural therapy for schizophrenia*. Hove: Lawrence Erlbaum.

Klosterkötter, J., Hellmich, M., Steinmeyer, E. M., and Schultze-Lutter, F. (2001). Diagnosing schizophrenia in the initial prodromal phase. *Archives of General Psychiatry*, *58*, 158–164.

Kuipers, E., Garety, P., Fowler, D. F., Dunn, G., Bebbington, P., Freeman, D., and Hadley, C. (1997). London-East Anglia randomised controlled trial of cognitive-behavioural therapy for psychosis. *British Journal of Psychiatry*, *171*, 319–327.

Larsen, T. K. (2002). The transition from the premorbid period to psychosis: How can it be described? *Acta Psychiatrica Scandinavica Supplementum*, *106*, 10–11.

Larsen, T. K., Bechdolf, A., and Birchwood, M. (2003). The concept of schizophrenia and phase specific treatment: Psychological treatment in pre-psychosis and non-responders. *Journal of the American Academy of Psychoanalytic and Dynamic Psychiatry*, *31*, 209–228.

Lewis, S. W., Tarrier, N., Haddock, G., Bentall, R., Kinderman, P., Kingdon, D., and Drake, R. J. (2001). A randomised controlled trial of cognitive behavior therapy in early schizophrenia. *Schizophrenia Research*, *49* (Suppl.), 263.

Lieberman, J. A., Tollefson, G. D., Schulz, C., Zipursky, R., Sharma, T., Kahn, R. S., et al. (2005). Antipsychotic drug effects on brain morphology in first-episode psychosis. *Archives of General Psychiatry*, *62*, 361–370.

McGlashan, T. H. (2001). Psychosis treatment prior to psychosis onset: Ethical issues. *Schizophrenia Research*, *51*, 47–54.

McGlashan, T. H., Zipursky, R. B., Perkins, D., Addington, J., Miller, T. J., Woods, S. W., et al. (2003). The PRIME North America randomized double-blind clinical trial of olanzapine versus placebo in patients at risk of being prodromally symptomatic for psychosis. I: Study rationale and design. *Schizophrenia Research*, *61*, 7–18.

McGlashan, T. H., Zipursky, R. B., Perkins, D., Addington, J., Miller, T. J., Woods, S. W., et al. (2006). Randomized, double-blind trial of olanzapine versus placebo in patients prodromally symptomatic for psychosis. *American Journal of Psychiatry*, *163*, 790–799.

McGorry, P. D. (2005). Early intervention in psychotic disorders: Beyond debate to solving problems. *British Journal of Psychiatry*, *187* (Suppl. 48), s108–s110.

McGorry, P. D., Yung, A. R., Phillips, L. J., Yuen, H. P., Francey, S., Cosgrave, E. M., et al. (2002). Randomized controlled trial of interventions designed to reduce the risk of progression to first-episode psychosis in a clinical sample with subthreshold symptoms. *Archives of General Psychiatry*, *59*, 921–928.

Margolese, H. C., Chouinard, G., Kolivakis, T. T., Beauclair, L., Miller, R., and Annable, L. (2005). Tardive dyskinesia in the era of typical and atypical antipsychotics. Part 2: Incidence and management strategies in patients with schizophrenia. *Canadian Journal of Psychiatry*, *50*, 703–714.

Mason, O., Startup, M., Halpin, S., Schall, U., Conrad, A., and Carr, V. (2004). Risk factors for transition to first episode psychosis among individuals with 'at-risk mental states'. *Schizophrenia Research*, *71*, 227–237.

Maurer, K., Könnecke, R., Schultze-Lutter, F., and Häfner, H. (2000). Early recognition inventory. Unpublished manual and instrument, Mannheim, Germany.

Maurer, K., Horrmann, F., Schmidt, M., Trendler, H., and Häfner, H. (2004). The early recognition inventory: Structure, reliability and initial results. *Schizophrenia Research*, *67* (Suppl. 1), 34.

Meyer, S. E., Bearden, C. E., Lux, S. R., Gordon, J. L., Johnson, J. K., O'Brien, M. P., et al. (2005). The psychosis prodrome in adolescent patients viewed through the lens of DSM-IV. *Journal of Child and Adolescent Psychopharmacology*, *15*, 434–451.

Miller, T. J., McGlashan, T. H., Rosen, J. L., Somjee, L., Markovich, P. J., Stein, K., and Woods, S. W. (2002). Prospective diagnosis of the initial prodrome for schizophrenia based on the Structured Interview for Prodromal Symptoms: Preliminary evidence of interrater and predictive validity. *American Journal of Psychiatry*, *159*, 863–865.

Morrison, A. P. (2001). The interpretation of intrusions in psychosis: An integrative cognitive approach to hallucinations and delusions. *Behavioural and Cognitive Psychotherapy*, *29*, 257–276.

Morrison, A. P., French, P., Walford, L., Lewis, S. W., Kilcommons, A., Green, J., et al. (2004a). Cognitive therapy for the prevention of psychosis in people at ultra-high risk. *British Journal of Psychiatry*, *185*, 291–297.

Morrison, A. P., French, P., Walford, L., Lewis, S., Kilcommons, A., Green, J., et al. (2004b). A randomised controlled trial of cognitive therapy for prevention of psychosis in people at ultra-high risk. *Schizophrenia Research*, *67* (Suppl. 1), 7.

Morrison, A. P., French, P., Lewis, S. W., Roberts, M., Raja, S., Neil, S. T., et al. (2006). Psychological factors in people at ultra-high risk of psychosis: Comparisons with non-patients and associations with symptoms. *Psychological Medicine*, *36*, 1395–1404.

Morrison, A. P., French, P., Parker, S., Roberts, M., Stevens, H., Bentall, R. P., and Lewis, S. W. (2007). Three-year follow-up of a randomized controlled trial of cognitive therapy for the prevention of psychosis in people at ultra-high risk. *Schizophrenia Bulletin*, *33*(3), 682–687.

Nuechterlein, K. H. and Dawson, M. E. (1984). A heuristic vulnerability/stress model of schizophrenic episodes. *Schizophrenia Bulletin*, *10*, 300–312.

Overall, J. E. and Gorham, D. R. (1962). The Brief Psychiatric Rating Scale. *Psychological Reports*, *10*, 799–812.

Phillips, L. J. and Francey, S. M. (2004). Changing PACE: Psychological interventions in the pre-psychotic phase. In P. D. McGorry and J. F. Gleeson (Eds.), *Psychological interventions in early psychosis: A practical treatment handbook* (pp. 23–40). Chichester: Wiley.

Phillips, L. J., Addington, J., and Morrison, A. (2008). At Risk Mental State: Management. In H. J. Jackson and P. D. McGorry (Eds.), *Recognition and management of early psychosis: A preventive approach*. Cambridge: Cambridge University Press.

Pukrop, R., Schultze-Lutter, F., Ruhrmann, S., Brockhaus-Dumke, A., Tendolkar, I., Bechdolf, A., et al. (2006). Neurocognitive functioning in subjects at risk for a first episode of psychosis compared with first- and multiple-episode schizophrenia. *Journal of Clinical and Experimental Neuropsychology, 28*, 1388–4007.

Ruhrmann, S., Schultze-Lutter, F., and Klosterkötter, J. (2003). Early detection and intervention in the initial prodromal phase of schizophrenia. *Pharmacopsychiatry, 36* (Suppl. 3), s162–s167.

Schultze-Lutter, F., Wieneke, A., Picker, H., Rolff, Y., Steinmeyer, E. M., Ruhrmann, S., and Klosterkötter, J. (2004). The Schizophrenia Prediction Instrument, Adult version (SPI-A). *Schizophrenia Research, 70* (Suppl. 1), 76–77.

Sensky, T., Turkington, D., Kingdon, D., Scott, J. L., Scott, J., Siddle, R., et al. (2000). A randomised controlled trial of cognitive-behavioural therapy for persistent symptoms in schizophrenia resistant to medication. *Archives of General Psychiatry, 57*, 165–172.

Süllwold, L. and Herrlich, J. (1998). *Psychologische Behandlung schizophren Erkrankter*. Stuttgart: Kohlhammer Verlag.

Svirkis, T., Korkeila, J., Heinimaa, M., Huttunen, J., Ilonen, T., Ristkari, T., et al. (2005). Axis I disorders and vulnerability to psychosis. *Schizophrenia Research, 75*, 439–446.

Valmaggia, L. R., van der Gaag, M., Tarrier, N., Pijnenborg, M., and Slooff, C. J. (2005). Cognitive-behavioural therapy for refractory psychotic symptoms of schizophrenia resistant to atypical antipsychotic medication: Randomised controlled trial. *British Journal of Psychiatry, 186*, 324–330.

Warner, R. (2005). Problems with early and very early intervention in psychosis. *British Journal of Psychiatry, 187* (Suppl. 48), s104–s107.

Wells, A. (1997). *Cognitive therapy of anxiety disorders: A practice manual and conceptual guide*. Chichester: Wiley.

Yung, A. R. and McGorry, P. D. (1996a). The initial prodrome in psychosis: Descriptive and qualitative aspects. *Australian and New Zealand Journal of Psychiatry, 30*, 587–599.

Yung, A. R. and McGorry, P. D. (1996b). The prodromal phase of first-episode psychosis: Past and current conceptualizations. *Schizophrenia Bulletin, 22*, 353–370.

Yung, A. R., Phillips, L. J., McGorry, P. D., McFarlane, C. A., Francey, S., Patton, G. C., and Jackson, H. J. (1998). The prediction of psychosis: A step towards indicated prevention. *British Journal of Psychiatry, 172* (Suppl. 33), 14–20.

Yung, A. R., Phillips, L. J., Yuen, H. P., McGorry, P. D., Francey, S. F., and McFarlane, C. A. (2003). Psychosis prediction: 12 month follow-up of a high risk ('prodromal') group. *Schizophrenia Research, 60*, 21–32.

Yung, A. R., Yuen, H. P., McGorry, P. D., Phillips, L., Kelly, D., Dell'Olio, M., et al. (2005). Mapping the onset of psychosis: The Comprehensive Assessment of At

Risk Mental States (CAARMS). *Australian and New Zealand Journal of Psychiatry, 39,* 964–971.

Zimmermann, G., Favrod, J., Trieu, V. H., and Pomini, V. (2005). The effect of cognitive behavioral treatment on the positive symptoms of schizophrenia spectrum disorders: A meta-analysis. *Schizophrenia Research, 77,* 1–9.

Zubin, J. and Spring, B. (1977). Vulnerability: A new view of schizophrenia. *Journal of Abnormal Psychology, 86,* 103–126.

Chapter 8

Integration of psychotherapy in concept change within a culture – India

Ishita Sanyal

Introduction

Since the WHO studies of the 1970s it has generally been accepted that the prognosis for those with schizophrenia in developing countries has been better than for those in developed countries. India is often cited as one such developing country. However, since the mid 1970s India has developed considerably and through technology and globalization has become one of the economic powerhouses of the twenty-first century. This development has seen rapid change at every level in Indian society, and as such India is an interesting place to look at how treatment of schizophrenia and mental illness has developed alongside economic development and how cultural change has impacted on this. This chapter will describe one programme in India which is trying to address the needs of those with mental illness while taking into account the role of culture, social system, community, and family support systems.

India: some context

An adequate description of India is beyond the scope of a single chapter. India, the world's most populous democracy with a population of over one billion people, is a massive and varied country of distinct regional, religious and cultural differences. Therefore to place some context on discussion in this chapter, this section will try to describe some of the aspects of Indian culture which are common to many parts of the country and which are important to understand in terms of treatment of and challenges to treating, schizophrenia and other mental illnesses. In particular we will try to describe aspects of society and family which are important, as well as the effects of globalization on India and Indians.

Society and family

Family is of great importance in Indian society, and traditionally has been the centre of people's lives. However, the role of immediate and extended families is changing, as are the roles within the family. For example the role of women is undergoing great change. The traditional patriarchal family system is no longer the automatic norm. Now women are taking part in every sphere of life, earning money, representing communities, as well as managing homes. But for many women who have to juggle different societal roles and expectations, the cost of the juggling is that they often suffer from both physical and mental problems thereafter.

Young people in India also face conflict due to two diametrically opposite value systems. The traditional one based around being a respectful person in a family context and which valued knowledge, character, personality and patience, and the new one of consumerism where a person is judged more by his or her material possessions.

On 24 November 2000 Americans celebrated 'Buy Nothing Day' to draw attention to the intense effects of consumerism. However, countries like India with rapidly developing economies are becoming lucrative markets for new business groups. The time is not far off when it seems that India will celebrate 'Buy Everything Day'! For young people who constitute 50–60 per cent of the population of India these two forces, traditional and consumerist, create great strain. This leads to two groups readily visible all over the country – that of 'Rock and Roll' and the poor and frustrated hankering for making their life 'Rock and Roll'. As seen in other places, rampant consumerism puts traditional family values in danger. In striving to make their lives better, young people often move away from the family and social structure that could support them should they develop mental illness, a development that becomes more likely as they are exposed to the stresses of a consumerist ideology in which you can never have your appetites sated.

Effects of globalization

While India may have become one of the preferred global business destinations, quality of life for most people is not advancing at the same rate.

Globalization has had an uneven effect in India. While some people have profited greatly, the majority still live in slums and rural areas where living conditions are often well below average. In the same way, while literacy rates have increased, health literacy and especially mental health literacy has not. This affects not only lay people but also doctors and other professionals. Mental health literacy is a requirement not only for people in general but also for doctors both in rural and in urban areas.

Developments in the field of science and technology have revolutionized human life at a material level. But in actuality, this progress is only superficial; underneath modern men and women are living in conditions of great mental and emotional stress even in developed and affluent countries.

People suffer from the changed outlook of today's life; change in attitude, expectations, craving for material gain, conflict amongst the old traditional values and the changed modern morals and value systems create an enormous problem amongst the young population in India. People now crave for leisure and luxury and the quest for knowledge has changed into a quest for acquiring tools to get material pleasure. Social capital, support systems, and joint family setups are dispersing very quickly in India. Many of the youth of today, compared to their parent's generation, are materially successful, confident about their career but often suffer from conflict, anxiety and depression as they fail to cope with their own increased expectations from life and conflict due to changed moral values.

Turning Point

Description

In the mid 1990s, if people in Kolkata (formerly Calcutta) wanted to access a rehabilitation service for mental health problems they had to go to the National Institute of Mental Health and Neuroscience (NIMHANS) in Bangalore, which is nearly 2000 kilometres away. Due to the difficulties caused by distance, there was little chance of follow-up appointments and it was more or less impossible to continue treatment for most people. At the same time, as with people experiencing mental illness anywhere, people with mental illness in India suffered a number of frustrations. These included the failure to contribute productively to the family, frustration due to the loss of all their expectations for themselves, and loneliness caused by their withdrawal from the outer world. In the urban population, although some family members can provide economic support and treatment to their affected family members, their endeavours fail to improve the cognitive functioning, motivation and functional level of the person concerned. This often leads to reinforcing the belief that mentally ill people are always a burden on their family. Though they stay within the four walls of the family, they fail to get their due respect and rights.

To address the lack of a local service to help people with psychotic illnesses Turning Point was started in Kolkata a number of years ago. The aim was to provide a service which would address the symptomatic elements of illness but importantly address the functional elements also with the goal of helping the individual become a fully participating and productive member of the community. In this section of the chapter I will discuss the challenges that were faced in establishing our service. Following that I will describe the programme we have established and then talk about the way in which we are now using technology to further that programme.

Challenges

In establishing Turning Point we faced four main challenges. These were the challenge of introducing a mental health service and dealing with stigma in the local community, low mental health literacy misattributing the cause of mental illness to parents, particularly mothers, dealing with the family-based Indian culture when most of what we had to guide us comes from more individualized western culture, and ensuring that we enhanced the economic capabilities of our clients because of the low availability of welfare.

Local community

There can be great stigma associated with mental health interventions in India. Thus it is important to get the support of the local community in establishing and helping to run an organization for mentally ill people. Without this support the basic task of finding premises may prove to be an insurmountable obstacle. Locals sometimes start protesting against having such an organization in their area and make efforts to close it down. Even if the organization gets a location, such adverse local feeling may make it difficult to continue. Therefore there is a need for much local liaising to smooth the road before starting any organization in India. If properly motivated and made aware, the community can help a lot in the operation of the organization. Involvement of the community in programmes of the mental health centres helps the community to understand the affected members in a better way and help them in their journey to successful recovery.

Low mental health literacy

Because of low mental health literacy in India, parents are blamed for mental illness in their children. While this is valid for both parents, it is especially true for mothers. While both parents are often stigmatized by society, fathers, other relatives, and even the person with mental illness will all blame the mother for the onset of illness. As a result, the mother often suffers from depression, anxiety and even psychotic problems. During intervention for the affected child, intervention for the proper mental health of the mother is also needed. Where either the mother or both parents are experiencing these problems, it adversely affects their ability to help their family members. Thus special support is needed for parents. Parents in India are very emotionally involved with their children. They believe that the success or failure of children is the result of their efforts. In this typical Indian culture, parents feel guilty if a child is not established in life or is suffering from any disease or disorder. Special attention must be paid to the mothers as they are the most neglected, most victimized in the family. In particular there are three areas that need to be challenged when helping women in this situation: first, that she must always give in to others and fulfil her needs only in relation to theirs, rather than that of self-fulfilment, second, that she must always be connected to others and cannot survive outside marriage, motherhood and family, and third, that she must always behave in a responsible manner and deny her emotions and feelings.

Interdependent Indian culture versus independent western culture

Unlike western culture, Indian culture believes in interdependence not in independence. Interdependence is a way of life in India. People help others in need and at the same time get help and support during the time of crisis. Emotionally, it is very difficult for an Indian to believe 'I am alone' as the Indian culture and life is surrounded by relatives and family members. Therefore, any intervention centre needs to see the individual as part of a larger system of family and community and treatment goals need to be consistent with this larger view.

Economic needs

For people with schizophrenia or other mental illnesses in India, getting economic resources or assistance from the government is near to impossible. Thus, an important part of the rehabilitation process is helping people find a way to earn a livelihood. Research in India also shows that in the urban population the most important need for people suffering from mental illness is employment. In India the government provides employment reserved for all other disability groups apart from mental illness. Moreover people refuse to give jobs to people who have ever suffered from any mental illness. A person once recovered, if not given an employment opportunity, may get depressed or due to added stress, relapse. A therapist should think not only about short-term relief from symptoms, but also about the wider functional needs of the person. This is possible through vocational training and through proper selection of placement after the training. So a centre dealing with people with mental illness must have a long-term plan for their vocational training and economic rehabilitation, so that they can again start earning and become a productive member of the society. At the time that we were starting Turning Point the vocational training facilities that were available were limited to bookbinding, food processing, and some handicraft works only. There was no provision of training that would fulfil the intellectual needs of the person concerned.

The Turning Point programme

Any given therapy practised worldwide often proves to be inadequate to meet the growing needs of the affected individual. Integration of different techniques, keeping in mind the specific needs of the individual in terms of cultural and religious backgrounds needs to be undertaken.

The programme that we use consists of a number of elements. These are designed to address different areas of need of the people who come to our centre. The different areas of our programme are designed to aid the person with mental illness to return to participating in the community, both socially and vocationally.

Physical exercises

Many of the people who come to our centre suffer from apathy, lack of drive and prefer to remain in their bed. They have little initiative for any physical exercises. It remains difficult for professionals and family members to make them perform the regular physical exercises.

A rehabilitation programme must have exercise in its schedule at the beginning of the day. Regular exercise helps to overcome apathy. It also helps people to be more physically fit and thus avoid some of the physical ailments which may affect people with psychosis later on in their lives.

News session

A person suffering from illness generally loses contact with the outside world; friends and family members start thinking that the person with illness is not interested in the 'real' world. As the person with illness withdraws they have less and less on which to draw to communicate with people about. For example they may seldom watch news or go through the newspaper.

News Session in the centre helps them to come in contact with current events in the world. It is also a socialization exercise which models interaction in society where people often talk about what is happening in sport or politics, for example. Sharing of news by the members of rehabilitation centre aids clients to re-establish knowledge of the world. This helps them to gain confidence while communicating with outsiders. This is important because as they recover, people with psychotic illnesses can believe that they are less smart than other people and this can adversely affect their self-esteem and reinforces isolation.

Group games

It has been seen in studies of patients suffering from dementia, that it is helpful if they remain active in works which activate the brain. Group games are specially designed to improve concentration and memory, and thus help to regain their ability to do productive work.

Games and role modelling

Games and role modelling of communication help to overcome shyness and the tendency to withdraw. Systematic exposure to situations requiring interaction with others, with a supportive figure from the rehabilitation centre, can help them to gain confidence and start communicating with outsiders. Once gaining confidence, they too can interact and communicate freely with other people.

Vocational training

Vocational training and rewards in the form of remuneration increase motivation. At Turning Point, it was observed that the women of the centre gained confidence, had increased motivation and increased functional level once they started getting remunerated for their work. Vocational training especially suitable for men was introduced, which increased their motivation and functional level also.

Other therapies

In addition the centre utilizes family interventions and supportive and cognitive therapy approaches. These therapies are often adapted to suit the cultural context. For example fear of failure can be addressed not only through cognitive behaviour therapy but also through including some Indian philosophy which may remind the person with illness that one only 'has the control over his activities and not on the result or output'.

Due to paucity of the organized care, families have always been a part of mental health care throughout the history of India. Whether this was by choice or due to lack of facilities it is difficult to conclude, although family involvement in care continues to be a preference. Families need to have several areas addressed in the interventions with them. These include:

- high level of expectations and critical comments or too little expectation and over-protection
- over-involvement
- problems related to long-term treatment
- lack of understanding of residual symptoms
- problems related to marriage
- rehabilitation.

Self-help groups

As the relatives and family members do not have an understanding of the problem of mental illness due to lack of mental health literacy, formation of self-help groups can be a great support at times of crisis. A mother of an affected child narrates her story where she got the help from the self-help group:

My son went away from our house. I was extremely worried. My husband kept aloof as always. It was the members of the self-help group who were with me 24 hours a day till my son returned back. They assisted me to take help from the police, enquire in the hospitals etc. I think they acted like my family members.

Role of technology

At Turning Point we have also started to use computers as part of our rehabilitation efforts. Computers have the ability to act as the bridge between the persons suffering from mental illness and society in general. The affected person also gains confidence and courage as they gain control over the machine. Using computers and the internet allows for many areas of intervention as is detailed below.

Awareness

Lack of mental health literacy is a large problem confronting those with mental illness and those who wish to help them in a recovery-oriented way. Like many people, those with illness and their families often believed that there is no cure for mental illness, and that life cannot get better. This led to feelings of hopelessness and helplessness among family members. These feelings led in turn to increased stress and anxieties, which led to higher levels of expressed emotions.

As generally the family members in India are supportive – gaining adequate knowledge and information about the illness through specific reliable websites on the internet instils hope in them. It also reduces their level of anxiety and stress and helps them to provide adequate support and motivation to the affected family member. Moreover, the information about other families throughout India helped to form self-help groups where they feel free to discuss about the problem without shame and discomfort.

The person with mental illness also develops new hopes by exploring these websites, and this often helps them to regain the courage to work at their recovery. The stories of recoveries from all over the world give much needed inspiration. As they are often written by those who have recovered, they have a credibility that psychiatrists and psychologists don't. Awareness of the possibility of recovery, along with vocational training and rehabilitation helps them to gain back needed confidence and start their life anew.

Psychoeducation

Psychoeducation is very important for both the family and the person concerned to get a true understanding of the problem, learn coping strategies, crisis management, and skills for handling delusions and hallucinations.

India is a vast country and due to lack of adequate funds it is often nearly impossible to carry on psychoeducation programmes of the magnitude that is needed. However, much of this information is available on the internet and this provides a cheap way for large numbers of people to access it. As they do they are able to discuss what they are learning with others.

Accessing professional advice

Compared to the magnitude of the problem of mental illness in India the number of professionals available is limited. To fill in the gap, the computer proves to be an effective solution. Through using the internet the advice of psychiatrists and psychologists can be given. Though we have not been able to have a web-camera, we have been able to keep a link between Turning Point and some renowned psychiatrists and international groups. This has allowed us to ask for and receive help and advice on a range of issues.

Reducing the stigma

One of the most common stereotypes of mental illness is that people suffering from mental illness are either dangerous or do not possess intelligence and rationality. Consequently, general society often wants to segregate those with mental illness and sometimes their families from their so-called 'normal society'. Through information technology stigma can be reduced. The communities where awareness programmes are active have started to accept people with mental illness more freely now.

Affordable treatment opportunities

For running a rehabilitation centre for persons suffering from schizophrenia empathetic people from the community are given appropriate trainings through computers. This once again utilizes the online access we have with psychiatrists and psychologists. This method of training and using local people reduces the cost of treatment sharply.

Social rehabilitation

Due to stigma, due to hopelessness, due to fear of rejection – people with mental illness often try to avoid interacting with society. This creates a barrier. Computers can act as an effective tool to remove this barrier. A person feels free and safe to experiment with the computer. It creates a criticism-free atmosphere where they are learning to control a machine. These persons used to think that they have lost control of their life and so dare not to control others. Controlling a machine helps them to regain their self-confidence. As the computer is a modern gadget they feel proud to learn it. They get the pleasure and confidence that they too can learn something new, something valuable in life.

Interaction with other sufferers though the internet gives them a chance to socialize with others without being afraid of developing a negative self-image. Being overly sensitive, these persons are often afraid to meet anyone. They often fear that they may create a negative image in the eyes of others. Computers help them to interact and communicate freely. Once they gain back the lost confidence, they feel free to communicate directly with the society. This helps the social rehabilitation process.

Effects of vocational training

Work therapy is very beneficial in the case of people with schizophrenia, especially if they earn through it. The economic freedom adds value to their life and quality of life increases. Once they gain back confidence, these people act as a resource and inspiration for others in the vocational training programme. After their recovery, they too act as a teacher and give training to other people with mental illness and help in the process of rehabilitation.

Group therapy

Group therapy always promotes the feeling 'that my problem is not a unique one' and that 'I too can recover like others'. Information of recovery from sufferers throughout the world – often acts as group therapy session where they can chat and discuss their difficulties and search for a probable solution.

Two case examples from Turning Point

Case study: Kakoli

Kakoli, a woman of 25 years, joined our rehabilitation programme five years back. At that time establishing rapport was very difficult as she had many delusions and hallucinations and she would talk only about film stars and her 'interaction' with them. Completely aloof from reality she would never pay attention to the sessions at the rehabilitation centre. I even asked her mother to discontinue counselling sessions at that time. Her mother was sincere, having faith in the counselling and in the programmes offered by the centre. Later on, a good rapport was developed and Kakoli started engaging with the sessions. In the rehabilitation centre at first she appeared slow, with poor memory, low concentration and low functioning skills. In the vocational centre, it was very difficult for her to thread the needle with her trembling hands. However, the games to improve concentration and memory really showed an effect in Kakoli. Her memory increased a lot and she started to learn how to use the computer.

Her mother was very regular in the awareness programmes and tried to follow the suggestions given during family counselling sessions. She was active in the self-help group of parents and tried to help others in distress. Kakoli gradually gained confidence, became an expert in handicrafts and good in computer handling also. Not only that, but also she learnt to fight for her own human rights. She would always keep a close vigil on the remuneration that she was receiving for her work. She would go into every detail to be assured that the remuneration she was receiving was accurate.

Two years previously when her mother fell ill (she used to stay with her widowed mother) she was able to manage all the household chores, going to the market, to the bank, to hospital and also coming to the rehabilitation centre alone. At night, when I sometimes used to make a call to assure her that she can ask for help if required, she would thank us but tell us she did not need help.

Case study: Prakash

During counselling sessions, I put stress on motivating the person to do the work in their personal life and also at the rehabilitation centre. To increase motivation often we make use of his/her own cultural, religious, spiritual beliefs. Indian philosophy believes in 'Karma Yogi' where one could achieve 'Moksha' through Karma or work. This 'Moksha' implies peace and serenity within oneself which could be achieved by performing one's own tasks.

Prakash, a young aggressive man, came to my office and started narrating gleefully how he hits his family members without showing any sign of feeling guilty. In fact, I was apprehensive and was not willing to admit such an aggressive person to the rehabilitation centre until he overcame his aggression. His family members pleaded to give him a chance at least for a few days. Finding out the potentialities of each and every person at the initial stage and focusing him on those activities is in our planned schedule. Prakash was eager to learn to use the computer. He gained so much satisfaction and confidence during his computer training sessions that his aggression decreased a lot. During his counselling sessions, it was also easy to address that for his own benefit to learn the computer he needed to gain control, not only on the computer but also over his aggression. Prakash rapidly improved his management of his aggression and his skills on the computer. Eventually he joined our centre as a resource person in computers.

Challenges to the future in India

Having described our programme, I will conclude by listing some of the challenges that remain for mental health in India.

Making the benefits of modern psychiatry geographically and economically available to all sections of the population

In India, this challenge has been with us for a long time. The extension of mental health services through general hospitals and through primary health care network has only partly helped. Still the majority of the people living in rural areas and in the city slums have no easy access to modern psychiatric services. In recent years, the private sector has made significant progress and is greatly helping in the big cities but we must remember that nearly 40 per cent of the Indian population is so poor that public sector mental health system is their only hope.

Combining biomedical and psychosocial approaches in psychiatric practice

Fashions changed rapidly in twentieth-century psychiatry. From the one extreme of psychoanalysis and dynamic psychiatry of the 1940s and 1950s we have moved to the other extreme of biologically oriented psychiatry. Mass treatment with psychotropic drugs is hardly a solution to psychosocial problems of the society and it may itself run into problems. To combine the biological and the psychosocial in our understanding of human suffering, is our special double heritage and we must not give up one for the sake of the other.

Utilizing communication technology

Effective utilization of communication technology and the computer can bring an enormous change in the lives of persons suffering from mental illness.

Making psychiatry more relevant for Indian cultural needs

Perhaps no other civilization has looked at the human mind and its functions as intensely as we have done in India for the last 3000 years but still our contributions find no place in modern psychiatry. In the field of psychotherapy we have a very powerful message from Indian philosophy that there is a limit to manipulating the external world; ultimate happiness and peace comes by changing oneself rather than changing the world. It is good to record that during the last few decades Indian psychiatrists are putting across in scientific meetings their experiences with traditional approaches like yoga, meditation, etc. We should, however, not confine ourselves only to describe the uses of Indian techniques of psychiatry but we should also come forward with Indian ideas about the basic concepts in psychiatry.

Keeping balance between psychiatry and mental health

The practice of psychiatry is now not restricted to the diagnosis and treatment of mental disorders, but includes prevention of mental disorders and promotion of mental health as its legitimate field of interest and activities. This expanded vision of psychiatry is creating its own difficulties. In public mental health programmes we have to involve other health professionals also. Here we can successfully train the family members and affected individuals once recovered to help others in need and to promote awareness and preventive mental health.

Integrating psychotherapeutic thinking and practice into 'real world' settings

Chapter 9

An integrated treatment program for first-episode schizophrenia

Rachel Miller, Joanne McCormack and Serge Sevy

Introduction

In the real world of working with young people in treatment for schizophrenia for the first time there are individual, institutional and practical concerns that often make treatment complex. Each patient is a unique person and no recovery is the same. Symptoms at first presentation, developmental stage, socioeconomic level, intelligence, cultural and ethnic background, academic accomplishments, work experience, use of substances, history of trauma, duration of untreated psychosis, personal strengths, and family all vary widely. And while most young people we describe have few significant personality problems, some have antisocial, borderline or other difficult personality traits. All of these issues need to be addressed in treatment, even after the remission of symptoms (McGorry, 2005). There are many practical problems that interfere with the ideal treatment plan, such as lack of health benefits, unavailability of families, and inability to get transportation to treatment. Institutions may be unable to provide the many services needed by first-episode patients. For example, in the United States medical coverage often determines the location of treatment, resulting in a dispersion of patients over wide geographical areas so that it is logistically difficult to develop programs or groups for first-episode treatment.

In this chapter, we describe an integrated treatment program developed over a period of years for young people coming into treatment for the first time for schizophrenia, schizophreniform disorder and schizoaffective disorder. In particular, we focus on a group of 79 patients enrolled in an ongoing first-episode study, many of whom presented with cannabis abuse and other significant treatment issues. In discussing integrative treatment we refer to treatment of co-occurring psychiatric disorders and substance abuse that is provided by one treatment team in order to address each disorder and its interactions (Mueser et al., 2003). Several studies, in fact, support the benefits of integrative psychosocial treatments for people with first-episode schizophrenia (Gleeson et al., 2003; Malla et al., 2002) and for people with first-episode and co-occurring substance abuse (Addington and Addington,

2001). Integration, as it has developed in the program we describe, offers a wide range of treatments and combines patients who do not use substances as well as those who do – an adaptation we will discuss in more detail in a later section. We focus treatment around a triad of insight, adherence and abstinence, which provides a model that permits us to maintain sight of the goals of treatment needed for optimizing recovery (Miller et al., 2005).

Within the framework of the Insight-Adherence-Abstinence model of treatment we utilize a combination of treatment approaches (Miller et al., 2005) as is the trend in treatments of schizophrenia today (Bachmann et al., 2003; Fenton and Schooler, 2000). This enables a range of problems to be addressed, including acceptance of illness, medication adherence, reintegration of self, building insight, improving coping skills, building social skills, decreasing cognitive deficits, addressing past trauma, returning to school or work, family problems, and abuse of substances.

Background

The New Onset of Psychosis (NOPS) psychosocial program has an 11-year history of working with young people coming into treatment for the first time for schizophrenia, schizophreniform disorder and schizoaffective disorder, hereafter referred to as schizophrenia for simplicity. The program was developed for the treatment of patients over the course of several first-episode schizophrenia studies taking place in the greater-metropolitan New York area. Young people were eligible for these research studies if they met the DSM-IV (American Psychiatric Association, 1994) criteria for schizophrenia, schizophreniform or schizoaffective disorder and were able to give informed consent. Once they enrolled in the respective studies, they were treated within the NOPS treatment program.

During the 11 years, there were 166 patients (87 in the first group and 79 in the second) who were followed under the auspices of the NOPS program. The psychosocial program changed over time in response to what we found effective in treatment and to changes in the patients' therapeutic needs. The first study (completed in 1999), which included treatment with antipsychotic medications, focused on biological aspects of schizophrenia. Patients were not accepted if they had substantial amounts of substance use that would affect the biologic measures of the study. For the second, ongoing study, patients abusing substances (excluding intravenous drugs) are eligible unless substance abuse is the primary cause of psychotic symptoms. As a result of the change in the inclusion/exclusion criteria there has been an increase in the number of patients with co-occurring substance abuse diagnoses. In the second study, upon which we are here focused, patients are initially randomized to either risperidone or olanzapine. If they do not respond or have significant side effects, their medicine is changed based on the best clinical judgment of the treating psychiatrist.

Integrated treatment

In addition to the integrated model of treatment for schizophrenia and co-occurring substance abuse, integration of treatment occurs on multiple levels: organizational structure, patient population, treatment modalities, treatment orientations, and research with clinical care.

Organizational structure

Treatment is organized around a continuous care team, consisting of two psychiatrists, a senior social worker and social work interns. The team follows patients from initial hospitalization to day program and on to outpatient treatment. This requires cooperation from the inpatient, day program and outpatient departments.

Patient population

All treatment groups are fully integrated without regard to age, sex, socio-economic factors, religion, marital status, ethnicity or history of substance abuse. Patients range in age from 16 to 38 years, with an average age of 23; there were 54 males and 25 females. This is a diverse ethnic group with 38 Black/African American, 22 Caucasian, 9 Hispanic, 7 Asian and 3 mixed. Many patients were born in the United States but others are immigrants from a variety of countries including Jamaica, Haiti, Russia, India, China, Central and South America, Philippines, Croatia, Poland and Korea. Of the 79 patients, 69 were never married, 4 are married and 6 are separated or divorced.

Treatment modalities

Patients are treated with antipsychotic medications in accordance with the protocol of the study. Additional medications are provided as needed. Psychosocial treatment includes individual and family treatment, patient groups, family groups, and family groups that include patients. The focus of individual treatment takes into account the phase of illness. Individual sessions are especially important during the early weeks of treatment when patients require help maintaining hope that they will improve and encouragement to stay the course of treatment. Once patients are able to leave the unit (usually at two weeks), they are encouraged to join the NOPS daily group, which takes place a short distance from the inpatient unit. This morning group provides the core of the treatment program from which patients later move into the NOPS outpatient groups. The connections made with peers in this group are strong and appear to help patients stay in treatment when they are transferred to different levels of care. Family treatment usually involves parents but in several cases we are working with husbands, wives, or other significant people in the lives of patients. Treatment for families begins during the first weeks of treatment, gradually shifting from individual family meetings to group modality for psychoeducation and problem-solving groups.

Treatment orientations

Therapy programs have evolved to integrate a broad range of treatment orientations, including such approaches as training in social skills and coping strategies, cognitive therapies, supportive therapies and psychoeducation (Bachmann et al., 2003). While these approaches are useful, the therapeutic relationship is essential. The treatment program, with its team of professionals, provides what Corradi (2004) describes as a 'holding environment' that allows patients to progress gradually. In agreement with Bachmann and colleagues, we believe it is most important that treatment be patient-centered and that the therapists 'exhibit emotional support, empathy, warmth, authenticity, transparency, and reliability' (Bachmann et al., 2003, p. 169).

For our patients it is recognized that we are treating a severe illness in people who are, foremost, human beings with their own unique personality and family problems, but whose thinking – at least initially – may be severely compromised by the effects of illness. For this reason, various approaches for understanding and attending to the problems of our patients are necessary. Ego supportive treatments help build reality testing and coping skills. Behavioral and cognitive behavioral approaches are instrumental with substance abuse problems and improving adherence. Cognitive therapy is also helpful for decreasing problems with impulse control, mood reactivity, behavioral problems unrelated to psychosis, and distorted thinking about the self. Social skills building exercises and cognitive enhancement therapy assist with cognitive difficulties and reintegration (Bellack et al., 1997; Hogarty and Flesher, 1999; Miller and Mason, 2004). Psychoanalytic theory is informative for understanding the destabilization of the sense of self and for working with identity issues. Substance abusing patients benefit from the use of theories taken from the stages of change model and motivational enhancement therapy (Mueser et al., 2003; Velasquez et al., 2001).

Neurobiological theories also inform treatment. Recognizing the role of biology in the etiology, course of illness and medication treatments is the foundation for psychoeducation. Patients benefit greatly from understanding how the brain works, the role of neurons and neurotransmitters, and how medications work. This provides a way in which to understand what happened to them and what is required to improve.

Research with clinical care

Providing clinical care within the research setting is beneficial to both patients and the research program. Because patients are participating in a research program in which they have consented for treatment, they are able to access resources that are not available to the general patient population. Fee waivers are available for people ineligible for benefits and those awaiting benefits, a process that often takes 3–8 months or more when benefits are denied and appeals are made for Medicaid or Social Security benefits. Transportation is available for those who are unable to find alternative means for coming into treatment. In addition, the research department nurse and technician assist with urine testing and other laboratory needs. The research staff advises the social workers of any problems they identify during research interviews that may be important to treatment. (This is agreed to by each patient during the consent process and does not appear to pose any problems.) In return, the research program benefits from the ability of the psychosocial program to retain patients in treatment and provides opportunities to meet with patients for research purposes when they come in for their psychosocial treatments.

Obstacles to treatment

As previously discussed, first-episode patients have many difficulties; however, the following problems stand out as obstacles to recovery.

Drop-outs

Drop-out, a common occurrence for newly diagnosed clients, is a significant problem (Coldham et al., 2002; Verdoux et al., 2000). The importance of not dropping out of treatment is supported by research telling us that patients with a short duration of illness have a better prognosis and decreased likelihood for treatment resistant psychosis (Bustillo et al., 1999; Edwards et al., 1998). In our experience, two factors appear most important in assisting patients to stay in treatment: continuity of care, and the connection with peers in treatment groups.

Poor adherence with medication

Adherence to recommended medications is a significant difficulty in treatment of first-episode schizophrenia (Coldham et al., 2002; Gaebel et al., 2002). The reasons for poor adherence for our patients are varied and include problems accepting the diagnosis; poor memory; lack of family support; poor judgment due to substance abuse; complaints of side effects (particularly weight gain and sexual dysfunction); and poor insight. Acceptance of illness has been a difficult process for nearly all patients and is not specific to any ethnicity, socioeconomic group or gender. For most of our patients, once psychotic symptoms resolve, lack of insight appears to be related to defense mechanisms and the 'sealing over' process as described by several authors

(McGlashan et al., 1975; Tait et al., 2003). Very few patients with poor insight are adherent; however, there are some exceptions.

Peter remains isolative, continues to believe in an imaginary friend, and does not believe he has an illness. Nevertheless, he recognizes – although he is not sure why – that his medication is helpful to him, and he takes it regularly.

Adherence is an ongoing issue in treatment for the majority of patients. In fact, over time we came to recognize that most patients experiment with lowering or discontinuing medication – at least once. Research also informs us that relapse is highly associated with poor adherence and can be significantly reduced (Robinson et al., 1999). Psychotherapy and psychoeducation focus on building insight by helping patients understand as much as possible about schizophrenia and its treatment and supporting their ability to accept treatment.

Amy is an example of a young woman who lowered her dose of medication on her own. When symptoms of sleeplessness and withdrawal returned, she was encouraged to see this as an experiment from which she could learn how to recognize symptoms and better care for herself in the future.

Helping patients explore resistance to medication in group, individual and family settings is beneficial. Use of aids for remembering medication, especially the see-through weekly pill box, has been effective for many patients. Additionally, enlisting families and patients to accept family monitoring of medication for the first year by presenting this to patients as the clinician's instructions to the family eliminates much of the power struggle over medication and decreases family members' confusion about their role in monitoring medication.

Substance abuse

Research indicates that substance abuse compromises treatment for schizophrenia and therefore requires aggressive and early treatment (Swofford et al., 2000). At the beginning of treatment 40 (50 per cent) of the 79 patients met DSM-IV (American Psychiatric Association, 1994) criteria for substance abuse or dependence as follows: 4 alcohol only; 21 cannabis only; 10 cannabis and alcohol; 1 cannabis and cocaine; 1 cannabis, alcohol and cocaine; 1 cannabis, alcohol, cocaine and opioids; 1 cannabis, alcohol, cocaine and hallucinogens; and 1 cannabis, alcohol and hallucinogens.

Based on our observations that patients who continue to use do not do as well, and often much worse than those who abstain, stopping all use is now a target of treatment. For this reason we integrate a prevention and treatment program into all patient groups. Explaining the risks of continued use is initiated with patients as early as the first days of treatment and continues to be reinforced throughout the continuum.

Motivation for abstinence, usually built on connecting past behaviors and their consequences (Mueser et al., 2003), presents a particular difficulty. First-episode patients do not have a history of relapse and recovery upon which to build motivation. Some stop using immediately because they believe their symptoms are due to substance abuse. However, this generally leads to the 'logical' conclusion that if they stop using substances the symptoms will not return; therefore, they no longer need medication.

Russell is a 20-year-old man who used marijuana and one ecstasy pill a month prior to coming for treatment. He did not return to using substances and had an excellent recovery. Therefore, he and his family decided that substances were responsible for his previous symptoms and he stopped medication. This led to a severe exacerbation of symptoms and a decline in his capabilities. Although he stabilized, he became lethargic and unmotivated, sleeping much of the day and unable to function in school. His family then blamed this on his medication and insisted on a reduction in medications that again led to an increase in symptoms.

Another dilemma in treatment is that newly recovering patients do not always have the insight or judgment necessary to think through decisions about substance use or its consequences. If they start using substances again, their symptoms worsen and the cycle continues. In order to address these problems, treatment focuses on the three core issues of insight, adherence and abstinence (Miller et al., 2005).

- *Insight:* developing an understanding of the illness and the benefits of adherence and abstinence.
- *Adherence:* working with the team on finding the best medications and taking those medications regularly.
- *Abstinence:* avoiding cannabis and other substances. Using no alcohol if alcohol abuse existed or only minimum alcohol if there was no history of alcohol abuse.

Initially we organized special groups for substance using patients, but we found patients did not do well. Therefore, we changed our model, integrating using and non-using patients, which appears to be more effective. Weekly urine testing was also introduced as part of the treatment plan – like getting weighed at a diet group – to be started as soon as patients moved out of the inpatient unit.

Negative symptoms and cognitive functioning

Patients with schizophrenia are often disorganized and struggling with impairments of concentration and memory (Addington et al., 2003). Within this group of patients, preliminary analysis shows that 21 patients suffered ongoing prominent negative symptoms of affective flattening, low energy, low drive and poor motivation. However, it appears most patients benefit from help with simple skills such as keeping a 'to do' list of activities and learning to prioritize and to break tasks into smaller steps. Patients are encouraged to begin reading for short periods and gradually increase their readings and the complexity of the material.

For patients returning to school, study skills are demonstrated and reviewed. Poor social skills, another frequent difficulty, are addressed with skill building exercises and practice in becoming interactive with peers. In group treatment, patients begin with mirroring exercises and using 'who, what, when, where and why/how' questions to increase the content of discussions. Eye contact is approached from the viewpoint of improving communication. In addition to helping patients connect with peers, friends and family, these skills help patients to be able to verbalize their thoughts and feelings regarding their illness and treatment in order to work through the many difficult psychological issues with which they are faced (Miller and Mason, 2004).

Shame, guilt and stigma

With few exceptions, first-episode patients struggle with feelings of shame regarding their illness. Usually this is closely tied to the stigma that society places on people with severe mental illnesses. Young people, who are often feeling they can no longer live up to their internalized ideal selves, may feel sad, angry and hopeless. Patients also often experience guilt, in particular when they believe drug use caused their illness; when they were aggressive during the psychotic episode; and when discontinuing medication leads to relapse. Feelings of shame can lead to depression and suicidal ideation. By addressing feelings of shame and guilt early in treatment, patients are often able to avoid serious depression and feelings that life is no longer worth living. Group treatment has been the superior modality in helping patients to accept themselves and their illness (see Woodhead, Chapter 14 in this volume). Patients are assisted to verbalize feelings associated with shame and guilt. Discussion focuses on understanding stereotyping, stigma, and self-stigmatizing; normalizing past aggressive behavior as due to the 'chemical imbalance' (only when aggressive behavior was in fact due to acute symptoms of psychosis); and learning to utilize mistakes for future motivation and planning (Miller and Mason, 2005).

Ongoing symptoms

Within the first 12 weeks of treatment 44 per cent of the patients responded on olanzapine and 54 per cent responded on risperidone, where response was defined as significant improvement on positive symptoms (i.e., delusions, hallucinations, thought disorder, and bizarre behavior) (Robinson et al., 2005). Those patients who did not adequately respond went on to try other medications – with varying degrees of success. Patients undergoing medication changes require significant support for themselves and their family members. Both group and multi-family groups were instrumental in providing hope and support.

Bart is an example of a young man who failed to respond to olanzapine, risperidone and fluphenazine before being started on clozapine. For more than a year his modest dose of clozapine caused him to sleep 15 hours daily and left him so tired he was unable to function when he was awake. The groups helped him and his mother to cope with the ongoing symptoms – and to avoid his return to poly-substance use – throughout the first year and the debilitating side effects of the second year, until gradually he recovered.

When patients do respond to treatment, the resolution of delusions is a gradual process. For example, we find that in the case of religious delusions there is a shift from full delusions to residual delusions, to ideation, and finally freedom from delusions (Miller and McCormack, 2006). During this period patients are receiving group therapy that attends to helping patients develop insight. This therapy uses a combination of psychoeducation and cognitive behavioral approaches and helps patients to process issues of shame, stigma and identity that may make them vulnerable to depression during the recovery period.

In working with our patients, we find that even after delusions have cleared, people who have a long duration of psychotic symptoms often maintain patterns of automatic thinking connected to delusions. Eye contact remains poor after years of paranoid thinking, or as is the case with one young man, when anxious he automatically returns to prior behaviors such as checking windows.

Jill, who previously heard voices telling her to kill herself, continued to have these thoughts when the psychosis lifted. Many patients are helped by the explanation that their thoughts and behaviors were learned during their psychotic state and can now be relinquished using various distraction and replacement techniques. Jill, for example, learned to catch herself and purposefully think, 'I'm a good person'.

Note that treatment utilizes many of the techniques of cognitive behavioral treatment (CBT), but treatment is integrated into the ongoing supportive setting (rather than manualized) so that other issues may be addressed as necessary.

Weight gain

Weight gain is the side effect that is experienced most widely by the patients in this group. During the first 16 weeks of treatment, approximately 50 per cent of the patients experienced a weight gain in the range 12–15 per cent and even higher if they also took divalproex (Robinson et al., 2005). Weight gain not only is an important health concern but also leads to self-esteem issues related to body image changes. To ameliorate this problem, a healthy diet and exercise module was added.

Personality traits

When patients come into treatment they sometimes present with personality problems, which may disappear as psychotic symptoms remit. However, there are patients whose maladaptive personality traits persist despite the improvement in their psychotic symptoms.

Ben is an example of a young man with many antisocial traits. This 21 year old was a gang leader on parole when he came into the hospital experiencing delusions and hallucinations. His only resource was an elderly, sick grandparent who had raised him when his mother was unable to do so due to her own illness. Before becoming ill, Ben had a gun, committed crimes, used drugs and hurt people. A year later his symptoms were responding well to medication and abstinence, but his personality characteristics required ongoing psychotherapy. Surprisingly, as with a number of other young males in this group with similar backgrounds, his regression into psychosis appears to have allowed him to make a therapeutic attachment so that he was able to begin to trust and try to make changes in his behavior.

Similarly, Larry is a young man who made a bomb threat when psychotic and continued, after remission of psychotic symptoms, to make suicidal gestures when angry. He was able to utilize a combination of CBT to recognize his triggers and dynamic therapy to better understand his emotional state.

Lack of family supports

Much of the literature regarding treatment of first-episode patients focuses on family treatment; however, a significant number of patients in the study being described do not have family available to participate in treatment. The causes vary: family members are dead, live at a distance, are medically or mentally ill, have transportation problems, or are unable to leave work. These patients not only lack the emotional support families usually provide, but also lack help with obtaining benefits, filling prescriptions, getting to appointments and taking medication. Intensive case management services are available and have proven effective in providing emotional and practical supports. Within our area these services are offered by outside agencies that provide a caseworker who maintains weekly contact with the patient and works collaboratively with the treatment team.

Trauma and family dysfunction

While a thorough discussion of trauma therapy for first-episode patients is beyond the scope of this chapter, some patients do come into treatment with a history of early trauma. In agreement with Read and Ross (2003), in such cases psychotherapy is necessary. When addressing troubling issues such as family dysfunction and past trauma, we maintain an empathic, non-judgmental and accepting stance. We also find it is essential to wait until patients are stable. A careful balance is then required to help patients verbalize feelings without becoming depressed, a difficulty we have addressed by helping patients build awareness of the effect of thoughts on their mood and behavior and by helping them recognize their ability to choose to be different from troubling family members. Appropriate coping skills are then reinforced.

Larry is an example of a 21-year-old man whose anger at abandonment by his father at a young age was complicating treatment. He was a good student until high school when he began to spend time with a group that abused alcohol and marijuana and accosted people for money. There were long periods of time when he was neither depressed nor using substances; however, his behavior changed and psychotic symptoms developed. Throughout the first year of treatment, he struggled with his anger at his father, who refused to speak to him. By helping him to recognize how his anger led to irritability and antisocial behaviors, Larry's mood became less reactive. Further, he was able to differentiate himself from his father and develop ideals that he began to integrate into his personality. At two and a half years into treatment, Larry is without psychotic or mood symptoms, has good relationships with his mother, stepfather and sister, has a girlfriend, is able to travel independently, completed his high school equivalency diploma, and is preparing for a new program that will lead to training in mechanics. Although the primary focus has been on Larry's insight, adherence to treatment and abstinence from substances, it was necessary to address the family issues that placed him at risk for substance abuse, depression and subsequent relapse.

Discussion

At study entry there were 79 patients; 11 patients left the study during the first 6 months (5 remained in treatment outside the study and 6 discontinued all treatment). Following the first 6-month period, drop-out rates appeared to lessen, with 8 leaving treatment during the remainder of the 3 years of the study, and only 3 of these patients not receiving treatment elsewhere. It should be noted that this is an ongoing study and 11 patients have not yet completed the full 3 years, although all have participated for more than 1 year. To date the drop-out rate is 24 per cent from the study, or 11 per cent if we recognize that 10 of the 19 who left the study went to treatment else-where. The 10 patients who transferred to other treatment did so for a variety of reasons, including moving from the area or not being interested in being in research. Similar drop-out rates in a program for first-episode substance abuse patients are reported at 20 per cent by Addington and Addington (2001). Gaebel et al. (2002) reported a 56–63 per cent drop-out rate for first-episode patients enrolled in a 2-year study of medication treatment strategies. Given the difficulties with first-episode patients dropping out of treatment, it appears this program has been helpful in retaining patients in treatment.

At initial entry into the study 40 of the 79 patients were past or current users of substances. As noted in Table 9.1, 33 had active substance abuse problems at the time of study entry: 23 met criteria for a current abuse or dependence diagnosis at the time of entry and 10 were not currently using, but only because of psychotic symptoms or incarceration. At the end of 1 year of treatment there were 64 patients in study treatment; 6 of the patients who

Table 9.1 Substance abuse at 12 months (n = 79)

	At baseline (gender)	No use at 12 months	Occasional use at 12 months	Meeting criteria for abuse or dependence at 12 months	Drop-outs
Patients with no history of substance abuse problems	39 (17F, 22M)	30	1	0	9
Patients with resolved substance abuse problems	7 (3F, 4M)	6	1	0	0
Patients with active substance abuse problems	33 (5F, 28M)	10	4	13	6

Note: F = female; M = male

left treatment had a history of substance abuse and 9 had no history of substance use. Among the group that was initially identified with active substance abuse problems, many continued use during the first year with 13 of the 33 using substances at the end of 52 weeks.

It should be noted that while these findings indicate low drop-out rates and a decrease in substance use, patients were enrolled in a medication study that did not research psychosocial interventions. Psychosocial interventions changed over time in an effort to improve treatment. There was no randomization to an experimental group and a control group, and no claims of evidence-based efficacy can therefore be made.

Conclusion

Focusing on the triad of insight, adherence and abstinence provides treatment with a foundation for integrating interventions to meet individual needs. This approach to treatment does not disregard the many problems of first-episode patients but asks, 'What are the difficulties unique to each patient that impede insight, adherence and abstinence.' Different problems require different treatment modalities and a variety of treatment orientations as outlined in Table 9.2.

Therapy for first-episode schizophrenia patients remains complex due to the nature of the illness, the developmental stage of adolescence during which people often begin treatment, and the many different needs of each individual. In addition, the social and financial supports vary widely, as do the life experiences of individuals. It is our impression that most first-episode patients and their families are fearful of being grouped with chronic patients, and that much of our success is a result of having a designated first-episode program. For providers it is not always possible to offer specialized first-episode groups, but the importance of this is an area that we believe needs to be studied and addressed. Over the 11 years of adapting the program to the patients' needs, we have made many changes. Today we believe we are more successfully helping patients adhere to treatment, abstain from substances, and reclaim their lives. Nevertheless, the quest to improve psychosocial treatments is one that requires we be open to integrating new interventions and to utilizing research to evaluate effectiveness in the real world.

Acknowledgments

Supported by grants MH60004 (Preventing Morbidity in First Episode Schizophrenia) and MH41960 (Hillside Center for Intervention Research in Schizophrenia) from the National Institute of Mental Health, Bethesda, MD, USA; grant DA015541 from the National Institute on Drug Abuse; and by grant RR018535-01 (North Shore-Long Island Jewish Research Institute

Table 9.2 Integrating treatment interventions to individual needs

Drop-out Supportive therapy Group therapy Family therapy Intensive case management	*Negative and cognitive symptoms* Skills building Communication enhancement Cognitive enhancement Behavioral therapy
Adherence with medication Psychoeducation Cognitive behavioral therapy Behavioral therapy Family psychoeducation	*Shame, guilt and stigma* Psychoeducation Supportive therapy Cognitive behavioral therapy
Poor insight Medication Psychoeducation Cognitive behavioral therapy Supportive therapy	*Ongoing psychotic symptoms* Medication Supportive therapy Cognitive behavioral therapy Coping skills training
Substance abuse Psychoeducation Motivational therapy Stages of change Cognitive behavioral therapy Behavioral therapy	*Personality traits* Cognitive behavioral therapy Ego supportive therapy
	Lack of family supports Practical services Intensive case management
	Trauma and family dysfunction Cognitive behavioral therapy Stabilizing identity Coping skills training

General Clinical Research Center) from the National Institutes of Health, Bethesda, MD, USA.

References

Addington, J. and Addington, D. (2001). Impact of an early psychosis program on substance use. *Psychiatric Rehabilitation Journal, 25*, 60–67.

Addington, J., Brooks, B. L., and Addington, D. (2003). Cognitive functioning in first episode psychosis: Initial presentation. *Schizophrenia Research, 62*, 59–64.

American Psychiatric Association (APA) (1994). *Diagnostic and statistical manual of mental disorders* (4th ed.). Washington, DC: APA.

Bachmann, S., Resch, F., and Mundt, C. (2003). Psychological treatments for psychosis: History and overview. *Journal of the American Academy of Psychoanalysis and Dynamic Psychiatry, 31*, 155–176.

Bellack, A. S., Mueser, K., Gingerich, S., and Agresta, J. (1997). *Social skills training for schizophrenia: A step-by-step guide*. New York: Guilford.

Bustillo, J. R., Lauriello, J., and Keith, S. J. (1999). Schizophrenia: Improving outcome. *Harvard Review of Psychiatry*, 6, 229–240.

Coldham, E. L., Addington, J., and Addington, D. (2002). Medication adherence of individuals with a first episode of psychosis. *Acta Psychiatria Scandinavica*, 106, 286–290.

Corradi, R. B. (2004). Medical psychotherapy of schizophrenia: A dynamic/supportive approach. *Journal of the American Academy of Psychoanalysis and Dynamic Psychiatry*, 32, 633–643.

Edwards, J., Maude, D., McGorry, P. D., Harrigan, S. M., and Cocks, J. T. (1998). Prolonged recovery in first-episode psychosis. *British Journal of Psychiatry*, 172 (Suppl. 33), 107–116.

Fenton, W. S. and Schooler, N. R. (2000). Evidence-based psychosocial treatment for schizophrenia. *Schizophrenia Bulletin*, 26, 1–3.

Gaebel, W., Janner, M., Frommann, N., Pietzcker, A., Kopcke, W., Linden, M., et al. (2002). First vs multiple episode schizophrenia: Two-year outcome of intermittent and maintenance medication strategies. *Schizophrenia Research*, 53, 145–159.

Gleeson, J., Larsen, T. K., and McGorry, P. (2003). Psychological treatment in pre- and early psychosis. *Journal of the American Academy of Psychoanalysis and Dynamic Psychiatry*, 31, 229–245.

Hogarty, G. E. and Flesher, S. (1999). Practice principles of cognitive enhancement therapy for schizophrenia. *Schizophrenia Bulletin*, 25, 693–708.

McGlashan, T. H., Levy, S. T., and Carpenter Jr., W. T. (1975). Integration and sealing over: Clinically distinct recovery styles from schizophrenia. *Archives of General Psychiatry*, 32, 1269–1272.

McGorry, P. (2005). Royal Australian and New Zealand College of Psychiatrists clinical practice guidelines for the treatment of schizophrenia and related disorders. *Australian and New Zealand Journal of Psychiatry*, 39, 1–30.

Malla, A. K., Norman, R. M., Manchanda, R., McLean, T. S., Harricharan, R., Cortese, L., et al. (2002). Status of patients with first-episode psychosis after one year of phase-specific community-oriented treatment. *Psychiatric Services*, 53, 458–463.

Miller, R. and McCormack, J. (2006). Faith and religious delusions in first-episode schizophrenia. *Social Work in Mental Health*, 4 (4), 37–50.

Miller, R. and Mason, S. E. (2004). Cognitive enhancement therapy: A therapeutic treatment strategy for first-episode schizophrenia patients. *Bulletin of the Menninger Clinic*, 68, 213–230.

Miller, R. and Mason, S. E. (2005). Shame and guilt in first-episode schizophrenia and schizoaffective disorders. *Journal of Contemporary Psychotherapy*, 35, 211–221.

Miller, R., McCormack, J., Sevy, S., and Robinson, D. (2005). The insight-adherence-abstinence triad: An integrated treatment focus for cannabis using first-episode schizophrenia patients. *Bulletin of the Menninger Clinic*, 69, 220–236.

Mueser, K. T., Noordsy, D. L., Drake, R. E., and Fox, L. (2003). *Integrated treatment for dual disorders: A guide to effective practice*. New York: Guilford.

Read, J. and Ross, C. A. (2003). Psychological trauma and psychosis: Another reason why people diagnosed schizophrenic must be offered psychological therapies. *Journal of the American Academy of Psychoanalysis and Dynamic Psychiatry*, 31, 247–268.

Robinson, D. G., Woerner, M. G., Alvir, J. M., Geisler, S., Koreen A., Sheitmen, B., et al. (1999). Predictors of treatment response from a first episode of schizophrenia or schizoaffective disorder. *American Journal of Psychiatry, 156*, 544–549.

Robinson, D. G., Woerner, M. G., Patel, R. C., Sevy, S. M., Gunduz-Bruce, H., Napolitano, B., et al. (2005). Comparison of olanzapine and risperidone treatment for first episode schizophrenia: Four month outcomes. Poster presentation at International Congress on Schizophrenia Research, Savannah, Georgia.

Swofford, C. D., Scheller-Gilkey, G., Miller, A. H., Woolwine, B., and Mance, R. (2000). Double jeopardy: Schizophrenia and substance use. *American Journal of Drug and Alcohol Abuse, 26*, 343–353.

Tait, L., Birchwood, M., and Trower, P. (2003). Predicting engagement with services for psychosis: Insight, symptoms and recovery style. *British Journal of Psychiatry, 182*, 123–128.

Velasquez, M. M., Maurer, G. G., Crouch, C., and DiClemente, C. C. (2001). *Group treatment for substance abuse: A stages of change therapy manual*. New York: Guilford.

Verdoux, H., Lengronne, J., Liraud, F., Gonzales, B., Assens, F., Abalan, F., et al. (2000). Medication adherence in psychosis: Predictors and impact on outcome. A 2-year follow-up of first-admitted subjects. *Acta Psychiatrica Scandinavica, 102*, 203–210.

Chapter 10

The importance of the treatment alliance in bipolar disorder

Lesley Berk, Craig Macneil, David Castle and Michael Berk

Introduction

> I flailed against the sentence I felt he had handed me. He listened to my
> convoluted, alternative explanations . . . He was very tough, as well as
> very kind, and even though he understood more than anyone how much I
> was losing – in energy and vivacity, and originality – by taking medica-
> tion, he never was seduced into losing sight of the overall perspective of
> how costly, damaging and life threatening my illness was . . . He treated
> me with respect, a decisive professionalism, wit, and an unshakable belief
> in my ability to get well, compete and make a difference.
>
> (Jamison, 1997, p. 87)

Bipolar disorder is a chronic illness that affects about 1.5 per cent of adults
(Craighead et al., 2002). Despite pharmacological treatment, there is still a
high relapse rate and subsyndromal symptoms impede functional recovery
between episodes (Fagiolini et al., 2005). Quality of life for people with
bipolar disorder may be even worse than for those with unipolar disorder
(Yatham et al., 2004). The suicide rate in bipolar disorder is 12 times higher
than the general population (Harris and Barraclough, 1997). Recognition of
the burden of this disease has led to an integration of different psychosocial
and pharmacological treatments aimed at reducing relapse. A common thread
in all such interventions is the treatment alliance.

The diathesis-stress model provides the theoretical base for integrating
psychosocial coping skills and medication to maximize outcomes in bipolar
disorder. Positive outcomes from a growing number of randomized controlled
trials of different psychosocial approaches such as individual cognitive behavioural models (Cochran, 1984; Lam et al., 2003; Scott et al., 2001), individual
prodrome management (Perry et al., 1999), group psychoeducation (Colom
et al., 2003), and family therapy (Miklowitz et al., 2000) highlight the potential utility of these adjunctive approaches in real life settings. Maximizing the
treatment alliance may assist in translating the efficacy of pharmacological
and psychosocial interventions into effectiveness in everyday clinical practise.

This chapter adopts an integrative framework to highlight potential ways in which the alliance may enhance outcome in bipolar disorder.

What do we mean by a treatment alliance?

The concept of the alliance developed from different psychotherapeutic approaches. Freud (1938) expanded his initial conceptualization of the therapeutic alliance, beyond that of the positive transference relationship, to include an acknowledgement of the real relationship between therapist and patient, and Greenson (1965) extended this idea to include the 'working alliance'. Rogers (1951) identified important humanistic therapist qualities (positive regard, genuineness, warmth and empathy). Bordin's (1979) definition of the treatment alliance emphasized the working alliance (agreement about the tasks and goals of treatment) and the quality of the bond between clinician and patient. A transtheoretical conception (Wolfe and Goldfried, 1988) of the alliance may apply across different treatment modalities, although its application may be altered by the different goals and tasks encapsulated by different treatments.

Proponents of cognitive behavioural therapy and pharmacological interventions recognized that the alliance may facilitate the 'competent delivery' of treatment (Waddington, 2002). The alliance in pharmacological treatment has evolved from one that prioritized the authority of the doctor in 'disease management' to a more collaborative relationship recognizing the active role of the patient (Berk et al., 2004). This move was facilitated by research into social cognitive models stressing patient's self-determination (Horne and Weinman, 1998) in a climate of legal accountability and the practical demands of ongoing care for chronic illness. These developments influenced the idea of a 'collaborative practice model' in bipolar disorder, which includes a process whereby the clinician and patient reach a concordance about the 'definition of problems' and set collaborative goals and strategies for achieving these goals (Bauer and McBride, 2003, p. 123).

Social psychology has highlighted the complexity of the alliance, pointing out the influence of both patient and clinician characteristics and the interaction between them (Safran and Segal, 1990). While focusing on Bordin's definition, we acknowledge the complexity of these variables and their potential contribution to maximizing the alliance in bipolar disorder.

Evidence of the relationship between alliance and outcome

Research shows that the treatment alliance affects outcome across diverse mental illnesses and treatment approaches (Frank and Gunderson, 1990; Keijsers et al., 2000; Weiss et al., 1997). Horvath (2005) reports that across reviews the alliance–outcome correlation in psychotherapy has been moderate but consistently significant (ranges 0.22–0.29) with clients' assessment of the alliance being more predictive than therapists' or observers', and more stable over time.

It has been suggested that patient characteristics and prior improvement may be confounds that detract from links between alliance and outcome but some studies have controlled for such factors (Barber et al., 2000; Burns and Nolen-Hoeksema, 1992). Hentschel (2005) points out that results of meta-analyses on the impact of the alliance on outcome confirm that the alliance has a significant moderate impact on outcome but that it needs to be understood in interaction with other variables.

To date there have been few studies on the treatment alliance in bipolar disorder. Cochran and Gitlin (1988) studied the importance of patient attitudes and intentions in predicting adherence status in 48 outpatients with bipolar disorder. They found psychiatrists' support of lithium treatment was a strong influence on adherence, raising awareness of the importance of this interaction.

Scott and Tacchi (2002) hypothesized that adherence is more likely to occur in bipolar disorder if the individual perceives a concordance between his/her experience of symptoms and their personal meaning, and the explanation provided by the treating clinician. They developed 'Concordance Therapy' which utilized a 'Cognitive Representation of Illness' model, adapted from Leventhal's Self Regulation Theory (Horne and Weinman, 1998). In their model, health-related behaviour involves a dynamic interaction between cognition, emotion, coping behaviour and appraisal of outcomes rather than a single rational decision, and medication adherence may be enhanced by concordance with the physician and appropriate cues to action. A small open pilot study (n = 10) conducted over 6 months with people with bipolar I disorder, highlighted the potential of such an intervention to enhance adherence to lithium (Scott and Tacchi, 2002).

Attunement between patient's support seeking and clinician's support in giving verbal and non-verbal behaviours predicted improvement in depression in a sample of 31 depressed patients, a few of whom had bipolar disorder (Geerts et al., 1996). The robust association between a good alliance and positive impact on depressive episodes (Keijsers et al., 2000) may be linked to the role of interpersonal factors in the aetiology of depression (Sergin, 2000) and the positive influence of social support (L. Johnson, et al., 2003). In bipolar disorder poor social support has been associated with the risk of relapse of both depressive and manic episodes (L. Johnson et al., 2003).

Satisfaction with one's clinician was associated with a better adaptation to diagnosis, improved coping and fewer feelings of shame and anger in the National Depression and Manic-Depression Association survey (Hirshfeld et al., 2003). The longitudinal STEP-BD study of 1000 people with bipolar disorder found that satisfaction with care was mediated by hope and resulted in improved functionality (Morris et al., 2005). Tyrrell et al. (1999) reported that a strong alliance with case managers was associated with better quality of life, satisfaction with relationships, and improved functionality in 54 clients with serious mental disorders, 8 of whom had bipolar disorder. In bipolar disorder, social maladjustment is a strong predictor of affective episodes (Staner et al., 1997). Tyrell et al. (1999) recognized the potential of the alliance to disconfirm unconstructive interpersonal strategies and to contribute to social adjustment.

In summary, there is robust evidence supporting the link between the treatment alliance and outcome in mental disorders. Most studies in bipolar disorder tend to have small or mixed samples and have not utilized available methods for assessing the alliance at different points in treatment or considered the myriad of confounding variables. They do raise the possibility of the importance of the alliance in enhancing adherence and benefits that may arise from increased acceptance and hope. These limited studies point to an impact on symptomatic and functional outcome. More research is needed not only to assess the impact of the alliance on outcome in bipolar disorder, but also to better understand how this variable may be enhanced to augment everyday clinical practice. Future research needs to take into account the complexity of mediating variables that influence the alliance, including patient factors, the therapists' contribution, and the demands of the illness.

Patient characteristics

Despite the global evidence linking alliance and outcome, there is little evidence of factors that influence the quality of the alliance in specific disorders (Hentschel, 2005). Patient characteristics such as hostile-dominant interpersonal problems and personality (Connolly Gibbins et al., 2003; Zuroff et al., 2000) have been associated with the alliance and psychotherapy outcome across a number of disorders. The impact of symptom severity on the alliance is controversial, with some studies (Hersoug et al., 2002) finding severity to be associated with worse alliance and others finding no such correlation (Connolly Gibbons et al., 2003).

In bipolar disorder, besides the severity of symptoms, the type of symptom (mania/hypomania, depression, mixed) may influence the individuals interpersonal functioning reverberating on the alliance. Subsyndromal symptoms, rapid cycling and comorbidity with other disorders such as substance abuse may influence the alliance. Attention may need to be given to dysfunctional attitudes and unrealistic expectations that could detract from the sustainability of the bond between patient and clinician (Berk et al., 2004). Neuropsychological impairment in bipolar disorder, even during remission (Martinez-Aran et al., 2004) may influence the individual's ability to attend, concentrate and remember, thus impacting on the building of the alliance. Duration since diagnosis may also play a role, with first episode requiring specific attention to engagement and acceptance issues.

Bernd et al. (2005) studied the impact of interpersonal factors on the alliance across psychodynamic, psychoanalytic and cognitive behavioural therapy in 714 patients, nearly half of whom had affective disorders. They found that interpersonal problems at intake did not necessarily have long-term effects on the alliance and a poor initial alliance could be reversed during the course of treatment. Patients' characteristics may signal required changes in clinicians' behaviour to engage the patient and maintain the alliance as it focuses on the goals of treatment.

How could the alliance enhance outcome in bipolar disorder?

In this section we draw on research and clinical practice to suggest ways in which the clinician may develop and use the alliance to support the goals of integrative treatment in bipolar disorder. 'Collaborative empiricism' (Beck et al., 1979) emphasizes the importance of a collaborative relationship in which patient and clinician are active partners in a shared exploration aimed at symptom reduction. For such a strategy to work, the patient needs to be engaged as an active collaborator. Engagement of the patient and clinician in psychotherapy (Keijsers et al., 2000) and pharmacotherapy (Priebe and Greyters, 1995) has been considered to be vital to the building of a secure alliance to enhance outcome.

In bipolar disorder, engagement in a strong treatment alliance may augment treatment by facilitating the exchange of vital information between clinician and patient and by increasing treatment adherence. In addition the alliance may decrease demoralization and enhance functionality.

Exchanging information

Common to all treatment interventions in bipolar disorder is a strong emphasis on informing the patient about the illness and treatments to facilitate collaborative self-management of illness (Bauer and McBride, 2003). Results of the large GAMIAN-Europe/BEAM survey (Morselli et al., 2004), aimed at understanding the burden of bipolar illness, found that there was an improvement in quality of life and adherence to medication over recent years in those people with bipolar disorder who were better informed about their illness and its treatment.

McGorry and McConville (1999) point out the vulnerability of people with psychotic disorders, especially early in treatment when receiving information about their illness. Insight into the reality that one has a severe mental illness may be associated with a fall in self-esteem, and demoralization. Denial may be a way of protecting oneself from the cognitive dissonance experienced when trying to integrate the idea of a stigmatized illness with one's usual self-concept. Thus, too much information especially if the individual is symptomatic or recently diagnosed, may enhance anxiety and acceptance difficulties. Information may need to be delivered in a way that is sensitive to the meaning the illness has for the individual and utilizes the individual's language at different points in treatment. The aim is to engage the individual in an alliance that assists with the exchange of information.

A survey by Lewis (2005) reiterated the need for information and the urgency of improved communication between doctor and patient in preventing some of the less desirable outcomes associated with bipolar disorder. Patients claimed that the long delay before receiving the correct diagnosis and hence treatment for bipolar disorder (about 10 years), may be avoided by doctors really listening to their patients and asking targeted questions (about previous mania/hypomania). Out of 69 per cent of patients who had suicidal thoughts, only 49 per cent discussed these thoughts with their doctor. More than a third claimed that they did not feel that their doctors really took their symptoms seriously. A treatment alliance that is patient centred and encourages communication may contribute to the collaborative management of the illness.

Adherence to treatment

A small number of studies on the doctor–patient alliance in bipolar disorder highlight the potential of the treatment alliance to influence adherence to medication (Cochran and Gitlin, 1988; Scott and Tacchi, 2002). Poor medication adherence is a primary cause of the efficacy–efficiency gap in the pharmacological treatment of bipolar disorder. Rates of long-term non-adherence in bipolar disorder range from 20 to 66 per cent (mean of 41 per cent) and adherence is typically intermittent or partial (Lingham and Scott, 2002). Poor adherence is associated with a number of factors, some of which are amenable to change (Berk et al., 2004). Studies suggest that it is the fear of long-term side effects and negative beliefs about medication and the denial of the severity of the illness that undermines adherence (Scott and Pope, 2002). A participatory style of communication that incorporates patients' attitudes and experience was associated with improved satisfaction with antidepressant treatment and adherence in a prospective study of 100 outpatients with depression (Bultman and Svarstad, 2000) and is considered to impact on outcomes in physical illness (Van Dulmen and Bensing, 2002). Pope and Scott (2003) found a discrepancy between reasons patients with bipolar disorder gave for stopping prophylactic lithium and those reasons attributed to them by doctors. This highlighted the need for clinicians to elicit the patient's point of view and 'concerns about what having an affective disorder and taking medication says about them' (Pope and Scott, 2003, p. 287).

Sajatovic et al. (2005) conducted a qualitative study on outpatient attitudes towards the patient–clinician relationship and treatment adherence in bipolar disorder. Provider characteristics including collaborative prescription practices, the expertise and compassion of the clinician, and his/her ability to listen and be sensitive to patients' feelings were highlighted. Trusting the provider to assist with decision making when the patient was symptomatic was considered vital, raising the importance of flexibility of the alliance in its adaptation to individual needs.

In their guide to cognitive therapy for bipolar disorder, Lam et al., (2000) emphasized the importance of establishing trust in the alliance in bipolar disorder to develop a strong bond that anchors the patient to treatment in the various phases of illness. This requires that the patient believes that the clinician values the patient's perspective without necessarily colluding with it, and has the patient's best interests at heart. Trust is developed by the therapist being reliable, not only in terms of appointments but also in terms of the structure and boundaries of therapy. The therapist needs to maintain an equilibrium and constant perspective on the illness, the person behind the illness and the goals of therapy, despite the seductiveness of the patient's manic or hypomanic moods and the hopelessness of his or her depressions. The therapist can examine the corresponding emotions that the patient is generating in himself/herself as a means of distancing from the situation, gaining perspective and dissipating or using them to repair ruptures (Safran and Segal, 1990). If the patient has already moved too far into the episode of illness, strategies for hospital admission that have been agreed on when the patient was well, may be implemented without long-term damage to the alliance. The bond may be cemented by continuity of care aimed at long-term management of this chronic illness (Bauer and McBride, 2003). It is the strength of a continuous bond that allows for differences between patient and clinician that may augment the outcome of treatment in bipolar disorder.

Unlike medication adherence, adherence to psychosocial treatment has not been studied. A lifestyle focusing on maintaining regulation of circadian rhythms and regulating goal striving (S. L. Johnson, 2005) may be important in preventing manic relapse, but it may involve discipline and self-management and be contrary to personality and ambitions. In addition, destructive habits such as substance abuse may trigger episodes in a vicious cycle. However, such lifestyle choices may be hard to change particularly for those individuals who have come to rely on substance abuse as a form of self-medication.

Prodrome management is an adjunctive psychosocial strategy that has proven efficacy in reducing manic episodes (Perry et al., 1999). When people with bipolar disorder are becoming symptomatic, metacognitive capacity (recognition that thoughts, assumptions and beliefs are mental events and processes rather than reflections of objective truth) (Fennell, 2004) may be challenged. The ability to act contrary to one's mood may be compromised by the symptoms themselves. For example, a person who is becoming depressed may find it difficult to get out of bed in the morning, even if rationally she understands that it is the best thing to do. Similarly, the executive who has a deadline to meet and has been finding it difficult to sleep because he is becoming high, may find it hard not to follow his mood and work all night. A strong collaborative relationship with the clinician and/or significant others may bolster both motivation and insight at this time and assist in preventing relapse (Bauer and McBride, 2003).

It is apparent that some of the skills required to prevent relapse require self-control and discipline and disruption to goals and lifestyle and for some people the advantages of the illness may outweigh the disadvantages. Unlike the symptoms of depression, euphoric mania may be subjectively enjoyable. For some people, much productivity, socialization, creativity and success is associated with hypomania (Berk et al., 2004). Such individuals may see no need for change or treatment.

Enhancing an individual's readiness to change is part of a psychotherapeutic technique focusing on the patient's goals and values known as motivational interviewing (Rollnick and Miller, 1995). This technique requires an active, empathic patient-centred alliance. Instead of persuading or coercing the patient to adhere to treatment, the clinician 'elicits from the client and reinforces reasons for concern and change'. Such techniques, in the context of an alliance based on trust and respect, may help to increase motivation to manage bipolar illness.

An emphasis on individual reasons and choice as a means of motivating adherence to treatment may need to be adjusted to patient characteristics such as severity of symptoms and the requirements of involuntary treatment. Adams and Scott (2000) found that high dependency and a need for approval, coupled with external locus of control were typical of highly adherent patients with bipolar disorder. Such factors may enhance willingness to follow the advice of clinicians and may imply a preference for a more paternalistic approach (Berk et al., 2004). In bipolar disorder, it may be appropriate to adopt a flexible decision making style to take into account the needs of individual patients at different points in treatment. Consistency in approach may be safeguarded by a core focus on encouraging autonomy where possible; on the foundation of a strong supportive alliance that permits movement between models of decision-making.

Demoralization and functionality

Joiner et al. (2003) reported that the experience of bipolar disorder may be associated with hopelessness and lack of confidence. Scott and Pope (2003) found that negative self-esteem was a robust predictor of relapse in bipolar disorder. Daskalopoulou et al. (2002) suggested that low self-esteem lasting into remission from an episode was associated with suicidality, highlighting the importance of finding ways of raising self-esteem in bipolar disorder.

Hopelessness has also been associated with suicidality (Beck et al., 1979).

Priebe and Greyters (1995) found psychiatrists' initial optimism about outcome to be a significant predictor of treatment outcome in 63 depressed patients. The link between satisfaction with clinician and hope and its impact on improved functionality was evident in the STEP-BD study (Morris et al., 2005).

An alliance that conveys to the individual that he/she is a person with specific abilities and talents despite the illness may assist the patient in integrating the illness into his/her self-concept. Highlighting the individual's strengths and virtues has been associated with building resilience and self-efficacy (Seligman, 2002). It is not surprising that satisfaction with the clinician is linked with adjustment to bipolar illness and enhanced coping (Hirschfeld et al., 2003). An alliance with the vulnerable side of the patient, that entails empathy with the burden, loss and limitations associated with the illness, but also relates to the strengths and abilities of the person behind the illness, may promote self-esteem and hope. These gains may buffer the individual against the risk of relapse and suicide while encouraging functionality. In addition the healing of ruptures within the alliance may have beneficial effects on other relationships (Safran and Segal, 1990) improving social functioning.

Case study: Andrew

Some of these ideas are demonstrated in this case study of the early phase of psychotherapy with a person recently diagnosed with bipolar disorder. Andrew is a 19-year-old, first-year university student. He was admitted to hospital as an involuntary patient suffering typical symptoms of mania, and on discharge, remained disorganized, over-familiar, experienced ongoing irritability and mild grandiosity.

Andrew's therapist facilitated the transition to outpatient psychotherapy and continuity of care. Due to Andrew's agitation and concentration difficulties, the therapist often kept sessions fairly short during the acute phase. During the early phase of treatment it was believed that a 'hierarchy of needs' model would be most beneficial, with the focus initially being on practical issues, which was the area about which Andrew described most concern. Engagement was facilitated by this 'patient-centred' approach.

Andrew had little insight during the early stages of therapy, but recognized he had been 'a bit speedy'. The therapist used Andrew's own language to discuss symptoms and did not focus on psychoeducation until he was less symptomatic. Motivation to attend sessions was associated with his goal of getting help with paying a number of bills he had accumulated. This task became a collaborative effort and facilitated the setting up of an element of openness and trust in their relationship. It also had the effect of showing Andrew that the therapist respected his need to gain control over his life again.

As therapy progressed, Andrew was reasonably comfortable with sessions following an organized format. This would typically include starting each session with a brief review of the previous session, collaboratively setting an agenda, and recapping at the end of each session. Regular summarizing was felt to be extremely important in order for the therapist to be clear as to what Andrew had understood during sessions, and also to correct any misunderstandings. Typically the therapist would attempt to limit the content of sessions to two or three 'key messages' or issues, recognizing that Andrew would be unlikely to recall any more detail at this stage. Andrew did appear to find the structured approach to sessions containing, and described that he felt 'listened to' at his appointments.

Once his mental state became more settled, Andrew began to ask his therapist what had happened to him, and why he had needed to go to hospital. The therapist asked Andrew to offer his own explanation first. Andrew stated that he had been stressed about his university exams, had been sleeping poorly and wondered if it was relevant that he had taken amphetamines for the first time around one month previously to help him study. Interestingly, Andrew also stated that he had an uncle with 'manic-depression'. This opened a dialogue about symptoms of bipolar disorder and the stress vulnerability model and contributed to Andrew's insight into his personal triggers of his illness.

In discussing the explanatory model of bipolar disorder, the therapist was keen to incorporate Andrew's understanding as much as possible. The therapist generally took a tentative approach when making observations or expressing opinion, using expressions such as 'Andrew, I wonder if . . .', 'Can I check . . . out with you . . .?' This assisted in demonstrating the therapist's desire to understand Andrew and to establish a dynamic in which Andrew felt he was genuinely participating. The therapist attempted to answer any questions about the illness and presented a hopeful perspective on finding ways to manage the illness without providing unrealistic expectations about cure.

As the sessions progressed the focus was on boosting Andrew's growing competence in recognizing prodromes and risk factors associated with his bipolar disorder. Ambivalence about medication was discussed and motivational interviewing facilitated his active role in reporting side effects and making informed treatment decisions with his doctor. Time focusing on the illness was balanced by a strengths-based approach, asking Andrew about his interests and abilities. This assisted Andrew in separating himself from his illness and enhanced his self-esteem, hope and motivation to manage his illness to create a future identity that was acceptable to him. Eventually, Andrew began to identify realistic goals while maintaining lifestyle regularity and monitoring triggers of bipolar illness.

At session 9, Andrew asked if the therapist would go to a psychology-related social event with him and the therapist politely refused. Andrew missed the next session. The therapist addressed this rupture by taking ownership of refusing Andrew's request, and acknowledging that this may have been hurtful and the possible reasons for confusing the therapeutic relationship with being 'friends'. Andrew acknowledged that it had been hurtful and confusing given that he thought they got on well together, and he had lost a number of his previous friends, but that he accepted that it was a professional relationship. Andrew acknowledged that he might have been more 'pushy' than normal due to feeling that he was still feeling slightly 'speedy', and had also approached two girls he did not know to ask them out.

This approach seemed to assist Andrew to have more realistic expectations, as the therapist had not handled the situation 'perfectly'. It demonstrated a helpful model of conflict resolution, where personal and emotionally important issues could be discussed openly, something Andrew said was often difficult within his family. This incident also impacted on his social functioning as it facilitated discussion about how to approach people with requests for social contact, something about which Andrew had previously been anxious and had lacked confidence.

Comment

This case study highlights the importance of the engagement process, taking into account individual variables such as symptom status, neuropsychological difficulties, age and stage of treatment. Trust was facilitated by the therapist's reliability and understanding of the patient's perspective of the illness balanced by his ability to remain professional and clear about the goals of treatment. Continuity of approach and maintaining structure and boundaries was aimed at the competent delivery of treatment. Sensitivity to the appropriateness of timely psychoeducation and providing a perspective that includes both the illness and potential ways of controlling it, facilitated integration into the self-concept. This was combined with an open recognition of the struggles and strengths of the person behind the illness and the realistic possibilities inherent in trying to manage illness and engage in life. The bond was strong enough to withstand differences of opinion and ruptures, which were used to enhance treatment goals.

Conclusion

Given the morbidity and mortality associated with bipolar disorder and the efficacy–effectiveness gap of pharmacological treatment, it is essential to explore changeable factors that may enhance integrative treatment. In bipolar disorder the building of a strong alliance may facilitate a number of treatment goals such as the exchange of information, adherence to treatment, acceptance of illness, hope and self-efficacy and constructive interpersonal strategies, which may effect symptomatic, functional, quality of life outcomes and reduce suicide.

Certain patient variables including symptom status, time since diagnosis, expectations and neuropsychological impairment may be relevant in bipolar disorder. Corresponding to these variables, certain clinician behaviour may be more appropriate at a particular point in therapy, raising the idea of the clinician as 'an authentic chameleon' (Hentschel, 2005). However, continuity is maintained by an underlying focus on enhancing autonomy and collaborative management of illness and maintaining a connection that can withstand essential differences and ruptures between clinician and patient. Given the need for regularity in other aspects of life (Frank et al., 2000), the consistency and reliability of the clinician's approach and the structure of treatment may be particularly important in bipolar disorder. An unexplored area is the extent to which clinician support may mimic informal support in its impact on outcome, and if this is mediated by other factors such as self-esteem (S. L. Johnson et al., 2000).

Research is needed to corroborate and refine these preliminary suggestions and to determine how clinician and patient characteristics and behaviours and their interaction with each other and the illness, in the different phases of treatment, may link the alliance with real life outcomes in bipolar disorder. Research that focuses on more detailed discrimination of disorder specific relevant variables and multiple measures of longitudinal treatment may assist in overcoming the 'homogeneity myth' associated with the treatment alliance and contribute to real life practice (Hovarth, 2005).

References

Adams, J. and Scott, J. (2000). Predicting medication adherence in severe mental disorders. *Acta Psychiatrica Scandinavica*, *10*, 119–124.

Barber, J. P., Connolly, M. B., Crits-Cristoph, P., Gladis, L., and Siqueland, L. (2000). Alliance predicts patients' outcome beyond in-treatment change in symptoms. *Journal of Consulting and Clinical Psychology*, *68*, 1027–1032.

Bauer, M. S. and McBride, L. (2003). *Structured group psychotherapy for bipolar disorder: The Life Goals Program*. New York: Springer.

Beck, A., Rush, A., Shaw, A., and Emery, G. (1979). The therapeutic relationship: Application to cognitive therapy. In A. Beck, A. Rush, B. Shaw, and G. Emery (Eds.), *Cognitive therapy of depression*. New York: Guilford.

Berk, M., Berk, L., and Castle, D. (2004). A collaborative approach to the treatment alliance in bipolar disorder. *Bipolar Disorders*, *6*, 504–518.

Bernd, P., Bauer, S., Horowitz, L. M., and Hans, K. (2005). The relationship between interpersonal problems and the helping alliance. *Journal of Clinical Psychology*, *61*, 415–430.

Bordin, E. (1979). The generalisability of the psychoanalytic concept of the working alliance. *Psychotherapy: Theory Research and Practice*, *16*, 252–260.

Bultman, D. C. and Svarstad, B. L. (2000). Effects of physician communication style on client medication beliefs and adherence with antidepressant treatment. *Patient Education and Counselling*, 40, 173–185.

Burns, D. D. and Nolen-Hoeksma, S. (1992). Therapeutic empathy and recovery from depression in cognitive behavioural therapy: A structural equation model. *Journal of Consulting and Clinical Psychology*, 60, 441–449.

Cochran, S. D. (1984). Preventing medical non-compliance in the outpatient treatment of bipolar affective disorders. *Journal of Consulting and Clinical Psychology*, 52, 873–878.

Cochran, S. D. and Gitlin, M. J. (1988). Attitudinal correlates of lithium compliance in bipolar affective disorders. *Journal of Nervous and Mental Disease*, 176, 457–464.

Colom, F., Vieta, E., Martínez-Arán, A., Reinares, M., Goikolea, J. M., Benabarre, A., et al. (2003). Randomized trial on the efficacy of group psychoeducation in the prophylaxis of recurrences in bipolar patients whose disease is in remission. *Archives of General Psychiatry*, 60, 402–407.

Connolly Gibbons, M. B., Crits-Cristoph, P., de la Cruz, C., Barber, J. P., Siqueland, L., and Gladis, M. (2003). Pre-treatment expectations, interpersonal functioning, and symptoms in the prediction of the therapeutic alliance across supportive-expressive psychotherapy and cognitive therapy. *Psychotherapy Research*, 13, 59–76.

Craighead, W. E., Miklowitz, D. J., Frank, E., and Vajk, F. C. (2002). Psychosocial treatments for bipolar disorder. In P. E. Nathan and J. M. Gorman (Eds.), *A guide to treatments that work* (pp. 240–248). New York: Oxford University Press.

Daskalopoulou, E. G., Dikeos, D. G., Papadimitriou, G. N., Souery, D., Blairy, S., Massat, I., et al. (2002). Self-esteem, social adjustment and suicidality in affective disorders. *European Psychiatry*, 17, 265–271.

Fagiolini, A., Kupfer, D. J., Masalehdan, A., Scott, J. A., Houck, P. R., and Frank, E. (2005). Functional impairment in the remission phase of bipolar disorder. *Bipolar Disorder*, 7, 281–285.

Fennell, M. J. V. (2004). Depression, low self-esteem and mindfulness. *Behaviour Research and Therapy*, 42, 1053–1068.

Frank, A. and Gunderson, J. G. (1990). The role of the therapeutic alliance in the treatment of schizophrenia. *Archives of General Psychiatry*, 47, 228–236.

Frank, E., Swartz, H. A., and Kupfer, D. (2000). Interpersonal and social rhythm therapy: Managing the chaos of bipolar disorder. *Biological Psychiatry*, 48, 593–604.

Freud, S. (1938). An outline of psycho-analysis. In J. Strachey (Ed. and Trans.), *The standard edition of the complete psychological works of Sigmund Freud* (Vol. 23, pp. 141–207). London: Hogarth Press.

Geerts, E., Bouhuys, N., and Van den Hoofdakker, R. H. (1996). Nonverbal attunement between depressed patients and an interviewer predicts subsequent improvement. *Journal of Affective Disorders*, 40, 15–21.

Greenson, R. (1965). The working alliance and the transference neurosis. *Psychoanalytic Quarterly*, 34, 155–181.

Harris, E. C. and Barraclough, B. (1997). Suicide as an outcome for mental disorders: A meta-analysis. *British Journal of Psychiatry*, 170, 205–228.

Hentschel, U. (2005). Therapeutic alliance: The best synthesizer of social influences on the therapeutic situation? On links to other constructs, determinants of its effectiveness, and its role for research in psychotherapy in general. *Psychotherapy Research*, 15, 9–23.

Hersoug, A. G., Monsen, J. T., Havik, O. E., and Hoglend, P. (2002). Quality of early working alliance in psychotherapy: Diagnosis, relationship and intrapsychic variables as predictors. *Psychotherapy and Psychosomatics*, *71*, 18–27.

Hirschfeld, R. M., Lewis, L., and Vornik, L. A. (2003). Perceptions and impact of bipolar disorder: How far have we really come? Results of the national depressive and manic-depressive association 2000 survey of individuals with bipolar disorder. *Journal of Clinical Psychiatry*, *64*, 161–174.

Horne, R. and Weinman, J. (1998). Predicting treatment adherence: An overview of theoretical models. In L. B. Myers and K. Midence (Eds.), *Adherence to treatment in medical conditions* (pp. 25–50). London: Harwood Academic.

Horvath, A. O. (2005). The therapeutic relationship: Research and theory. *Psychotherapy Research*, *15*, 3–7.

Jamison, K. R. (1997). *An unquiet mind*. London: Picador.

Johnson, L., Lundström, O., Åberg-Wistedt, A., and Mathé, A. A. (2003). Social support in bipolar disorder: Its relevance to remission and relapse. *Bipolar Disorders*, *5*, 129–137.

Johnson, S. L. (2005). Mania and dysregulation in goal pursuit: A review. *Clinical Psychology Review*, *25*, 241–262.

Johnson, S. L., Meyer, B., Winett, C., and Small, J. (2000). Social support and self-esteem predict changes in bipolar depression but not mania. *Journal of Affective Disorders*, *58*, 79–86.

Joiner, T. E., Vohs, K. D., Rudd, M. D., Schmidt, N. B., and Petit, J. W. (2003). Problem-solving and cognitive scars in mood and anxiety disorders: The sting of mania. *Journal of Social and Clinical Psychology*, *22*, 192–212.

Keijsers, G. P., Schaap, C. P., and Hoogduin, C. A. (2000). The impact of personal patient and therapist behaviour on outcome in cognitive-therapy: A review of empirical studies. *Behaviour Modification*, *24*, 264–297

Lam, D. H., Jones, S. H., Hayward, P., and Bright, J. A. (2000). *Cognitive therapy for bipolar disorder: A therapist's guide to concepts, methods and practice*. Chichester: Wiley.

Lam, D. H., Watkins, E. R., Hayward, P., Bright, J., Wright, K., Kerr, N., et al. (2003). A randomised controlled study of cognitive therapy for relapse prevention for bipolar affective disorder. *Archives of General Psychiatry*, *60*, 145–152.

Lewis, L. (2005). Patient perspectives on the diagnosis, treatment, and management of bipolar disorder. *Bipolar Disorders*, *7* (Suppl. 1), 33–37.

Lingham, R. and Scott, J. (2002). Treatment non-adherence in affective disorders. *Acta Psychiatria Scandinavia*, *105*, 164–172.

McGorry, P. D. and McConville, S. B. (1999). Insight in psychosis: An elusive target. *Comprehensive Psychiatry*, *40*, 131–142.

Martinez-Aran, A., Vieta, E., Reinares, M., Colom, F., Torrent, C., Sanchez-Moreno, J., et al. (2004). Cognitive function across manic or hypomanic, depressed, and euthymic states in bipolar disorder. *American Journal of Psychiatry*, *161*, 262–270.

Miklowitz, D. J., Simoneau, T. L., George, E. L., Richards, J. A., Kalbag, A., Sachs-Ericsson, N., and Suddath, R. (2000). Family-focused treatment of bipolar disorder: 1-year effects of a psychoeducational program in conjunction with pharmacotherapy. *Biological Psychiatry*, *48*, 582–592.

Morris, C. D., Miklowitz, D. J., Wisniewski, S. R., Giese, A. A., Thomas, M. R., and Allen, M. H. (2005). Care satisfaction, hope, and life functioning among adults with bipolar disorder: Data from the first 1000 participants in the Systematic Treatment Enhancement Program. *Comprehensive Psychiatry*, *46*, 98–104.

Morselli, P. L., Elgie, R., and Cesana, B. M. (2004). GAMIAN-Europe/BEAM survey. II: Cross-national analysis of unemployment, family history, treatment satisfaction and the impact of the bipolar disorder on life style. *Bipolar Disorders*, *6*, 487–497.

Perry, A., Tarrier, N., Morris, R., McCarthy, E., and Limb, K. (1999). Randomised controlled trial of efficacy of teaching patients with bipolar disorder to identify early symptoms of relapse and obtain treatment. *British Medical Journal*, *16*, 149–153.

Pope, M. and Scott, J. (2003). Do clinicians understand why individuals stop taking lithium? *Journal of Affective Disorders*, *74*, 287–291.

Priebe, S. and Greyters, T. (1995). The importance of the first three days: Predictors of treatment outcome in depressed in-patients. *British Journal of Clinical Psychology*, *34*, 229–235.

Rogers, C. (1951). *Client-centered therapy*. New York: Houghton Mifflin.

Rollnick, S. and Miller, W. R. (1995). What is motivational interviewing? *Behavioural and Cognitive Psychotherapy*, *23*, 325–334.

Safran, J. and Segal, Z. (1990). *Interpersonal process in cognitive therapy*. New York: Basic Books.

Sajatovic, M., Davies, M., Bauer, M. S., McBride, L., Hays, R. W., Safavi, R., and Jenkins, J. (2005). Attitudes regarding the collaborative practice model and treatment adherence among individuals with bipolar disorder. *Comprehensive Psychiatry*, *46*, 272–277.

Scott, J. and Pope, M. (2002). Nonadherence with mood stabilizers: Prevalence and predictors. *Journal of Clinical Psychiatry*, *63*, 384–390.

Scott, J. and Pope, M. (2003). Cognitive styles in individuals with bipolar disorders. *Psychological Medicine*, *33*, 1081–1088.

Scott, J. and Tacchi, M. J. (2002). A pilot study of concordance therapy for individuals with bipolar disorders who are non-adherent with lithium prophylaxis. *Bipolar Disorders*, *4*, 386–392.

Scott, J., Garland, A., and Moorhead, S. (2001). A pilot study of cognitive therapy in bipolar disorders. *Psychological Medicine*, *31*, 459–467.

Seligman, M. E. P. (2002). *Authentic happiness*. Milsons Point, NSW: Random House.

Sergin, C. (2000). Social skills deficits associated with depression. *Clinical Psychology Review*, *20*, 379–403.

Staner, L., Tracy, A., Darmaix, M., Genevrios, C., Vanderelst, M., Vilane, A., et al. (1997). Clinical and psychosocial predictors of recurrence in recovered bipolar and unipolar depressives: A one-year controlled prospective study. *Psychiatric Research*, *69*, 39–51.

Tyrrell, C. L., Dozier, M., Teague, G. B., and Fallot, R. D. (1999). Effective treatment relationships for persons with psychiatric disorders: The importance of attachment states of mind. *Journal of Consulting and Clinical Psychology*, *67*, 725–733.

Van Dulmen, A. M. and Bensing, J. M. (2002). Health promoting effects of the physician-patient encounter. *Psychology, Health and Medicine*, *7*, 289–300.

Waddington, L. (2002). The relationship in cognitive therapy: A review. *Behavioral and Cognitive Psychotherapy*, *30*, 179–191.

Weiss, M., Gaston, L., Propst, A., Wisebord, S., and Zicherman, V. (1997). The role of the alliance in the pharmacological treatment of depression. *Journal of Clinical Psychiatry, 58*, 196–204.

Wolfe, B. E. and Goldfried, M. R. (1988). Research on psychotherapy integration: Recommendations and conclusions from an NIMH workshop. *Journal of Consulting and Clinical Psychology, 56*, 448–451.

Yatham, L. N., Lecrubier, Y., Fieve, R. R, Davis, K. H., Harris, S. D., and Krishnan, A. (2004). Quality of life in patients with bipolar I depression: Data from 920 patients. *Bipolar Disorders, 6*, 379–385.

Zuroff, D. C., Blatt, S. J., Sotsky, S. M., Krupnick, J. L., Martin, D. J., Sanislow, C. A., and Simmens, S. (2000). Relation of the therapeutic alliance and perfectionism to outcome in brief outpatient treatment of depression. *Journal of Consulting and Clinical Psychology, 68*, 114–124.

Chapter 11

Fragmentation, invalidation and spirituality

Personal experiences of psychosis – ethical, research and clinical implications

Jim Geekie and John Read

Introduction

> I was 150 per cent convinced it was spiritual voices. Then I get told by the teacher it was not. Then I get told one minute it's a psychotic breakdown. Then I get told you're not hearing them. Then I get told it's your own mind talking to itself. Then I get told it's your higher self. I don't know quite frankly what to believe. You know, do I have to keep coming here every time I hear what I think is a spiritual voice?

The quote above, from a client of a first-episode psychosis (FEP) service struggling to make sense of her experience of psychosis, captures several of the themes explored in this chapter on the individual's experience of psychosis: a sense of fragmentation of self, of being invalidated by others and a quest for spiritual meaning. The quote raises two important questions regarding psychotic experiences: what are we to make of them and what should we do about them? Clearly, for this individual and others who have such experiences, as well as for those working clinically in this field, these are not mere academic questions. Rather, they are questions which are both profoundly philosophical (regarding the meaning of experience) and pragmatic (how to respond to these experiences). Both the philosophical and the pragmatic are of central importance to any discussion on the nature and meaning of psychosis as evidenced by research such as that by Wagner and King (2005) who found that existential needs (the search for meaning and the need for spirituality) are the most pressing needs identified by those who have psychotic experiences.

In this chapter our focus is on the individual's experience and understanding of psychosis, as expressed in routine clinical meetings with one of us (Jim Geekie) in his role as clinical psychologist with a FEP service in New Zealand. We begin by outlining our theoretical framework, before considering findings and implications from our research into understandings of psychotic experiences.

To begin, it is necessary to comment on the language used in this chapter. It is with some reluctance that we use the term 'psychosis', a term used predominantly by clinicians and researchers, which expresses their particular interests and approaches, which may not be congruent with the perspectives of those with first-hand knowledge of psychosis. Terms such as 'psychosis' and 'schizophrenia' seem to privilege professional conceptualizations of the experience over client conceptualizations. As argued elsewhere (Geekie, 2004) our position is that 'psychosis' and 'schizophrenia' are, essentially, synonymous with 'madness', 'insanity' and other lay terms. To avoid privileging one discourse over another we will use these terms interchangeably, in the hope that this helps express the range of perspectives that one can bring to bear on these experiences.

The literature on psychosis is characterized by a range of competing positions aimed at explaining the nature and causes of madness. For example, in the scientific literature, we find a plethora of powerful and persuasive positions adopted vis-à-vis psychosis, ranging from biological and genetic explanations (Carpenter and Buchanan, 1995; Gottesman, 1991), to neuropsychological (Frith, 1992), psychological (Bentall, 2003), psychodynamic (Karon, 1999), existential/philosophical (Sass, 1992) and traumatogenic (Read et al., 2001). Others, such as Boyle (1990) have argued that the notion of 'schizophrenia' is fundamentally flawed and should, therefore, be disregarded. This list by no means exhausts the range of theories currently proffered to account for madness. Our purpose here is merely to note that the professional literature is characterized by this variety of theories, rather than to evaluate their relative merits.

Similarly, in the lay literature, we find a diversity of opinions expressed by those who have personal experience of psychosis, as well as by family members or carers of people who experience psychosis and members of the general public (Jorm et al., 1997; Read and Haslam, 2004). Lay perspectives tend to favour psychosocial over biological explanations of causality, whereas professional perspectives generally emphasize biological causal factors (Read et al., 2004: Sharfstein, 2005).

This diversity of opinion on what madness is (and what causes it) is nowhere more pronounced than in first-person accounts of madness. Here, we find a vast range of ways of explaining the nature and causes of the experience. Given that these are personal accounts of a wide array of experiences, it is perhaps inevitable that this literature contains such diversity. While many first-person accounts of psychosis (for example, MacDonald, 1960; McLean, 2003) do acknowledge the existence (and merits and failings) of professional perspectives, the reverse is rarely the case. Indeed, one could, on reading the scientific literature alone, easily conclude (erroneously in our minds) that those who have the most intimate experience of madness have little to contribute to understandings of the nature and possible causes of the experience. This position is epitomized by the notion of 'insight': it is commonplace for the client's understanding to be seen as not only inaccurate and irrelevant but as another expression of the pathology of psychosis (Beck-Sander, 1998;

Jaspers, 1963), thus disqualifying the client from making any meaningful contribution to understandings of madness.

Cross-culturally, we find a wide range of understandings of psychotic-like experiences. Locally, within New Zealand, this is clearly illustrated with the indigenous people of the country, the Maaori, whose approaches to health in general and mental health in particular place greater emphasis on 'spiritual' matters (such as respecting, and being open to messages from, ancestors) as well as relationships within and between the family and the wider community (Durie, 1999, 2001; see also Herewini, Chapter 6 in this volume). A full discussion of approaches to madness found cross-culturally is not possible here; for the purposes of this discussion it is sufficient to note that the diversity of understandings of psychosis extends beyond the western world.

This diversity, both within the scientific literature on schizophrenia and between scientific approaches and other perspectives (lay, first-person accounts and cross-cultural) is not inherently problematic; indeed there are significant clinical and theoretical advantages to be derived from the existence of multiple, competing attempts to explain madness. However, there are also some problems with the current situation, including the marginalization of voices other than those of the dominant groups (clinicians and researchers) in the field. Creating greater integration while maintaining (even celebrating) diversity may reduce this marginalization of alternative perspectives, and provide a wider range of legitimate understandings of psychotic experiences.

Essential contestedness as a basis for integration

Achieving integration will require us, momentarily at least, to step outside the debate regarding madness in order to consider the nature of the debate itself. It is our contention, as argued elsewhere (Geekie, 2004), that we should consider the debate regarding the nature and causes of madness to be an intrinsic and inevitable aspect of the meaning of madness/schizophrenia. That is, we should consider schizophrenia to be an 'essentially contested concept' (Gallie, 1955–1956). Following Wittgenstein's (1953) position that to appreciate the true meaning of a term we should look to how that term is actually used, rather than how it is formally defined (for example, in a dictionary or a diagnostic manual), we argue that 'schizophrenia' is now, and always has been, used in a 'contested' fashion. Thus, we propose, disagreements regarding its nature *constitute* the meaning of schizophrenia. It is in the very nature of madness that its exact meaning will be disputed. From this position, there is not, indeed *cannot*, be a final resolution to this debate; rather, multiple, competing perspectives are the stuff of what schizophrenia is made.

We do not mean to endorse a laissez-faire position of any theory of schizophrenia being of the same value as any other. Our position is that we must recognize the differences between theories. However, rather than endless and ultimately fruitless debates regarding which theory is the 'true' one, we may need to develop different criteria by which to evaluate theories of madness. We propose a pragmatic approach to the evaluations of theories (both lay and scientific) on grounds such as which aspects of the complex experience of madness they best illuminate, and whose perspective (client, clinician, researcher etc.) they best represent. Similarly, we could evaluate theories in terms of the humanitarian and practical implications which follow from the perspective, such as implications for treatments, and how helpful or otherwise these particular practical implications are. This may also force us to consider the reasons why we adopt the particular theory we do, given the plethora of theories available to us (Read and Hammersley, 2006). In short, if we recognize that no single theory of schizophrenia on its own will unlock all the mysteries of madness, this may allow us to better embrace the notion that our understandings of madness may always be incomplete and partial, but that madness is better illuminated by a plurality of perspectives, each with different merits, failings, and practical implications, and each reflecting distinct positions from which to shed light upon 'schizophrenia'. Recognition of plurality may facilitate increased integration, or at least acceptance, of the various perspectives and ultimately lead to greater understandings and improved treatment approaches for these sometimes distressing experiences.

Research into first-hand experiences of psychosis

We will now discuss our research into how clients of a FEP service convey their experiences of psychosis in clinical meetings with their psychologist. This is naturalistic research involving qualitative analyses of recordings of psychotherapy sessions between clients of a FEP service and Jim Geekie, in his role as clinical psychologist. Clients who had already engaged in psychotherapy and who were keen to explore the meaning of this experience were invited to participate in the research. It was explained that accepting or declining would have no implications for ongoing psychotherapy (or for the client's relationship with the clinical service), nor would the format or content of the meetings be altered to suit the aims of the research. To avoid the risk of clients feeling coerced, those under the Mental Health Act were not invited to participate. Recordings of sessions were transcribed and subsequently analysed to look for emergent themes. Fifteen individuals participated, eleven male and four female. All were under the FEP team and had current, or recent, psychotic experiences. Ten participants were 'Pakeha' (New Zealanders of European descent), two Maaori, three Pacific Islanders and two Asian (some participants identified with more than one cultural orientation). In total, sixty-two recordings were made.

Grounded theory (Glaser and Strauss, 1967), a qualitative method designed to facilitate the development of new theoretical constructs 'grounded' in data (such as interview material), was used for the analysis. This approach places emphasis on research participants' own accounts of the phenomena investigated (Pidgeon, 1997), and as such is well suited to the present research.

Grounded theory involves identifying common themes in the interview material, which are 'coded' by the researchers. Initial stages of coding generally give rise to 'lower level' descriptive categorization. Descriptive categories from the present research can be found in an earlier report (Geekie, 2004). Grounded theory predicts that the process of analysis, which involves the researchers immersing themselves in the data and continually reviewing and revising the coding system will lead to the emergence of more abstract, theoretical categories which capture the 'core' of the data. It is this level of analysis that we present here, where we will outline three 'core' categories or 'constructs' (Kelly, 1955). These are theoretical constructs in that their development involves a considerable degree of abstraction from the data. To be clear, these constructs did not 'jump out' at us from the data: rather, they emerged from our analysis of the interview material and, as such, they represent *our* best efforts at making sense of the participant's subjective experience of psychosis.

These three constructs are: 'invalidation–validation', 'fragmentation–integration' and 'spirituality' (see Table 11.1). Two of these are 'bipolar', with the opposite poles being identified (in keeping with Kelly's theory), whereas the third, 'spirituality', does not easily fit within this structure. The first two constructs relate broadly to participants' expression of what it feels like to be psychotic, and which factors they view as implicated in this experience, whereas 'spirituality' relates more to the framework of meaning within which the participant locates the experience.

Expressing the first two constructs as bipolar will, we hope, emphasize the notion that these relate to processes which are essentially dimensional in nature, with one end being 'negative' and the other more 'positive'. It is rare

Table 11.1 The lived experience of psychosis

Construct	Definition	Range
Invalidation–validation	Loss of faith in ability to accurately construe experience and to convey this to self/others.	Relationships with self and others.
Fragmentation–integration	Loosening of connections between aspects of experience; sense of wholeness 'fragmented'; loss of self-harmony.	Experience of self, the interpersonal world, and the physical world.
Spirituality	Tendency to place psychosis in metaphysical context, with existential/moral significance; reflective, or constitutive, of relationship between individual and universe.	Meaning/significance of psychosis to individual.

in the professional literature to acknowledge that, for some individuals, some psychotic experiences are viewed in a 'positive' way. Yet, for the participants in this research, this was indeed the case at times.

Invalidation–validation

Definition

The notion of losing faith in one's ability to accurately perceive or construe experience and to convey one's understanding to self and others. This construct incorporates aspects of Shotter's (1981) notion of 'authoring' as well as Kelly's (1955) concept of 'validation' (the capacity to make accurate predictions). 'Invalidation' refers to the sense of having one's 'authorship' over experience challenged, threatened, or undermined.

Scope

This construct covers relationship with self and (faith in one's own capacity to accurately construe experience) and relationships with others (the sense that others have faith in one's ability to author experience).

Perhaps one of the most profound aspects of having had a psychotic episode is expressed through the lack of trust that participants developed in their own ways of being in the world (or 'personal ontology') as well as their own ways of making sense of the world ('personal epistemology'). Our impression here is that the philosophical/existential assumptions which we all make regarding Being and Knowing, but which remain largely if not wholly unquestioned and implicit, are called into question. Here, we find parallels to philosophical accounts of psychosis articulated by the likes of Sass (1992).

The threat of feeling that one's way of being in the world has been invalidated is expressed by Moana,[1] a Polynesian woman.

Moana comments: 'I find it really, really hard to go back to the way I used to think, where imagination was just imagination.'

Similarly, Andrew, a European man in his early twenties, reports that he can no longer trust even his own emotions: 'It's not that I'm incapable of feelings. It's just that I don't know if my feelings are fake or not.'

The sense that one's personal epistemology may no longer be valid was also a source of distress.

This was conveyed by Spencer, a young Maaori man who, when asked what he found most distressing about his experience of psychosis, replied 'doubting myself, doubting my own judgements'.

Diane, a European woman in her late thirties who had begun to hear voices which she initially understood as revealing important truths, struggled with the loss of trust in her own perceptions, asking, 'What the hell am I supposed to believe? I can't even trust myself any more.' She saw this predicament as an inevitable consequence of having had a psychotic episode: 'Suddenly finding what they thought was real isn't – that would frighten or disturb anyone.' She was left pondering the question of how she could come to trust her judgements again: 'How in the future am I going to know what's real and what isn't?'

Two participants articulated the full impact of invalidation on the person.

Angus, who experienced psychosis just as he was finishing university, notes: 'The realization that it was a dream or a made up reality makes you lose the foundation, and you don't know what to believe any more.'

Similarly, Vincent, in his late thirties, reflecting on his experience of psychosis, comments: 'That's sort of shaken my belief system and my direction in life, my purpose. Sort of like my belief system, my self, my personality, you know.'

At the other end of the validation–invalidation construct, we find expression of the importance of finding one's voice and being able to 'author' one's own experience of psychosis. This was communicated forcibly, but not without humour, by Angus.

Angus, having just patiently perused the contents of a *What is psychosis?* brochure, notes 'Yeah, that's all very good, but I need to make my *own* sense of the whole thing'.

Angus was not alone in expressing the need to develop a *personal understanding* of the experience, rather than simply adopt a ready-make explanation.

Sarah, who understood her experience in terms of illness, still found this explanation insufficient: 'I mean I want to find out why it has happened and why it has happened to *me*.'

The importance of telling one's story is also stressed by Carter, who was eager to express his story and to have it witnessed, both in therapy and by others in his life.

Carter welcomed the opportunity to document this on tape, both for his own reflection as well as for sharing with friends and family: 'I've got to tell the story. Got to summarize it on this tape here.'

Many participants complained that they felt others discounted them, denying them the right to author their own experience. Some complained that this was tantamount to feeling invalidated as a person.

Indeed, Jerome used this exact terminology in expressing his situation: 'Well, my experiences aren't being validated as real. All my close friends have almost written me off. Because it's almost like I am a lost cause. They see me as cracked.'

This sense of being discounted by others is echoed by Bill.

Bill reports that with friends and family he feels he no longer has a voice: 'I feel almost unheard and not accepted.'

One consequence of this invalidation is to be denied the opportunity to enter into discussions regarding the meaning of the experience.

Sarah discovered this when she tried to have such a conversation with her husband, a process she considered vital to her recovery: 'We spoke about it a couple of times, but he says, "Don't think about it and try to get better as soon as possible".'

Finally, an interesting take on being invalidated was provided by Stanley.

Stanley reported that even his voices (auditory hallucinations) discounted his story-telling capacity by telling him he was crazy (and thus not in a position to author his experience): 'The voices have also said I'm schizophrenic.'

Fragmentation–integration

Definition

A sense of a loosening (or, less often, tightening) of connections and associations between aspects of experience, relating to a sense of 'wholeness', and the notion that through psychosis this can become 'fragmented', or, at the other end of the construct, that there can be a sense of 'integration'. Commonly, fragmentation is associated with of a loss of harmony, whereas integration is associated with sense of well-being.

Scope

The experience of 'fragmentation–integration' is evident in the experience of self, the interpersonal world, and the physical world. Participants conveyed a sense of feeling that their experience of self was fragmented, including experiencing oneself as being discontinuous over time, with, in particular, a feeling that the pre-psychotic self was quite different from the current self.

Michael, a young Pakeha man, comments: 'I don't know if all this is normal or not. I can't remember what I used to be like. I can't remember anything about what life was like before.'

Participants expressed a sense of feeling fragmented, with aspects of self being experienced as 'out-of-sync' with each other.

This is captured by Jerome: 'I feel like everyone's doing their thing. Everyone's got a place, but I haven't got a personality or anything. I'm not in sync with my personality, or my self, or anything.'

A similar sentiment is expressed by Janet, a young European woman, who, in considering her position in the world, complains simply, yet profoundly, 'Like, I don't know if I belong here, or what.'

This fragmentation is mirrored in the experience of the interpersonal world. The most obvious manifestation of this was conveyed by those who felt more distanced from family and friends, as if out of reach of loved ones, giving rise to a sense of isolation, of psychological aloneness, even when in the company of others.

This is captured in the following quote from Moana: 'It's kind of with the psychosis I feel I don't fit in, into what everyone else is doing, in just relating what they do and that. I feel out of place.'

Participants also spoke about their relationship to the world being disjointed or fragmented, giving rise to feeling removed from the physical world around them.

Michael expresses this: 'But, with me it was like nothing, no involvement at all. Like everything I see around me is a movie, and I'm not part of it. I'm not part of it.'

Paul reports a similar feeling and comments on the associated despair: 'Yeah, it was really extreme. You just feel detachment. You just don't feel a part of anything. You feel like maybe you'll go to the building and jump off.'

At the other end of this construct, we have a sense of integration, a feeling of increased 'connectedness'. Though rarer than fragmentation this was, nonetheless, an important component of the experience for some.

Moana notes that at one point during her psychotic episode, everything suddenly seemed to fit together in a coherent fashion: 'It was so logical, it just all came together in such a logical way. It explained everything and anything.'

Paul also conveys an overwhelming sense of connectedness between self and world: 'I felt like I was so connected to everything. To the air, like to the clouds and stuff, and to music.'

The same individual may describe psychosis in ways which suggest both fragmentation and integration. One possibility, consistent with the stories related in this study, is that different stages of psychosis are characterized by different aspects of this construct. Specifically, florid psychosis (and possibly the pre-psychotic period) seems more associated with a sense of integration, whereas in the post-psychotic phase, self and world feel in a more fragmented state.

Spirituality

Definition

Viewing the experience of psychosis in broadly 'spiritual', though not necessarily religious, terms, i.e., a tendency to place the psychotic experience in a metaphysical context where it is considered to reflect something of existential or moral significance for the individual (e.g., relating to the nature of 'good' and 'evil' or to the spiritual purpose of life).

Scope

This construct relates specifically to the meaning/significance that the individual attaches to, or derives from, the experience of psychosis.

Viewing the experience of psychosis as spiritual was of central importance to the participants, although in a range of different ways. The struggle to find personal meaning in the experience was a central theme permeating much of the participants' exploration of the experience, consistent with Wagner and King's (2005) findings that existential concerns are of the highest priority to this client group. The search for the spiritual significance or implications of the experience went beyond material explanations for causes of the experience. Participants in the study had a wide range of explanations of what may have caused the experience (see Geekie, 2004 for more details) including biological, psychological and environmental factors. However, these explanations of causality, which may have helped answer the question of *how* the experience came about, did not seem to quell the need to answer the pressing concern of *why* the psychosis occurred, and what this experience implied for the nature of the individual's world. This aspect of the experience, so noticeable in our research, is largely absent from professional literature on psychosis; although there are some exceptions to this, they remain on the periphery of the literature (e.g., Clarke, 2001; Fallot, 2001; Randal and Argyle, 2005). This, we believe, epitomizes the gulf between the scientific literature and the first-hand lived experience of psychosis.

Jerome expresses the conviction that his experience of psychosis must be understood within a spiritual context, when, reflecting on his previous floridly psychotic state, he explains, quite simply 'There's a whole spiritual story surrounding all of this.'

Moana found herself often uncertain as to whether or not she should try to eliminate her psychotic experiences, given that she saw these experiences as more than, or different from symptoms of illness: 'But, I keep thinking, what is that? What if it's my soul?'

Moana expressed strong, and, in this context, understandable ambivalence about treatment for her psychosis (although this did not translate into non-compliance with medication).

As a young Polynesian woman, Moana's thoughts about her experience often convey cultural understandings of the experience, particularly in the domain of spirituality.

For example, Moana considers that her experience of psychosis may relate to suffering of her ancestors in the after life: 'And then you think, what kind of stuff has happened to our ancestors after they've gone into the after life?' Similarly, reflecting on a friend's experience of psychosis, she notes: 'Apparently, he'd slept under some Maaori carvings, and one of them was, you know, dark, and so he'd been possessed.'

Clearly, cultural factors are of great significance in the meanings ascribed to the experience of psychosis (see Durie, 1999, 2001 for a discussion; see also Herewini, Chapter 6 in this volume). This is an avenue rich in potential for future research.

A common aspect of participants' spiritual concerns was seeing the experience in terms of good versus evil.

Dominic, who had experienced both auditory and visual hallucinations with violent content, finds it difficult to escape the conclusion that having had these experiences means that he himself is evil: 'From a spiritual perspective, I'd have to say that the universe has told me that I'm bad or something.'

Others express this struggle as a literal battle that they feel personally engaged in, with huge impact on their life.

As Moana explains: 'I'm finding it really hard to become religious, because I feel like on a psychological level, I'm battling with God and the Devil.'

Differentiating between psychotic experiences and spirituality was a consideration of many participants. This was at times posed in a way which invited a joint inquiry.

As Andrew asks: 'What's the difference between a psychotic breakdown, or psychotic voices and a spiritual experience?'

Others express their conviction that making such a differentiation is, in fact, impossible.

Diane comments: 'How do you differentiate between a true schizophrenic and a true spiritual experience? You can't.'

This question is of great practical importance. How one construes experience determines the ways one might consider appropriate in dealing with it.

Nearing discharge from our service, and having been free of voices for about a year, Spencer, who had strong spiritual beliefs, wonders how he should respond to any voices he might hear in the future: 'There's all these unanswered questions, like, every time I hear a voice, is it my own mind making it up? What is spiritual? What is not spiritual?'

Analysis of the psychotherapy sessions showed that each participant, without exception, expressed spiritual concerns regarding their experience of psychosis. Although the emphasis placed on the spiritual dimension varied, this was nonetheless a crucial component of the experience for participants, and as such something to which clinical services must give serious thought.

Ethical, research and clinical implications

Ethical implications

We believe that the main ethical implications from our research relate to the importance of ensuring that the basic human right of 'authoring' experience (Shotter, 1981) is not denied to those who experience psychosis. We recognize that, in practice, this can be a difficult task given the, at times, unusual nature of psychotic experiences. However, we believe that services can be more sensitive than they have traditionally been to the client's right to author their own experience. Similarly, we believe there is an ethical case to be made for broadening the gates of our 'scientific' understandings of psychotic experience to allow those with first-hand lived experience of psychosis to participate more fully in the dialogue regarding this experience.

Research implications

Our research findings are tentative, needing further exploration before we could confidently comment on their utility. One way in which this could be done would be to develop operational definitions and instruments (such as questionnaires) which would allow quantification of the three constructs outlined above as well as investigation of a range of issues, including the reliability and validity of the constructs in capturing important aspect of the experience of psychosis. Were such validation forthcoming, this would open up the possibility of exploring if, and how, these constructs relate to other variables such as type of presentation, gender, culture etc.

Clinical implications

Clinical implications from our research include the need for services to *routinely* attend to the meaning of the experience for the client and to make provision for *mutual* exploration of this, including attending to the *philosophical* aspects of the experience (such as personal ontology and personal epistemology).

Validation–invalidation

There is a risk that services may, inadvertently, replicate the experience of invalidation for clients. This could include for example, informing the client that he or she simply does not accurately understand his or her experience ('you lack insight'). On a more subtle level, challenging how the client construes the experience runs the risk, if done insensitively, of further undermining the client. Challenges to the client's explanatory model (Kleinman, 1988), however well intentioned, may be experienced as further invalidation. Mutual, respectful exploration of the meaning of psychosis, within the context of a trusting relationship and with recognition of the plurality of perspectives on schizophrenia may reduce this risk.

Genuine collaboration in exploring the experience may be a requirement here. This may necessitate a shift on the part of clinicians, away from the position of believing that we already *know* what the experience means to recognizing that we bring one way of understanding psychosis, but that this is but one among many useful and valid ways of construing psychosis. If clinicians were to embrace the notion of 'essential contestedness', this may reduce the risk of invalidating the client in clinical encounters.

Another clinical implication is the need to address some of the fundamental implications of the client feeling invalidated, in particular the client's loss of faith in his or her own ways of perceiving and making sense of the world. Interventions need to help the client identify ways of reliably checking out perceptions and understandings of experience, particularly where these are associated with distress for the client. This may involve encouraging the client to use trusted individuals (possibly including the therapist) to test out perceptions: where there is congruence between the client's and the trusted individual's perceptions or understandings, this may help the client build confidence in his or her own perspective. Other ways of evaluating perceptions and understandings of experience may include considering some of the practical implications of adopting a particular position or developing 'behavioural experiments' to test out competing understandings. If this process of evaluation takes place within a trusting relationship, this may make less threatening the re-evaluation of certain perceptions without risking a sense of invalidation of self: that is, the therapeutic relationship may validate the client's sense of self while simultaneously allowing the client to test out perceptions and understandings of the world. In our clinical service, we have developed a 'storytelling' group, with the explicit purpose of promoting the notion of client as author of his or her experience.

Fragmentation–integration

Clinical services should endeavour to encourage integration (or reintegration) and avoid amplification of the process of fragmentation. The current set-up of early intervention services (with a time-limited involvement with clients) runs the risk of replicating fragmentation for some clients who may need longer than the time offered by such services (usually around two years). Greater flexibility regarding duration of time the service is involved with clients may help overcome this problem. Within the clinical service where the current research was undertaken, this point has been taken on board, with the service now extending its availability to up to three years where indicated. It may be that to fully tackle this situation, and reduce the risk of 'refragmentation', early intervention services need first to identify those clients for whom this risk appears significant and to endeavour to offer ongoing support to those individuals for whom time-limited interventions may be contra-indicated. This could be achieved by some early intervention staff also having clinical time dedicated to working longer term with clients.

A service which has a cohesive philosophy adopted by all members of the team may model integration (provided, of course, the philosophy is not too narrow to allow for a range of understandings of psychosis). Similarly, therapeutic interventions which encourage integration within the client, and/or the family may be particularly useful. Here essential ingredients may be a reliable and enduring relationship with the clinician and therapeutic interventions which facilitate integration (such a focusing on and developing sense of self; noticing connections between life experiences and psychosis, etc.). Integration can also be promoted through family work which addresses these issues as well as working more closely with the individual's peer group and attending to occupation.

One way of addressing some of the issues above in a clinical setting may be through the use of the philosophical inquiry (Clayton, 1996) method: a process of philosophical reflection, designed to encourage clearer analytic skills through the guided exploration of philosophical issues We have trialed this in Auckland, where we have run joint clinician-consumer facilitated philosophical inquiry groups for FEP clients, with feedback from participants being encouraging (Burdett, 2001; Burdett and Geekie, 2003).

Spirituality

We believe that this is the aspect of psychosis most neglected by clinicians and researchers. A significant difference may be made were services simply to acknowledge spirituality as an important and legitimate aspect of the experience for clients and to provide an opening for this to be discussed safely, without risk of further invalidation. Mutual exploration of such issues may enhance the relationship between service and client as well as point to avenues of intervention that would otherwise be overlooked. Services may also consider using outside agencies, such as chaplaincy services, or other appropriate experts in the particular form of spirituality of concern to the client, where the service recognizes that the client's spiritual musings lie beyond their level of expertise.

Conclusions

We have outlined our research into the individual's experience of psychosis, and proposed three constructs which help convey how participants in our research relate their experience of psychosis. We hope these constructs are true to the lived experience of the client (feedback from clients supports this view) as well as having utility for clinicians and researchers in the field of psychosis. We hope these constructs help shed light on the nature of psychosis and that this will help illuminate the way for all of us engaged in the business of making sense of madness. We express our gratitude to the participants in this research and leave the final words to Moana, with whose sentiments we agree entirely.

'I keep thinking how can something like that happen and not have meaning?'

Note

1 All names and other identifying features have been changed to protect identity of participants (although all quotes are verbatim).

References

Beck-Sander, A. (1998). Is insight into psychosis meaningful? *Journal of Mental Health*, *7*, 25–34.

Bentall, R. P. (2003). *Madness explained*. London: Allen Lane.

Boyle, M. (1990). *Schizophrenia: A scientific delusion?* London: Routledge.

Burdett, J. (2001). Using group philosophical inquiry as a means of promoting recovery for people who experience mental illness. Unpublished MA dissertation, Deakin University, Victoria, Australia.

Burdett, J. and Geekie, J. (2003). Philosophical inquiry groups for clients of a first episode psychosis service. Paper presented at Fourteenth ISPS Symposium, Melbourne, Australia, September.

Carpenter, W. T. and Buchanan, R. W. (1995). Schizophrenia: Introduction and overview. In H. I. Kaplan and B. J. Sadock (Eds.), *Comprehensive textbook of psychiatry* (6th ed., Vol. 1, pp. 889–902). Baltimore, MD: Williams and Wilkins.

Clarke, I. (Ed.) (2001). *Psychosis and spirituality: Exploring the new frontier*. London: Whurr.

Clayton, C. (1996). *PETE: The practice of philosophical inquiry as a therapeutic experience*. Lymington: Owl of Minerva.

Durie, M. (1999). Mental health and Maori development. *Australasian and New Zealand Journal of Psychiatry*, *33*, 5–12.

Durie, M. (2001). *Mauri Ora: The dynamics of Maori health*. Oxford: Oxford University Press.

Fallot, R. D. (2001). Spirituality and religion in psychiatric rehabilitation and recovery from mental illness. *International Review of Psychiatry*, *13*, 110–116.

Frith, C. D. (1992). *The cognitive neuropsychology of schizophrenia*. Hillsdale, NJ: Lawrence Erlbaum.

Gallie, W. B. (1955–1956). Essentially contested concepts. *Proceedings of the Aristotlian Society*, *16*, 167–198.

Geekie, J. (2004). Listening to what we hear: Clients' understandings of psychotic experiences. In J. Read, L. M. Mosher and R. Bentall (Eds.), *Models of madness: Psychological, social and biological approaches to schizophrenia* (pp. 147–160). Hove: Brunner-Routledge.

Glaser, B. G. and Strauss, A. L. (1967). *The discovery of grounded theory*. Chicago, IL: Aldine.

Gottesman, I. I. (1991). Schizophrenia genesis. New York: Freeman.

Jaspers, K. (1963). *General psychopathology*. Manchester: Manchester University Press.

Jorm, A. F., Korten, A. E., Jacomb, P. A., Christensen, H., Rodgers, B., and Pollit, P (1997). Public beliefs about causes and risk factors for depression and schizophrenia. *Social Psychiatry and Psychiatric Epidemiology*, *32*, 143–148.

Karon, B. P. (1999). The tragedy of schizophrenia. *General Psychologist*, *34*, 1–12.

Kelly, G. A. (1955). *The psychology of personal constructs, volumes I and II*. New York: Norton.

Kleinman, A. (1988). *The illness narratives: Suffering, healing and the human condition.* New York: Basic Books.

MacDonald, N. (1960). Living with schizophrenia. *Canadian Medical Association Journal, 82,* 218–221.

McLean, R. (2003). *Recovered, not cured: A journey through schizophrenia.* Crows Nest, NSW: Allen and Unwin.

Pidgeon, N. (1997). Grounded theory: Theoretical background. In J. T. E. Richardson (Ed.), *Handbook of qualitative research methods for psychology and the social sciences* (pp. 74–85). Leicester: BPS Books.

Randal, P. and Argyle, N. (2005). 'Spiritual emergency' – a useful explanatory model? A literature review and discussion paper. *Spirituality and Psychiatry Special Interest Group of the Royal College of Psychiatrists: Publications Archive.* http:// www.rcpsych.ac.uk/college/sig/spirit/publications/

Read, J. and Hammersley, P. (2006). Can very bad childhoods drive us crazy? Science, ideology and taboo. In J. O. Johannessen, B. V. Martindale and J. Cullberg (Eds.), *Evolving Psychosis: Different stages, different treatments* (pp. 270–292). Hove: Brunner-Routledge.

Read, J. and Haslam, N. (2004). Public opinion: Bad things happen and can drive you crazy. In J. Read, L. R. Mosher and R. P. Bentall (Eds.), *Models of madness: Psychological, social and biological approaches to schizophrenia* (pp. 133–145). Hove: Brunner-Routledge.

Read, J., Perry, B. D., Moskowitz, A., and Connolly, J. (2001). The contribution of early traumatic events to schizophrenia in some patients: A traumatogenic neurodevelopmental model. *Psychiatry, 64,* 319–345.

Read, J., Mosher, L. R., and Bentall, R. P. (2004). *Models of madness: Psychological, social, and biological approaches to schizophrenia.* Hove: Brunner-Routledge.

Sass, L. A. (1992). Heidegger, schizophrenia and the ontological difference. *American Psychologist, 5,* 109–132.

Sharfstein, S. (2005). Big pharma and American psychiatry: The good, the bad and the ugly. *Psychiatric News, 40* (16), 3.

Shotter, J. (1981). Vico, moral worlds, accountability and personhood. In P. Hellas and A. Lock (Eds.), *Indigenous psychologies: The anthropology of the self* (pp. 265–284). London: Academic Press.

Wagner, L. C. and King, M. (2005). Existential needs of people with psychotic disorders in Porto Alegre, Brazil. *British Journal of Psychiatry, 186,* 141–145.

Wittgenstein, L. (1953). *Philosophical investigations.* Oxford: Basil Blackwell.

Chapter 12

Psychosocial interventions in clinical practice guidelines for schizophrenia

Eóin Killackey, Helen Krstev and John F. M. Gleeson

Introduction

There have always been treatments for mental illness. Evidence exists of early trepanning efforts, and through the ages other techniques have been used such as blood letting, confinement, dietary interventions, environmental interventions, talking therapies of various modalities, industrial therapies, insulin comas, and ice baths among many others that do not come so easily to mind. Often the means by which a particular treatment came into the canon of therapies was via a distinguished advocate teaching the technique to a group of people who would later propagate it. Alternatively, the view was held that only physicians, due to the serious nature of their work, would make the correct decision regarding treatments. For example in 1879, writing in the *American Journal of Insanity* (now the *American Journal of Psychiatry*) one author noted that in relation to treatment, doctors were people of such sober judgement and developed knowledge that 'all remedies whatever are at the disposal of practitioners to reject or employ them under the sole guidance of their own judgment' (Bodington, 1879, p. 453).

However well it may have directed selection of appropriate treatments in 1879, the 'sole guidance of [doctor's] own judgment' was ultimately recognized as being one of the restraints on patients receiving access to the best care. The reasons for this are probably many, but two key aspects must have contributed to this change. The first is a cultural shift across the course of the second half of the twentieth century, in which the automatic respect previously given to authority figures diminished. This is as true in medicine as it is in other parts of society. Second, the rise of technology has allowed for the broader and more rapid dissemination of information. For example, now, on the day a journal publishes results of a trial, those results are available to researchers all over the world. This sort of dissemination could not have been dreamt of even in the 1980s.

Although there had been calls for selection of treatments to be more scientifically based for some time (Cochrane, 1972), it was not until the 1990s that large steps were taken to make this a reality. First, in 1992 an article was published in the *Journal of the American Medical Association* in which the term 'evidence-based medicine' (EBM) was used for the first time (Guyatt et al., 1992). The article described that this new approach would be based on clinicians being able to access and appraise the literature in order to determine the treatments with the most evidence and then to use this to guide their practice. This was closely followed in 1993 by the establishment of the Cochrane Collaboration which set about systematically gathering and publishing evidence related to health.

Central to EBM is the randomized controlled trial (RCT). The RCT is seen as the best way to find out if one treatment is better than another comparison treatment. Obviously, the methodology of such a trial is important, and the choice of comparison trial is crucial. A trial with too poor a comparison condition will produce an inflated measure of the effectiveness of the intervention of interest. As data was gathered in the Cochrane Collaboration, and as more researchers outside this collaboration used similar methods to compile meta-analyses, the production of guidelines based on this evidence began as a way to inform clinicians of what the evidence indicated in their field of endeavour.

Clinical practice guidelines (CPG) for the treatment of schizophrenia began appearing in the mid 1990s and continue to be either produced or updated today (Gaebel et al., 2005). The idea of CPG is not that they are a how-to manual for clinicians, or that they should replace decision making necessary when dealing with an individual with their unique combination of issues (Lehman, 2006). Rather, guidelines provide clinicians with a condensed version of what is useful according to the best current evidence (Boyce et al., 2003). In their introduction to EBM, Guyatt and colleagues discussed a diligent evidence-based physician going to a computer to look up the literature on a particular disorder, going to the library to photocopy it, reading and then applying it (Guyatt et al., 1992). In 1992, when searchable databases were in their infancy, this was feasible in many settings, but the internet was still some time away from general usage, and the idea of the practitioner being able to download journal articles at their desk would have still seemed like science fiction. However, in 2007 the diligent clinician is inundated with information, having the choice of multiple databases to search from, instantly retrievable material (all the way back to volume 1 issue 1 in the case of the *American Journal of Psychiatry* for example) and an ever increasing number of journals indexed. Searching for literature has become a skill in itself. For example, at the time of writing, entering the term 'schizophrenia' on PsycInfo returned 77,604 peer reviewed journal articles. A busy clinician is unlikely to have the time necessary to sort through and determine which of these articles provides the evidence needed. Therefore development of a CPG uses a team of experts to gather and analyse the literature, grade it by quality and produce a statement of what the evidence says works (Boyce et al., 2003).

In a review of CPG for schizophrenia Gaebel and colleagues identified 27 sets of guidelines from 21 countries. They were able to access 24 of these and reviewed them on a number of domains including methodological quality, content, and the degree to which they have been implemented.

This chapter will explore the degree to which psychosocial interventions are featured in such guidelines, and will illustrate this with some specific references. The way in which guidelines have affected practice will be considered. Finally, there will be consideration of what may need to be done in order to increase the inclusion of psychosocial interventions in guidelines, and how this may be translated into the greater availability of these interventions for people experiencing psychosis and schizophrenia.

Guidelines and inclusion of psychological and psychosocial interventions

In the American Psychiatric Association's first edition of its guidelines for the treatment of schizophrenia (APA Working Group on Schizophrenia, 1997), there was a brief coverage of psychological therapies with more attention given to psychosocial interventions. In all two and a half pages was sufficient to cover psychosocial treatment. In the 2004 second edition there was considerably more space and a greater detail of consideration given to psychosocial interventions (APA Working Group on Schizophrenia, 2004). However, this raises the question of how many guidelines include psychological and psychosocial interventions and to what extent?

In a review of 24 guidelines from 18 countries, Gaebel and colleagues (2005) identified five psychosocial areas and described whether or not each guideline included recommendations about that area. The results are sobering for those who believe that psychosocial interventions are an important component of treatment. The results were that in terms of recommendations about family support 14/24 covered this; psychoeducational interventions 13/24; CBT 12/24; vocational rehabilitation 12/24; systems of community treatment 12/24. Nine of the guidelines made no recommendation about any psychosocial domain at all. In comparison all but two made a recommendation about the use of second generation antipsychotics as a first-line treatment in acute non-first episode. Other psychopharmacological areas were similarly covered (Gaebel et al., 2005). One of the reasons for concern given the low coverage of psychosocial interventions in these guidelines is that they can often inform policy which dictates which services governments will fund. For example in the UK if the National Institute for Health and Clinical Excellence (NICE) recommends a drug, the National Health Service has to fund that drug within three months (Hogg, 2002). Unfortunately the same obligation is not on the government for other therapies (Hogg, 2002).

To give an overview of the coverage of psychosocial interventions in guidelines, the top three guidelines, and one from the mid-range, according to Gaebel and colleagues (2005) will be used as examples. The determination of ranking was arrived at by subjecting all the guidelines in their review to analysis using the Appraisal Guideline Research and Evaluation Europe (AGREE) rating scale which assesses the quality of both what the guideline suggests and also how it was developed. It does this by measuring 23 items across 6 domains. The domains are: scope and purpose; stakeholder involvement; rigour of development; clarity and presentation; applicability; editorial independence (Gaebel et al., 2005). The three highest scoring guidelines were the NICE (2003) guidelines from the UK which were ranked first, the second edition guidelines from the American Psychiatric Association (APA Working Group on Schizophrenia, 2004), and the Royal Australian and New Zealand College of Psychiatrists (RANZCP) summary guidelines (McGorry et al., 2003) which ranked third. The mid-range guideline chosen is the Singapore Ministry of Health (2003) guideline.

The NICE guidelines consider the evidence around a number of core outcomes of interest. These are suicide, relapse, symptom reduction and remaining in treatment (NICE, 2003). One of the key advantages of these guidelines over others is that they consider psychological and psychosocial interventions separately. Thus in the psychological interventions sections there is consideration of CBT, cognitive remediation, counselling and supportive psychotherapy, family interventions, psychoanalytic and psychodynamic interventions, psychoeducation and social skills training. Obviously the guidelines come to different conclusions about each therapy and its application to the treatment of schizophrenia. Another good feature is that where appropriate there are recommendations for future research directions and also economic analyses. There is no sense in this guideline that psychological interventions are an afterthought.

The APA second edition guidelines (APA Working Group on Schizophrenia, 2004) are very different from the NICE guidelines and do consider psychological therapies as part of the psychosocial interventions. Additionally these guidelines consider a lesser range of therapies. In terms of therapeutic modalities that are covered there is CBT, cognitive remediation, family interventions, social skills training, psychoeducation and personal therapy. While these guidelines do state that psychosocial interventions should be a part of a treatment plan, they do not seem to be as well integrated as in the NICE guidelines. The APA guidelines are strong on the overall psychosocial domain, and argue that vocational, housing and other functional domains need further attention. Therapy, according to the future research directions, needs to be developed in conjunction with medication. Interestingly there is no mention, positive or negative, of psychoanalytic or psychodynamic therapies in the guidelines.

The full version (McGorry et al., 2005) of the summary RANZCP guidelines (McGorry et al., 2003) was released too late to be included in the review of Gaebel et al. (2005), but will be the basis for consideration in this chapter. In the interests of transparency it should be disclosed that one of us (Eóin Killackey) was also an author of these guidelines. The guidelines provide clear phase-by-phase discussions of which psychosocial interventions are usefully utilized in a given phase of illness. However, they do not make a clear distinction between psychological and psychosocial interventions. Therapies that are considered include CBT, cognitive remediation, family intervention, social skills training, compliance therapy, psychoeducation and psychodynamic therapy. Each of these is reviewed and recommendations are given for future research directions.

The Singapore guideline differs considerably from the others. While it includes some psychological and psychosocial interventions, it does not review these in any depth. More tellingly, these guidelines make recommendations about which measures are important for clinical audits to measure. Because it is assumed that these are published by the Singapore Ministry of Health, these recommendations will be important in official determinations of what constitutes adequate care for people with schizophrenia in Singapore. Therefore it is disappointing that the provision of psychological or psychosocial interventions are not mentioned in the clinical audit parameters (Singapore Ministry of Health, 2003).

It can be seen that despite some criticism (Barker and Buchanan-Barker, 2003), a number of guidelines have developed quite rapidly in a little over a decade, and some are already on their second editions (APA Working Group on Schizophrenia, 2004; Canadian Psychiatric Association, 2005; Lehman et al., 2004). More importantly, the guidelines which are recognized as being of better quality do include a variety of psychological interventions for schizophrenia and make recommendations about the appropriateness of these in the treatment of schizophrenia. However, unless these various guidelines are actually utilized in everyday practice and have some effect there, all they are is well intended, well researched but ultimately useless documents. The next section of the chapter will consider to what extent guidelines in general affect practice and more specifically, the extent how much recommendations about psychological and psychosocial interventions are implemented.

Do guidelines influence practice? What the literature says

As Gaebel et al. (2005) noted in their review, many countries and organizations have produced their own sets of guidelines, such that in the review there were more guidelines than countries represented. This has led to the suggestion that there is a lot of needless replication in the production of these guidelines as most of the evidence used is international and rarely do the makers of guidelines have access to data about specific ethnic subgroups (Leucht et al., 2006). However, in response it has been pointed out that while most of the data is international, and even where it is not (e.g., USA) it is not usually broken into ethnic subgroups, most guideline makers are asking different questions of the data informed by their local needs (Gaebel and

Weinman, 2006). If this is the case it would be expected that there would be evidence of the adoption of the local guidelines in each area. Further, this evidence could be expected because of the nature of EBM. That is, a systematic approach to appraising what works and what doesn't. This should apply to guidelines and their implementation as much as it does to individual treatments (Pilling and Price, 2006).

In 1998 when the PORT guidelines were first produced (Lehman et al., 1998a) it was discovered that very few patients had access to effective treatments. The original PORT guidelines are somewhat dated now but the results of this are interesting. They found that of outpatients 45 per cent had access to psychotherapy, 10 per cent to family therapy, 10 per cent to assertive community treatment and 22 per cent to vocational rehabilitation (Lehman et al., 1998b). In an article accompanying the new edition of the PORT guidelines, there is discussion of the low level of these rates and the difficulties of ensuring that where these therapies are provided, that what is provided is a high fidelity implementation (Essock et al., 2004; Torrey, 2004). Surveys of people with mental illness reveal that very few of them are gaining access to evidence based treatments (Hall, 2004).

The first comment that may be made is that there is not as much research concerning the implementation of guidelines as one might expect. Most of the existing research is concerned with adherence of practice to medication recommendations; little is concerned with recommendations about psychosocial or psychological interventions. In the research that does exist, there are references to implementation lagging behind the development of guidelines (Healy et al., 2004). A summary of what has been found shows that guidelines do not influence medication prescription practice even when prescribers are aware of the guidelines, and it is not because they are worried about cost (Healy et al., 2004). Further, a number of studies find that medication is not prescribed in line with guidelines in a large proportion of cases (Leslie and Rosenheck, 2004; Weinmann et al., 2005). Despite this, there are some large studies that indicate that overall more people than not are receiving medication in line with guideline recommendations (West et al., 2005). However, when it comes to psychological and psychosocial treatments, the results are, in line with the findings accompanying the PORT guidelines, not good.

In a national survey in the United States, West and colleagues found that:

> rates of conformance with the [PORT] guideline recommendations were significantly lower for psychosocial recommendations than for psychopharmacologic recommendations: for psychosocial recommendations rates ranged from 0 per cent to 43 per cent, whereas for psychopharmacologic recommendations rates ranged from 30 to 100 per cent.
>
> (West et al., 2005, p. 287)

Possibly the worst finding in this study was that of the consumers who were unemployed because of their illness, none had received a vocational intervention in the previous month. This is despite many guidelines consistently recommending that there is good evidence to support vocational interventions and recommending that they form a routine part of the treatment of schizophrenia.

So why is the situation so poor for psychological and psychosocial interventions in schizophrenia? One argument is that these interventions cost more money and so are not implemented and there is evidence that where there are budget cuts psychosocial programmes are victims of these before medication (Leslie and Rosenheck, 2004). However, for a number of psychological and psychosocial interventions there is now good economic data which shows that when implemented effectively these programmes pay for themselves (NICE, 2003). Of course the key condition is faithful implementation which is difficult, but not impossible to measure (Essock et al., 2004). Another argument is that there is no lobby group for psychological and psychosocial interventions in the way that there is for pharmaceutical interventions. Certainly there is more research about the latter (Killackey et al., 2006a) and often the methodologies required to run a medication trial and a psychotherapeutic trial are different. On the other hand, new psychological treatments do not generally have to be approved by a body such as the US Food and Drug Administration. One could argue that attaining such official sanction may lead to more investment in psychotherapeutic research.

One of the difficulties of implementing new psychological and psychosocial techniques is that it requires new learning on the part of the practitioner (Lehman, 2006). This is much more than is required of the clinician when a new medication comes onto the market, and it may be in itself a barrier, particularly where clinicians already have high caseloads and little time allocated to professional development. Again this may not be an obstacle when a therapy exists that clearly makes a difference and at the same time does not impose unreasonable learning requirements on clinicians. A good example of this is CBT, which has demonstrated efficacy for a number of disorders, has clear manuals for people beginning to practise, and does not make the same demands as other more traditional psychodynamic psychotherapies.

What is to be done?

Despite the development of guidelines, it would appear from the evidence that, at least in the case of psychological and psychosocial therapies, recommendations are not forming part of routine clinical practice. A number of areas need attention if the situation is to improve.

It would seem logical that there needs to be some consideration given to the barriers faced in implementing guidelines. In surveys most clinicians think that guidelines are a good idea, but despite knowledge about them, do not refer to them in practice (Healy et al., 2004). More research is needed to uncover what would make clinicians more likely to use guidelines. Similar work is required with administrators. Answers from this sort of research are likely to drive research required to meet these needs such as economic analyses of therapies which may convince administrators.

In order to match the rhetoric of non-pharmacological interventions as being vital alongside medication in the treatment of schizophrenia, the prominence given to psychosocial and psychological interventions in guidelines needs to improve. While some guidelines currently do this quite well, a number do not. The best guidelines at the moment in this regard are the NICE (2003) guidelines.

The evidence suggests that while the recommendations concerning medications are more often than not implemented, implementation is far from uniform. In the case of psychological and psychosocial interventions it is often non-existent. Therefore there must be recognition that the guideline development process does not end with the production of a document, but must continue through to dissemination and implementation. This has been recognized by the National Institute for Health and Clinical Excellence in the UK (Pilling and Price, 2006). At the launch of the NICE guidelines, implementation was the responsibility of users and not centralized. As a consequence it was haphazard. Because of this NICE established an evidence-based implementation process that is being trialled in various areas and which early indicators suggest is more effective than the previous approach (Pilling and Price, 2006).

The recommendations of guidelines can only be as extensive as the good research that there is on which to base them. There are real difficulties in conducting research trials of psychological interventions. Often the intervention needs to be very carefully described prior to the trial and people trained to provide it. Consumers may be reluctant to participate if they have already many commitments in terms of their recovering health. Often the intervention and follow-up periods will be longer than in medication trials, and at the end of all that the effect sizes may be small and publication in a top journal elusive. However, it is not impossible as some imaginative trials have shown (Álvarez-Jiménez et al., 2006), despite what may seem at times like insurmountable odds (Mario Álvarez-Jiménez, personal communication).

There has been a reasonable amount of pessimism in this chapter. However, this does not reflect that clinicians are providing poor service to clients, only that in the small literature that there is about guidelines and implementation, that the implementation component is overdue for more attention. The optimistic picture is that over and over people experiencing mental illness want psychological (Pilling and Price, 2006) and psychosocial (Killackey et al., 2006b) interventions because they recognize that they serve a need not met by medication alone. Therefore, it is important that there continues to be a determination to explore which interventions work and how they work and to communicate this to all of those interested in the integration of psychological and psychosocial interventions into the mainstream of treatment for people with mental illness.

References

Álvarez-Jiménez, M., González-Blanch, C., Vázquez-Barquero, J. L., Pérez-Iglesias, R., Martínez-García, O., Pérez-Pardal, T., et al. (2006). Attenuation of antipsychotic-induced weight gain with early behavioral intervention in drug-naive first-episode psychosis patients: A randomized controlled trial. *Journal of Clinical Psychiatry, 67*, 1253–1260.

APA Working Group on Schizophrenia (1997). Practice guideline for the treatment of patients with schizophrenia. *American Journal of Psychiatry. Special Issue: Practice Guideline for the Treatment of Patients with Schizophrenia, 154* (Suppl. 4), 1–63.

APA Working Group on Schizophrenia (2004). *Practice guideline for the treatment of patients with schizophrenia* (2nd ed.). Washington, DC: APA.

Barker, P. and Buchanan-Barker, P. (2003). Schizophrenia: The 'not-so-nice' guidelines. *Journal of Psychiatric and Mental Health Nursing, 10*, 374–378.

Bodington, G. F. (1879). An English view of restraint: Restraint in the treatment of insanity. *American Journal of Insanity, 35*, 452–465.

Boyce, P., Ellis, P., and Penrose-Wall, J. (2003). Introduction to the royal Australian and New Zealand College of Psychiatrists clinical practice guidelines series. *Australian and New Zealand Journal of Psychiatry, 37*, 637–640.

Canadian Psychiatric Association (2005). Clinical practice guidelines: Treatment of Schizophrenia. *Canadian Journal of Psychiatry, 50* (Suppl. 1), s1–s56.

Cochrane, A. L. (1972). *Effectiveness and efficiency: Random reflections on health services.* London: Nuffield Provincial Hospitals Trust.

Essock, S. M., Covell, N. H., and Weissman, E. M. (2004). Inside the black box: The importance of monitoring treatment implementation. *Schizophrenia Bulletin, 30*, 613–615.

Gaebel, W. and Weinman, S. (2006). Call for a European guidelines institute: Author's reply. *British Journal of Psychiatry, 188*, 193.

Gaebel, W., Weinmann, S., Sartorius, N., Rutz, W., and McIntyre, J. S. (2005). Schizophrenia practice guidelines: International survey and comparison. *British Journal of Psychiatry, 187*, 248–255.

Guyatt, G., Cairns, D., Churchill, D., Cook, D., Haynes, B., Hirsch, J., et al. (1992). Evidence based medicine: A new approach to teaching the practice of medicine. *Journal of the American Medical Association, 268*, 2420–2425.

Hall, L. L. (2004). Half-full but nearly empty: Implications of the schizophrenia PORT updated treatment recommendations. *Schizophrenia Bulletin, 30*, 619–621.

Healy, D. J., Goldman, M., Florence, T., and Milner, K. K. (2004). A survey of psychiatrists' attitudes toward treatment guidelines. *Community Mental Health Journal, 40*, 177–184.

Hogg, C. (2002). *Schizophrenia policy 'unworkable'.* Retrieved 19 March 2007, from http://news.bbc.co.uk/2/low/health/2246604.stm

Killackey, E., Álvarez-Jiménez, M., Cotton, S., Gleeson, J., and Jackson, H.

(2006a). Are we as biopsychosocial as we used to be? Preliminary findings from the literature in first episode (LIFE) project. *Acta Psychiatrica Scandinavica, 114* (Suppl. 431), 60.

Killackey, E. J., Jackson, H. J., Gleeson, J., Hickie, I. B., and McGorry, P. D. (2006b). Exciting career opportunity beckons! Early intervention and vocational rehabilitation in first episode psychosis: Employing cautious optimism. *Australian and New Zealand Journal of Psychiatry, 40*, 951–962.

Lehman, A. F. (2006). Editorial. Treatment guidelines: Caveat emptor! *Journal of Mental Health, 15*, 129–133.

Lehman, A. F., Steinwachs, D. M., and the Co-Investigators of the PORT Program. (1998a). Translating research into practice: The Schizophrenia Patient Outcomes Research Team (PORT) treatment recommendations. *Schizophrenia Bulletin, 24*, 1–10.

Lehman, A. F., Steinwachs, D. M., and the Schizophrenia Patient Outcomes Research Team. (1998b). Patterns of usual care for schizophrenia: Initial results from the Schizophrenia Patient Outcomes Research Team (PORT) client survey. *Schizophrenia Bulletin, 24*, 11–20.

Lehman, A. F., Kreyenbuhl, J., Buchanan, R. W., Dickerson, F. B., Dixon, L. B., Goldberg, R., et al. (2004). The Schizophrenia Patient Outcomes Research Team (PORT): Updated treatment recommendations 2003. *Schizophrenia Bulletin, 30*, 193–217.

Leslie, D. L. and Rosenheck, R. A. (2004). Adherence of schizophrenia pharmacotherapy to published treatment recommendations: Patient, facility, and provider predictors. *Schizophrenia Bulletin, 30*, 649–658.

Leucht, S., Stiegler, M., Rummel, C., Wahlbeck, K., and Kissling, W. (2006). Call for a European guidelines institute. *British Journal of Psychiatry, 188*, 193.

McGorry, P., Killackey, E., Elkins, K., Lambert, M., and Lambert, T. (2003). Summary Australian and New Zealand clinical practice guideline for the treatment of schizophrenia. *Australasian Psychiatry, 11*, 136–147.

McGorry, P., Killackey, E., Lambert, T., and Lambert, M. (2005). Royal Australian and New Zealand College of Psychiatrists clinical practice guidelines for the treatment of schizophrenia and related disorders. *Australian and New Zealand Journal of Psychiatry, 39* (1–2), 1–30.

NICE (2003). *Schizophrenia: Full national clinical guideline on core interventions in primary and secondary care.* London: Gaskell and the British Psychological Society.

Pilling, S. and Price, K. (2006). Developing and implementing clinical guidelines: Lessons from the NICE Schizophrenia Guideline. *Epidemiologia e Psichiatria Sociale, 15*, 109–116.

Singapore Ministry of Health (2003). *Schizophrenia: Clinical practice guideline.* Singapore: Ministry of Health.

Torrey, E. F. (2004). PORT updated treatment recommendations. *Schizophrenia Bulletin, 30*, 617–618.

Weinmann, S., Janssen, B., and Gaebel, W. (2005). Guideline adherence in medication management of psychotic disorders: An observational multisite hospital study. *Acta Psychiatrica Scandinavica, 112*, 18–25.

West, J. C., Wilk, J. E., Olfson, M., Rae, D. S., Marcus, S., Narrow, W. E., et al. (2005). Patterns and quality of treatment for patients with schizophrenia in routine psychiatric practice. *Psychiatric Services, 56*, 283–291.

Chapter 13

Families dealing with psychosis

Working together to make things get better

Ross M. G. Norman, Lori Hassall, Sharon Scott Mulder, Brenda Wentzell and Rahul Manchanda

Introduction

Psychotic disorders often have profound impacts on the families of those who are ill, necessitating various coping strategies (Addington et al., 2003; Scheme et al., 1998). In this chapter we shall discuss the potential role of families not only in the treatment and rehabilitation of their own relatives, but also in bringing about wider social change related to psychotic disorders.

What can families receive from the health care system?

There is a considerable literature helping families deal with the challenges and stressors they are experiencing as well as promoting the recovery of the ill person (Anderson et al., 1986; Falloon et al., 1984; McFarlane, 2004; Mueser and Gingerich, 1994). The underlying premise is that by educating and helping families, there will be a reduction in stress levels benefiting all family members and the ill person in particular. Education about the nature of the illness and its treatment should also help family members effectively support the recovery of the person.

The concerns of families are likely to depend partially on the symptoms of the ill person which can vary considerably. These include not only the more bizarre symptoms of the illness, but also social withdrawal, decreased motivation and self care as well as comorbid symptoms of mood, anxiety, substance use and abuse, etc. The extent to which any set of symptoms or behaviours causes distress in the family will also be moderated by the family's circumstances such as the constellation and supportiveness of family members, the age and demands of other individuals within the family, cultural beliefs, financial resources, the nature of employment of family members, level of tolerance for unusual behaviours and, of course, the amount of contact between the ill person and family. It has also been our experience that a family's previous experience with mental illness can also play a role in their level of distress. Those families who have experienced chronic mental illness in other family members may be less hopeful about the effectiveness of treatment when an additional family member becomes ill. Both quantitative studies and more qualitative and descriptive material indicate that the problems most commonly identified by families include a pervading worry about the future, concerns for the safety of the ill person; safety of the family (particularly if there is a perceived risk of violence on the ill person's part); embarrassment; lack of cooperation or initiative by the ill person in daily living; the responsibility for providing the ill person with help in transportation, finances, and household chores; the need for supervision; and interference with family members' own functioning and enjoyment of life (Beard and Gillespie, 2002; Gibbons et al., 1984; Jones and Jones, 1994). It should be noted that the literature on family concerns appears to have been derived largely from research on parents, spouses or partners. Our experience with initial stages of psychosis suggests that it is also important to better understand and address the concerns and needs of siblings of the ill person for whom the experience of the onset of psychosis in a brother or sister can be very upsetting.

The reactions and concerns of families when dealing with psychosis are likely to change over time (Baronet, 1999; Dixon et al., 2000). For this reason, it may not be appropriate to simply directly apply family interventions designed for longstanding illness when dealing with first episodes of psychosis (Dixon et al., 2000; Nugter et al., 1997). As part of the protocol in the Prevention and Early Intervention Program for Psychoses in London, Ontario, family members are given the opportunity to indicate in writing their primary concerns at the initiation of treatment and on at least a yearly basis thereafter. Coding and tabulation of responses show that concerns about positive psychotic symptoms such as hallucinations, delusions and bizarre behaviour and how they can be treated as well as issues related to reducing substance abuse and stabilization of immediate living circumstances dominate family concerns during the first several months of treatment. Over time as these immediate concerns are addressed, the primary concerns of family members tend to focus more on issues such as re-establishing personal relationships and a social network for the ill person, improving his or her general psychological health and self-esteem, and opportunities for return to school, work or other productive and meaningful activity.

Given that the challenges faced by families will be influenced by the ill person's symptoms and behaviours as well as family circumstances, family interventions are perhaps best seen as supporting the development of a practical repertoire or tool box of strategies to reduce stress, encourage problem solving and facilitate positive relations. Which specific elements of the intervention are most valuable will likely vary between families and over time. As with any effective and structured intervention, it is important to be able to effectively address at least some of the family needs as soon as possible in order to foster engagement. Detailed descriptions of clinical programs and related materials have been presented in articles, books and/or videos (e.g., Anderson et al., 1986; Falloon et al., 1984; Kuipers et al., 1992; McFarlane, 2004; Mueser and Gingerich, 1994; Norman et al., 2000). These typically include basic education about the nature of schizophrenia and developing skills to cope with associated challenges. Components often included in programs are outlined in Table 13.1. Skills development includes suggestions for anticipating and avoiding difficulties, coping with challenging situations and crises, and recognizing the importance of reacting verbally and non-verbally in ways that will modulate levels of stress for the family and ill person.

Home visits may be included as part of some family interventions. Such interventions are sometimes presented in a single family format and sometimes in multi-family groups. It has been argued that the multi-family format has advantages in developing mutual emotional support between groups and facilitates problem solving (McFarlane et al., 1995).

The context in which these interventions are usually provided is also important. Generally they are offered as part of a comprehensive and coherent program of pharmacological and psychosocial treatments, rather than as stand-alone interventions. Proponents of such programs emphasize that they are not 'family therapy' designed to bring about change in 'dysfunctional' families. There is considerable sensitivity by professionals and families to notions of family dynamics as being a cause of schizophrenia and related

Table 13.1 Components often included in structured family interventions

Education about psychotic disorders	• Nature and basis of symptoms which define psychotic disorders and are used for diagnosis • Common comorbid symptoms and difficulties • Understanding the individual's experience of these symptoms • Etiology and pathophysiology of psychotic disorders • Diathesis/stress model • Methods and effects of pharmacological and psychosocial treatment • Rehabilitation and reintegration • Early signs of relapse
Skills development	• Problem solving • Stress management • Coping with specific positive and negative symptoms • Dealing with substance use • Verbal and non-verbal aspects of effective communication • Maintaining household routines • Dealing with stigma • Re-establishing social connections • Supporting individual's vocational and educational opportunities • Aiding reintegration • Accessing community resources • Preventing and dealing with relapse • Preventing engulfment of individual and family (including siblings and children) by illness • Mutual help and support across families

disorders. Although there is evidence that childhood trauma may contribute to risk for psychosis (Read et al., 2005), models which assume that psychotic disorders are intrinsically tied to dysfunctional families have been largely discredited on empirical grounds. Nevertheless, our experience has been that such theories still have currency among some mental health service providers and public which adds to the distress of many families and can reduce their receptivity to being involved in clinical services for their ill family member (see Martindale, Chapter 3, and Couchman, Chapter 15 in this volume for extended discussions of this issue). Such sensitivities can also result in concerns about the concept of expressed emotion as a predictor of course of illness, although the latter is not explicitly postulated to be a cause of psychotic illness (Lefley, 1992). Historically the type of family interventions we are describing were often developed with the explicit intention of reducing the intensity of expressed emotion in targeted families, but more recently expressed emotion appears to be a less central part of the rationale for such work (Dixon et al., 2000), and such interventions seem to be providing information and skills development of potential relevance to most, if not all, families dealing with severe mental illness.

There is evidence that face-to-face structured interventions can reduce the distress and burden of families who participate (Falloon and Pedeson, 1985; Hazel et al., 2004). Several reviews and meta-analyses have documented their effectiveness in improving outcomes for the ill person across cultures (Dixon et al., 2000; Pilling et al., 2002; Pitschel-Walz et al., 2001). These benefits are not restricted to symptoms of psychosis and likelihood of hospitalization, but also include salutary effects on family burden and distress and the social and vocational functioning of the ill person. There are, however, several unresolved issues including identification of critical components, the role of reduction in expressed emotion (EE) as a mediator of effectiveness, the effectiveness of briefer or 'as needed' interventions, and the comparative advantages of single family versus multi-family approaches (Dixon et al., 2000; Huxley et al., 2000; Mueser and Bond, 2000; Pilling et al., 2002). Nevertheless, the overall efficacy of face-to-face family interventions is well established, and they are now included in best practice guidelines (e.g., Addington et al., 2005; Lehman et al., 2004a). Delivery of such interventions is particularly challenging when psychotic illness occurs in rural or other areas that do not have specialized programs for psychosis in close proximity. Under such circumstances there is the need to develop and evaluate innovative methods of providing services to families. Unfortunately, even when specialized clinical services are available, family interventions, like many other empirically validated psychosocial interventions, are not provided as often or effectively as they should be (Dixon, et al., 1999, 2000; Lehman, 2000; Lehman et al., 1998, 2004b; McFarlane et al., 2001; Resnick et al., 2005).

The Prevention and Early Intervention Program for Psychoses (PEPP) in London, Ontario provides a multifaceted approach to working with families.

The overall goals of PEPP include community outreach to identify and treat first-episode psychotic disorders as quickly as possible, engagement of clients and their families in a comprehensive treatment and recovery program, and advocacy both for the strengthening of early intervention services and reduction in unnecessary social disadvantage for those experiencing first-episode psychosis. Initial assessments can be accessed very quickly and treatment is initiated on either an outpatient or inpatient basis. The core of the clinical program is an assertive case management model which provides comprehensive assessment of the client's needs and utilizes medical and psychosocial interventions to initially treat the acute symptoms of psychosis and aid social and psychological recovery. The program is predicated on a diathesis-stress model of illness and emphasizes reducing vulnerability through pharmacological interventions, skills development, and interventions in the individual's environment. Emphasis is placed on developing a strong therapeutic relationship with the ill person and partnership with families. Delivery of service also involves working closely with a variety of community services, educational institutions, employers, etc. Details of the overall program are available elsewhere (www.pepp.ca; Malla et al., 2003).

Efforts to cultivate a working alliance with families are present from the time a client is initially assessed by PEPP. Consistent with several studies (e.g., de Haan et al., 2002; Helgason, 1990), we find family members to be the instigators of contact with our services more often than clients themselves. Whenever possible, families are an integral part of the initial assessment process. Developing a working alliance with families is of major importance to the case manager. The assessment addresses not only information from family members about clinical symptoms of the ill person, but also the impact of illness on family, their understanding of the illness and its treatment, and any circumstances that are likely to have an impact on treatment and recovery. One benefit of the early establishment of close contact with families is the facilitation of later discharge planning and transition from hospital to home for those patients who have to be hospitalized for their initial treatment. Case managers and other clinicians in the program can provide ongoing support to family members, instrumental assistance, home visits, referral to community services when required, etc., over several years.

More structured aspects of our work with families are based on an adaptation of the psychoeducation program initially developed by Anderson et al. (1986) in the context of patients with a longstanding chronic illness. This program has been adapted to better address the concerns of families who are dealing with a more recent onset illness and who are often relatively naive with reference to psychiatric illness and its treatment. For the convenience of families, the family psychoeducational workshop is offered on a weekend. The material covered emphasizes basic information about what is known about the causes of psychotic illness such as schizophrenia as well as the nature and mechanisms of treatment. The basic education component of family intervention generally leaves family members with a level of knowledge about psychotic illness that is *at the very least* the equal of most non-specialist physicians and mental health professionals. A second component of the workshop is designed to help deal with the challenges of having a family member with psychotic illness. It addresses such issues as adherence to medication, dealing with stigma, substance use, maintaining family routine, addressing negative symptoms, intimacy/sexuality, supporting the recovery of social and vocational functioning or return to school, possible signs of relapse, etc. Video-taped scenarios using staff and actors are used to model some of the common problems that arise and various methods of coping with them. The importance of both verbal and nonverbal communication is illustrated. Emphasis is placed on maintaining an emotional equilibrium and on a problem-solving approach that meets the needs of both family members and the ill person. A third element of the workshop involves first-person narratives from a family member and a client. During a relaxed lunch break, a member of the PEPP Parent Support Group speaks to the attendees about their family's experience with the illness and invites families to attend future support group meetings. The day ends with a presentation from a PEPP client who shares his or her story and describes what was helpful in terms of family support during the early days with the illness. These presentations are both realistic and encouraging, which instils a sense of hope for families, who are often feeling overwhelmed. The workshop is very interactive in nature and family members are encouraged to voice their concerns and ask questions. The ill clients are not invited to this workshop in order to allow a very open and candid discussion of concerns by family members. This workshop provides a good general introduction to material that will, according to the specific needs of clients and families, be readdressed over time in interactions with case managers and other clinical staff. In addition, the workshop provides an important opportunity for family members to interact informally with all the clinical staff and with other families who are dealing with similar challenges. Family members report they find the workshop significantly increases their knowledge about the illness and competence and confidence in dealing with the associated challenges. Evaluations of the workshop consistently show at least 85 per cent of participants find it has been very helpful in providing useful information about the illness, helping them develop needed skills and leaving them feeling more hopeful about the illness.

The coping approaches introduced in the initial multi-family workshop are also reinforced, according to each family's needs and circumstances, in multi-family groups that include both clients and family members. These usually involve four to six families and two clinician facilitators holding bi-weekly meetings over an 18-month period. The intervention, based on the work of McFarlane (2002), uses a focused problem-solving approach. McFarlane's multi-family intervention is designed to help families and clients reduce anger, anxiety, confusion and social withdrawal and to promote effective problem solving. The experience in PEPP has supported the hypothesis that such groups are particularly effective because they increase social support for the family, reduce feelings of stigmatization, provides a forum for sharing experiences and mutual assistance (McFarlane, 2004). Evaluations completed by those attending these groups show that 80–90 per cent of attendees find the experience enjoyable, supportive and useful. All attendees report using the problem-solving techniques provided in the group and see the group as having had a positive effect on their family relations.

Families of clients within PEPP have also organized a family support group. The PEPP Parent Support Group is an integral part of the program. Below we will outline several of the benefits this group has provided for PEPP, families and the community. In the current context, it is important to note in addition to providing support to one another through regular group meetings, this group has been the foundation for a network of informal supportive relations between PEPP family members that occur on a daily basis in person, by telephone, and through email.

There are, of course, many challenges in working with families. As noted above, psychotic illness often has its onset at a time when families would, even under the best of circumstances, be dealing with the many issues that can be associated with a young person developing his or her own identity and independence. The presence of a psychotic illness can complicate such processes. Issues of confidentiality, autonomy versus parental control, mutual respect, vacillation between engagement or involvement and disengagement or distancing, and dealing with feelings of guilt (often unintentionally fostered by society and health care providers) offer many challenges. Not all families become participants in the recovery process. There are cases where clients do not want their families to be involved or families wish to distance themselves. Our approach to such cases is to make sure families are aware of the support available. Even if circumstances mean that a family will not be collaborators in the treatment and recovery process, it is often possible to provide them with general information about psychotic illness and coping skills without infringing on consent, confidentiality and client privacy. Work with families can be very challenging, but its benefits are great. Having a common understanding of the nature of the illness and its treatment, reducing family stress and increasing their confidence and competence in providing support and coping with challenges, and giving them more opportunity to hold the program accountable for the nature of the services it provides, have all been of enormous benefit.

After a thorough review of first-episode studies, Ram et al. (1992) estimated an average likelihood of relapse of such patient within the first two years after remission of approximately 66 per cent which compares to less than 40 per cent within PEPP. Several factors probably contribute to that difference, but we believe that the existence of good working relationships with the families of many of our clients is an important one.

What can the health care system receive from families?

Families should no longer be seen primarily as a cause of psychotic illness or as a roadblock to recovery, but rather as potential collaborators and powerful partners in the treatment and recovery process. As noted above, the evidence is now clear that it is beneficial for the mental health care system to work with families in providing clinical services (Dixon et al., 2000; Pilling et al., 2002; Pitschel-Walz et al., 2001). There are, however, many challenges in providing care and support to those with psychotic illness that occur outside the clinic. For instance, if optimal clinical services for psychotic disorders are to be developed and maintained there must be funding and political support. If psychosis is to be identified and treated early and if social recovery is to be successful there has to be social change. Our experience has been that families can often be more effective advocates for political support and social change than mental health professionals. While our recent experience in this regard has been primarily with respect to facilitating the early identification and treatment of psychosis, we feel certain that the experience of families has general implications for improving the lives of those with psychotic disorders. In particular families have been extremely valuable in providing much needed practical support, public education, and political advocacy.

In the context of PEPP, families have provided invaluable assistance in such roles as volunteer tutors for clients returning to school, assistance in finding employment for clients, development of a program website (www.pepp.ca), sitting on the PEPP Community Advisory committee and other hospital and community committees, public speaking, contributing to training for the police services, teacher's college and new first-episode programmes and services, organization of social activities for clients such as Christmas parties, outings, summer barbecues, etc., and fund raising. The parent support has donated equipment and supplies to aspects of the clinical program particularly concerned with social and vocational recovery. One major social event, PEPP's 'The Big Night' is a fundraiser that does much to create an image of celebration of hope and recovery for psychotic disorders. It features an elegant evening of dinner, dancing and an auction. Funds raised from these events are used to support client-centred activities within the program, but perhaps even more important is their role in potentially changing social attitudes towards psychotic disorders.

It is well documented that the stigma associated with mental illness in general, and psychotic illness in particular, poses many problems in both the lives of individuals with such illness and for funding and effective delivery of relevant services. Our experience in the field of early intervention for psychotic disorders has certainly been consistent with the formal literature in indicating that stigma can interfere with people seeking treatment and adhering to treatment, and that social discrimination can have a very negative impact on an ill person's psychological, social, and vocational/educational recovery. We have found the activities of family members to be helpful in addressing stigma. For example, the fundraising activities mentioned above have resulted in the profile of psychotic disorders as a cause for community support being raised considerably. Community fundraising breakfasts supported by local organizations have profiled PEPP alongside the Cancer Society and other widely supported health charities. 'The Big Night', which is entirely associated with early intervention for psychosis, has become a major annual social event attended by political and business leaders, professionals, local media personalities, program clients and family members and several hundred members of the public. Items auctioned for fund raising at this event include items contributed by elegant restaurants, boutique shops, and other businesses. One can purchase anything from a weekend at a resort to an evening's in-home entertainment by a classical violinist to spending a day with the fire department. Such activities by the parent support group help reduce the local stigma about psychotic illness.

Another important area of family participation is in education. As an example of this, family members and clients participate in teaching medical students during a one-week section of their curriculum devoted to psychotic disorders. In their evaluations, the students consistently identify the sessions with clients and family members as having a major impact on their appreciation of the experience and needs of those with psychotic illness and the effectiveness of various components of treatment. Family members have also been partners in the launch of a community campaign for early identification of psychotic disorders by distributing materials throughout the community, setting up information displays, participating in community forums generating hope and enthusiasm. Members of this group have accepted invitations to speak to community, family and mental health agencies throughout a wide geographical area. Members of the Parent Support Group were the focus of a video tape entitled *One Day at a Time*, developed by the Canadian Mental Health Association National Office, which provides practical advice, support and hope to families anywhere who are dealing with a psychotic disorder.

The advocacy by families has extended to lobbying for the greater availability of early intervention services for psychosis. Families have been vocal in lobbying members of the provincial and federal legislatures for better services for those with psychotic disorders. They have appeared before government panels reviewing health care priorities and met with key decision makers in health care policy. They have also been very active in ensuring support from the health care organization which sponsors PEPP around such critical issues as the availability of appropriate space in a non-stigmatizing location, protection of staff resources, etc.

The above examples of advocacy from families occurred within the context of a well developed early intervention clinical program. Other examples can be found in the context of the family experience of dealing with early psychosis without such clinical programs. One of us (Sharon Scott Mulder) has the experience of trying to find appropriate services for a child who developed a psychotic disorder in another part of Canada before the introduction of a specialized early detection and treatment program. That experience included difficulty accessing appropriate services for diagnosis and challenges in encouraging the ill family member to engage in treatment. Even when treatment services were accessed, there were inconsistencies in treatment approaches; poor community supports and dysfunctional communication between clinicians and family. These challenges were encountered within a context of stigmatization and relative social isolation and led to a search for other families in the region with similar experiences. With encouragement from the PEPP family support group, this resulted in the development in March 2000 of the Manitoba First-Episode Psychosis Family Support Group. The group then engaged in a systematic process of advocacy for the establishment of early intervention services in the Province of Manitoba including meeting with sympathetic members of the legislature and aides to the Premier and the Minister of Health, organizing a publicized walk to 'flag psychosis early', and being featured in the media about the need for early intervention services. As a result, by July 2002, the government allocated half a million dollars for the development of a new community based early intervention program for psychotic disorders – the Early Psychosis Prevention and Intervention Service (EPPIS), which developed as a partnership of families and professionals with parents serving on its steering committee.

What can families receive from one another?

The experience of the families in Manitoba illustrates the potential power of families in bringing about change in the health care system. It reflects an important way in which families working together can help one another. With modern communications, it is also possible for families to provide important mutual support across long distances. Canada is a large country with a relatively small population, so people are often without the specialized treatment and support programs that can be developed in more densely populated regions. The challenges of a family coping with a psychotic illness can be particularly overwhelming in such circumstances. An exciting development in recent years has been the emergence of a National Network of support for first-episode psychosis families across Canada. This was facilitated by the Canadian Mental Health Association, National Office with funding from Health Canada and built upon an informal network that had emerged as the result of activities by such groups as the PEPP Parent Support Group and the Manitoba First-Episode Psychosis Family Support Group.

Still in early stages of development, this National Network assists with the production of the newsletter *Family to Family* with circulation throughout Canada and internationally. Its members who are engaged in public awareness campaigns have developed educational and support materials for families that can be readily accessed, and continue to advocate for a national strategy for early intervention for psychosis. Just as important as these formal activities is the extent to which the group is able to provide informal support to families of those dealing with recent onset psychotic disorders. Because of the network, family members of individuals with onset of a psychotic disorder are able to access information, support and practical assistance, no matter where they live. In this way families looking for help in Newfoundland on the extreme east of the country have been provided support and information on findings services by members of the National Network living in Manitoba (thousands of kilometres away). In a similar fashion, a member of the family National Network in Ontario has been a great source of support and help to a family dealing with a first episode of psychosis far away in British Columbia. Members of the network have been able to locate the son of a family living in Winnipeg and provide assistance to the young man, who was homeless and suffering from untreated psychosis in Toronto. There are many such stories of the valuable contribution of this network in helping ill persons and their families through the use of electronic communication and personal contact.

What facilitates family advocacy and support?

There is probably no one single factor that guarantees families will undertake the types of initiatives described above. Among the factors that likely contribute are professionals accepting that, in general, the concerns of family members are understandable and legitimate and working with families in the delivery of clinical services is beneficial, if challenging. It is also important that all parties recognize that addressing the needs of those with psychotic illness and their families depends not just on clinical interventions, but social change. Important foci for advocacy result from identifying targets such as creation of new services and better support of existing services or changing social attitudes that interfere with recognition of illness and social reintegration. Families come to recognize they may have more power than clinicians in addressing political and social issues. Exercising this power can have immense positive effects for all concerned.

Effective and continuous advocacy requires optimism and hope. So it is important that families see reason for optimism that they can make a difference in reducing the debilitating aspects of mental illness and improving quality of life for individuals with such illnesses. The optimism generated by the rationale that early intervention programs may lead to better outcomes has likely been a crucial factor in motivating the family initiatives we have described. Anger and frustration can be important motivators of action, but the enthusiasm and impact are likely to be greater when evidence can be used as the basis for advocating for specific improvements. We have found that optimism about being able to improve outcomes for other individuals and families has been an important impetus for action even for families who have experienced a very poor course of illness.

Opportunities must also be available for families to meet one another and develop networks. If family members are meeting only with professionals, mutual support is much less likely to occur. Perhaps most important of all, someone from within the community of families has to take a leadership role and facilitate the development of a sense of cohesion and purpose for those who participate.

Conclusion

The perception of the family in relation to psychotic disorders has evolved from one in which families were seen as causes of psychosis to one in which families are seen as often being important mediators of the recovery of those with such illnesses. This has led to an increasing emphasis on providing education and support to family members. It may be that we are witnessing the evolution of yet another view of the family as an important source of mutual education and support and advocacy for the needs of those with early psychosis.

References

Addington, J., Codham, E., Jones, B., Ko, T., and Addington, D. (2003). The first episode of psychosis: The experience of relatives. *Acta Psychiatrica Scandinavica, 108*, 285–289.

Addington, D., Bouchard, R-H., Goldberg., J., Honer, W., Malla, A., Norman, R., et al. (2005). Clinical practice guidelines: Treatment of schizophrenia. *Canadian Journal of Psychiatry, 50* (Suppl. 1), s1–s56.

Anderson, C. M., Reiss, D. J., and Hogarty, G. E. (1986). *Schizophrenia and the family*. New York: Guilford.

Baronet, A. M. (1999). Factors associated with caregiver burden in mental illness: A critical review of the research literature. *Clinical Psychology Review, 19*, 819–841.

Beard, J. J. and Gillespie, G. (2002). *Nothing to hide: Mental illness in the family*. New York: New Press.

de Haan, L., Peters, B., Dingemans, P., Wouters, L., and Linszen, D. (2002). Attitudes of patients toward the first psychotic episode and the start of treatment. *Schizophrenia Bulletin, 28*, 431–442.

Dixon, L., Lyles, A., Scott, J., Lehman, A. F., Postrado, L. T., Goldman, H. H., et al. (1999). Services to families of adults with schizophrenia: From treatment recommendations to dissemination. *Psychiatric Services, 50*, 233–238.

Dixon, L., Adams, C., and Lucksted, A. (2000). Update on family intervention for schizophrenia. *Schizophrenia Bulletin, 26*, 5–20.

Falloon, I. R. and Pedeson, J. (1985). Family management in the prevention of morbidity of schizophrenia: The adjustment of the family unit. *British Journal of Psychiatry, 147*, 156–163.

Falloon, I. R. H., Boyd, J. L., and McGill, C. W. (1984). *Family care of Schizophrenia: A problem solving approach to the treatment of schizophrenia*. New York: Guilford.

Gibbons, J. S., Horn, S. H., Powell, J. M., and Gibbons, J. L. (1984). Schizophrenic patients and their families: A survey in a psychiatric service based on a DGH unit. *British Journal of Psychiatry, 144*, 70–77.

Hazel, N. A., McDonnell, M. G., Short, R. A., Berry, C. M., Voss, W. D., Rodgers, M. L., et al. (2004). Impact of multiple family groups for outpatients with schizophrenia on caregivers' distress and resources. *Psychiatric Services, 55*, 35–41.

Helgason, L. (1990). Twenty years' follow-up of first psychiatric presentation for schizophrenia: What could have been prevented? *Acta Psychiatrica Scandinavica, 81*, 231–235.

Huxley, N. A., Rendell, M., and Sederer, L. (2000). Psychosocial treatments in schizophrenia: A review of the past 20 years. *Journal of Mental and Nervous Disease, 188*, 187–201.

Jones, S. L. and Jones, P. K. (1994). Caregiver burden: Who the caregivers are, how they give care, and what bothers them. *Journal of Health and Social Policy, 6*, 71–89.

Kuipers, L., Leff, J., and Lam, D. (1992). *Family work for schizophrenia: A practical guide*. London: Gaskell.

Lefley, H. P. (1992). Expressed emotion: Conceptual, clinical and social policy issues. *Hospital and Community Psychiatry, 43*, 591–598.

Lehman, A. F. (2000). Commentary: What happened to psychosocial treatment in the way to the clinic? *Schizophrenia Bulletin, 26*, 137–139.

Lehman, A. F., Steinwachs, D. M., and the co-investigators of the PORT project (1998). Translating research into practice: The Schizophrenia Patient Outcomes Research Team (PORT) treatment recommendations. *Schizophrenia Bulletin, 24*, 1–10.

Lehman, A. F., Lieberman, J. A., Dixon, L., McGlashan, T. H., Miller, A. L., Perkins, D. O., et al. (2004a). Practice guidelines for the treatment of patients with schizophrenia. *American Journal of Psychiatry, 161*, 1–56.

Lehman, A. F., Kreyenbuhl, J., Buchanan, R. W., Dickerson, F. B., Dixon, L. B., Goldberg, R., et al. (2004b). The schizophrenia patient outcomes research team (PORT): Updated treatment recommendations 2003. *Schizophrenia Bulletin, 30*, 193–217.

McFarlane, W. R. (2002). *Multifamily groups in the treatment of severe psychiatric disorders*. New York: Guilford.

McFarlane, W. R. (2004). Family intervention in early psychosis. In T. Ehmann, G. W. MacEwan, and W. G. Honer (Eds.), *Best care in early psychosis intervention: Global perspectives* (pp. 213–220). Abingdon, UK: Taylor and Francis.

McFarlane, W. R., Lukens, E., Link, B., Dushet, R., Deakins, A., Newmarket, M., et al. (1995). Multiple-family groups and psychoeducation in the treatment of schizophrenia. *Archives of General Psychiatry, 52*, 679–687.

McFarlane, W. R., McNary, S., Dixon, L., Hornby, H., and Cimett, E. (2001). Predictors of dissemination of family psychoeducation in community mental health centres in Maine and Illinois. *Psychiatric Services, 52*, 935–942.

Malla, A. K., Norman, R. M. G., Scholten, D., and Townsend, T. (2003). A Canadian programme for early intervention for psychotic disorders. *Australian and New Zealand Journal of Psychiatry, 37*, 407–413.

Mueser, K. T. and Bond, G. R. (2000). Psychosocial treatment approaches for schizophrenia. *Current Opinion in Psychiatry*, *13*, 27–35.

Mueser, K. T. and Gingerich, S. (1994). *Coping with schizophrenia: A guide for families* Oakland, CA: New Harbinger.

Norman, R. M. G., Malla, A. K., and McLean, T. (2000). *Working together things can get better (Video and Booklet)*. London, Ontario: Janssen-Ortho.

Nugter, A., Dingemans, P., van der Does, J. W., Linszen, D., and Gersons, B. (1997). Family treatment, expressed emotion and relapse in recent onset schizophrenia. *Psychiatry Research*, *72*, 23–31.

Pilling, S., Bebbington, P., Kuipers, E., Garety, P., Geddes, J., Orbach, G., et al. (2002). Psychological treatments in schizophrenia. I: Meta-analysis of family intervention and cognitive behaviour therapy. *Psychological Medicine*, *32*, 763–782.

Pitschel-Walz, G., Leucht, S., Bauml, J., Kissling, W., and Engel, R. R. (2001). The effect of family interventions on relapse and rehospitalization in schizophrenia: A meta-analysis. *Schizophrenia Bulletin*, *27*, 73–92.

Ram, R., Bromet, E. J., Eaton, W. W., Pato, C., and Schwartz, J. E. (1992). The natural course of schizophrenia: A review of first episode studies. *Schizophrenia Bulletin*, *18*, 185–207.

Read, J., van Os, J., Morrison, A. P., and Ross, C. A. (2005). Childhood trauma, psychosis and schizophrenia: A literature review with theoretical and clinical implications. *Acta Psychiatrica Scandinavica*, *112*, 330–350.

Resnick, S. G., Rosenheck, R. A., Dixon, L., and Lehman, A.F. (2005). Correlates of family contact with the mental health system: Allocation of a scarce resource. *Mental Health Services Research*, *7*, 113–121.

Scheme, A. H., van Wijngaarden, B., and Koeter, M. W. J. (1998). Family caregiving in schizophrenia: Domains and distress. *Schizophrenia Bulletin*, *24*, 609–618.

Chapter 14

Therapeutic group work for young people with first-episode psychosis

Gina Woodhead

Introduction

Groups provide an opportunity to practise in vivo the social and coping techniques clients may have learnt in their individual therapy sessions. Group programme workers have observed that group participation can improve daily routines, independence, peer support and the quality of a client's life. Group work can also be an efficient method for providing information to multiple clients.

This chapter highlights the value of therapeutic group interventions within mental health settings, with particular reference to clients with first-episode psychosis. A search of the literature indicated a paucity of published research with this specific group of patients, so I have also selectively examined literature on psychosocial interventions with a variety of psychiatric populations in order to explore potential common benefits of group interventions.

Young people recovering from psychosis commonly experience a loss of social roles, status and confidence in social situations – therefore group work may be of particular relevance for this group of clients (Albiston et al., 1998). Group interventions can contribute significantly in assisting young people to overcome some of these obstacles. Participating in groups can provide a sense of belonging and encourage individuals to take risks and explore options within the peer group (EPPIC Statewide Services, 2000).

Macdonald et al. (2005) reported that young people recovering from a first episode of psychosis want the same social experiences as healthy young people. They want friendships and support and they want to participate in age-appropriate activities and roles. The authors noted that participating in a recovery group programme offered young people these opportunities. Edwards and McGorry (2002) argued that interventions for first-episode psychosis should focus upon symptom reduction and upon psychosocial domains. They recommended implementing a range of psychosocial strategies during recovery, including group-based interventions.

Evidence-based research on group work for severe mental disorders is limited (McDermott, 2003), and extremely scant in relation to the first-episode psychosis population (Penn et al., 2005). Penn and colleagues (2005) comprehensively reviewed twenty years of research on psychosocial treatment for first-episode psychosis clients. They identified research that covered a variety of psychosocial treatments including only three evaluations of group work. Of these, two entailed quasi-experimental designs, and no randomized controlled trials were found. These authors concluded that the available research demonstrated some benefits of group therapy, however, given the nature of these studies, they argued that findings needed to be interpreted with caution, and called for more randomized control trials.

McDermott's (2003) article reviewed ten years of outcome studies of group interventions for persons living with serious mental illness. She concluded that there was overall a poor research base in this area, suggesting that this may be in part due to the complexity of group interventions, which may have multiple efficacious components. McDermott (2003, p. 361) stated that 'there is a pressing need to enhance our research efforts, designing studies that combine quantitative, qualitative, and participatory methods at greater levels of rigour and sophistication'.

In the absence of research findings, my colleagues and I have also discussed the value of clinical observations when evaluating groups, especially when seeking feedback from participants who may have difficulties expressing themselves verbally or in writing. Although there is scarcity of research tackling the effectiveness of group interventions for the first-episode population, some studies have provided some indicative findings in support of positive outcomes for first-episode clients participating in therapeutic group programmes (Penn et al., 2005). Miller and Mason (1998), for example, reported that participation in therapeutic groups could reduce isolation, build confidence, encourage peer support and provide opportunities for psychoeducation.

Albiston et al. (1998) evaluated the impact of a group-based, psychosocial programme for young people recovering from first-episode psychosis at the Early Psychosis Prevention and Intervention Centre (EPPIC) in Melbourne, Australia. They compared 34 young people who attended the group programme with 61 EPPIC clients who had not attended. Their evaluation focused on premorbid adjustment, quality of life and negative symptoms. They found that the young people attending this group programme had a lower level of premorbid adjustment and showed a trend towards a higher level of negative symptoms at admission, compared with the control group of closely matched EPPIC clients. At six months, they found no significant differences between the groups. They argued that involvement in the group programme may have had a positive impact on this vulnerable subgroup of EPPIC clients by preventing deterioration and the development of disabilities during the so-called 'critical period' following first-episode psychosis (Birchwood and Macmillan, 1993).

Peer groups and social function

In a qualitative research project, Mackrell and Lavender (2004) examined the nature and trajectory of peer relationships for 12 young people recovering from early psychosis. They reported that participants identified becoming increasingly isolated from their peers during adolescence and before the acute psychotic episode, which further increased after the onset of psychosis. Interviews revealed that poor peer relationships in childhood often progressed into relationship issues and isolation in adolescence. In addition, the experience of difficult relationships may have been a factor influencing the development of psychosis. The authors concluded that an early intervention programme aimed at increasing resilience might enable young people to manage negative peer relationships. Finally, they proposed that acute services could develop peer group friendly environments aimed at building and maintaining peer relationships, this could include carefully managed therapeutic group programmes.

This research was congruent with the retrospective personal reflection presented by Chovil (2005). He recounted an insidious onset of first-episode psychosis during his early days at high school. Chovil described a gradual change and deterioration in his general functioning that commenced during the prodromal period. He recalled that he gradually lost his relationships over a nine-year period without anyone realizing he was ill. According to Chovil, this period can include increasing social isolation and lack of confidence, anxiety, academic struggle and failure, resulting in dropping out from school and a decreasing ability to remain employed. In his case this was also combined with a pattern of drinking alcohol and smoking marijuana to excess. Chovil (2005) stated that it is not enough to treat only the presenting symptoms of psychosis. He proposed that at a minimum, rehabilitation resources should be developed to maximize recovery and prevent relapse for these clients. In the light of Chovil's account of a deterioration in social function during prodrome, therapeutic group-work utilizing peer support to enhance self-confidence and social skills may be a useful early intervention option to address these issues.

Macdonald et al. (2005) also argued that group programmes provide young people with environments that support them to cope with the effects of psychosis. Their phenomenological study, which focused on social relationships, explored through interview the subjective experiences of six young people recovering from a first psychotic episode who were attending a group programme within their clinical service. The authors reported that some of these young people spent less time with old friends, with whom they often felt misunderstood. Also, in the aftermath of their psychosis, they believed that their friends perceived them differently. They found that the young people expressed a strong preference to spend time with people who had been through similar experiences. Furthermore, the authors reported that group members described a mutual understanding and trust and a perception of being accepted and safe in the group. In addition, participants described a willingness to discuss problems and personal issues with their peers in the group programme. Participating in problem solving, and giving and receiving advice and feedback were common experiences. The authors noted that group members highlighted the importance of camaraderie and optimism around recovery and they spoke of the value of support from others with a shared experience of psychosis.

On the basis of these findings, the authors concluded that opportunity for conversation, involvement in age-appropriate activities, problem solving, and opportunities for emotional ventilation are in keeping with the social experiences and goals of clients recovering from early psychosis. They suggested that a group programme with a supportive milieu and social contacts with understanding people can offer these opportunities.

Woodside et al. (2006) interviewed eight participants recovering from psychosis about their experiences of finding and keeping employment. Their findings suggested that achieving vocational success when recovering from severe mental health issues can be closely linked with feeling connected to peers in the workplace and they emphasized the importance of a supportive peer group. Therapeutic group programmes that address social issues in the workplace may assist clients with preparation for work.

These studies provide rich and meaningful data regarding the subjective experiences and the value of empathic peer relationships for young people with first-episode psychosis. However, more research is needed. Given the qualitative nature of some of these studies and the small sample sizes, the generalizability of findings to the first-episode population may be limited. More research utilizing a variety of designs is warranted in order to build a stronger evidence base.

Rationale for therapeutic group work for young people with first-episode psychosis

Francey (1999) argued that young people recovering from a first episode of psychosis represent a population with specific needs. She suggested that therapeutic group programmes, with an emphasis on utilizing peer support, encouraging social confidence and reinforcing desirable social skills are ideal treatments to assist with psychosocial recovery. However, as already highlighted, there are few empirical studies demonstrating the therapeutic value of group participation for young people recovering from first-episode psychosis.

EPPIC's manual for *Group work in early psychosis* (2000) presented a rationale for group work for the early psychosis population. It outlined how psychosis can delay the tasks of psychosocial development, which include identity formation, goal setting, individuation from parents, and the formation of close friendships with peers. It reported that participation in a therapeutic group can provide an environment where young people can share experiences and improve personal strengths and coping skills. It also argued that participation can foster an optimistic outlook and the mastery of appropriate developmental tasks.

Francey (1999) described how, for young people recovering from a first episode of psychosis, group interventions offer opportunities to address individual goals and needs, as well as mastering developmental tasks. She stated that groups can provide psychoeducation through peer sharing. This can include information about symptoms, medication and recovery, as well as factors that can be detrimental to recovery such as drug misuse. Francey argued that group work helps young people to develop and foster their independence in many life skills, for example, education, vocation and independent living skills. These life skills can be addressed through discussions and pre-vocational training (Albiston et al., 1998; Francey, 1999).

A quality assurance project evaluating an EPPIC drop-in group supported the value of group experience for some of the young people attending this service (Woodhead, 2004). Thirty-five group members completed a questionnaire to give feedback about the group and to explain their reasons for attending. Just over 70 per cent said that while opportunities to participate in fun and interesting activities provided the initial impetus for their attendance, the development of relationships with other young people going through similar issues maintained their involvement. Some individuals commented on the value of being accepted by others, and emphasized the instillation of hope and the increased sense of optimism through seeing others further along in their recovery.

McCay et al. (1996) reported similar results when they conducted a pilot study to evaluate a discussion-based group intervention for clients recovering from a first-psychotic episode. They stated that participants believed that receiving support and understanding from others with similar experiences was a beneficial and valuable opportunity. The authors reported that participants expressed a wish for ongoing contact with each other and a desire for relationships away from the treatment setting. Interestingly, at the conclusion of the formal group intervention, the members independently arranged a continuing, informal self-help group.

Miller and Mason (1998) stated that group work for the first-episode population is an effective way of building coping skills and addressing stress associated with receiving a diagnosis. Their group programme model integrates psychoeducation with clients' concerns.

The scant empirical findings, together with clinical experience, indicates that group programmes should be supportive in style, with a focus upon the building of strengths, coping skills and psychoeducation, utilizing techniques such as cognitive behaviour therapy (CBT) and supportive psychotherapy (Francey, 1999; McCay et al., 1996; Miller and Mason, 1998). Furthermore, psychological techniques and programmes have been developed specifically to assist with recovery from first-episode psychosis (see Francey, 1999).

Referral considerations

Group interventions may not be suitable for everyone. Participation in peer groups is complex and can be stressful (Mackrell and Lavender, 2004). Some young people may be overwhelmed by the demands of a group situation due to active positive symptoms, or they be unwilling to participate based on previous negative peer-related experiences. Sometimes the objectives of the group do not correspond with the goals of an individual. For these reasons and more, clinicians need to make careful decisions before referring their clients to groups. Group facilitators need to be clear about the group's objectives and the expectations of participants to increase the likelihood of positive outcomes. Facilitators must be aware of each individual's history and personal goals, and make careful decisions about the group's configuration. For example, a group that includes too many participants exhibiting behaviours that require close management can be difficult for a group facilitator to control. This may also impact negatively on the groups' development and functioning overall.

Screening and preparation for potential members are also essential. Toseland and Siporin (1986) reviewed clinical and empirical literature on when to recommend group treatment and indicated that group members should have personality attributes and capacities to enable them to participate. For example, group work may not be suitable for some clients due to their individual needs, symptoms, personality style, or certain antisocial behaviours.

Group leadership and facilitation

Group work aims to facilitate, utilize and monitor interactions between individuals in order to achieve the desired therapeutic objectives for individuals within a group environment. Groups should have clear goals, boundaries and rules, which should be clearly communicated to participants. The role of the group facilitator is a challenging one. They should be open, fair, demonstrate keen interest and respect for the participants and enjoy the group environment. Harper (2003, p. 27) stated that 'successful group facilitation is part science and part art'. The tasks include modelling, encouraging desirable behaviours, creating appropriate boundaries and setting limits. Although it can be challenging for facilitators to control all the variables of group interaction, it is important to encourage group members to join in the pursuit of healthy and positive behaviours and to actively discourage illicit drug taking or antisocial behaviours. Ongoing training and supervision for group facilitators is highly recommended.

Goals of young people

Albiston et al. (1998) audited 80 self-referral forms completed by young people attending the group programme. These forms were used by EPPIC staff to initiate the collaborative goal-setting process of: identifying an individual's personal goals, establishing performance indicators for the evaluation of outcome, and selecting the groups best suited to the individual's personal goals. These self-referral forms requested information regarding the current and desired outcomes across a range of domains, including social relationships, employment, accommodation, health, and self-image.

The data revealed that just over 80 per cent of the respondents identified a goal related to social relationships and the development of self-confidence. Half of the young people nominated a vocational or educational goal and the same number wished to increase their independence and develop new skills. More than one-third were concerned with their physical health, level of motivation, and the lack of structure and routine in their daily lives.

A quality assurance audit conducted within the EPPIC Group Programme in 2004 found similar results. The auditor accessed information collected over two years during initial introductory interviews regarding young people's personal goals and the groups they were interested in attending. She then compared this information with group referral forms completed by case managers. In total, the auditor reviewed information on 230 clients. Many of the young people indicated a wide variety of goals that they wished to address, and they selected multiple groups. At times, the goals underpinning a client's selection of groups were unclear.

In addition, the auditor found that 83 per cent of young people requested a group to assist them with their socializing. Goals included making new friends, being with people who would accept and understand them, feeling more confident around people, and learning and practising social skills; 76 per cent requested vocational or educational groups, indicating a desire to return to school or find a career. A high proportion of this subgroup requested assistance with finding employment and expressed a wish for structure and routine in their day; 66 per cent requested groups to improve their knowledge and understanding of mental health issues and to develop skills and strategies to deal with them, and 58 per cent wanted a creative group. They wished to learn new skills, develop new interests, and find ways to express their feelings. Music, art and creative writing were the most common activities requested.

The audit also indicated that case managers were aware of the desired goals of their clients. Furthermore, the client goals identified by case managers were strikingly similar to those listed by the clients on their self-referral forms. Case managers most often referred their clients to groups with a major socializing component. Groups with a major vocational and educational component, including time use, were the second most frequently requested, followed by psychoeducational and personal development groups. Groups assisting with creative opportunities were requested to a lesser extent.

EPPIC Group Programme staff also developed a database as part of quality assurance that aimed to describe the group programme population (Turner et al., 2004). Written referrals and initial assessments of 95 clients (with a mean age of 21.5 years) were recorded; 70 per cent were male with predominately schizophrenia-spectrum disorders. Nearly all of the clients had never married and almost 75 per cent were unemployed. Most of the young people lived at home with their families. The authors found that clients attending the EPPIC Recovery Group Programme were predominately poorly educated, unemployed males, with poor social and occupational functioning. In addition, a significant proportion of them were substance users. Hence, a group programme with a strong focus on improving social, occupational and vocational functioning was strongly indicated.

Group programmes

Miller and Mason (1998, 2001) recommended that group interventions support the overall management of psychosis, including the encouragement of medication compliance. Albiston et al. (1998) and Francey (1999) presented a description of the development and the essential elements and principles of the EPPIC Group Programme. Francey (1999) described how this group programme was included as a core ingredient of a multi-component service aiming to implement early intervention and preventative strategies for young people experiencing and recovering from a first episode of psychosis. The group programme provided a range of groups (at least 12 per week) designed to meet young people's goals and interests. The group programme aims to empower the recovering young person whilst focusing on their strengths and collaboratively defining goals. Because participants are adolescents and young adults, opportunities to complete developmental tasks are given priority. Treatment plans are developed collaboratively with individuals to ensure that the selection of groups is meaningful and that participants feel empowered by the experience.

Albiston et al. (1998) has previously described the format of the EPPIC Group Programme. The groups were organized into streams that match goals identified by clients. Thus, each stream includes a variety of different groups with a different focus, as outlined below.

The Social/Recreational Stream is offered in keeping with the high proportion of goals related to social or communication issues. This stream includes the drop-in group, outings, outdoor adventure, and sport groups. The groups in this stream encourage and provide opportunities for peer support, aim to build confidence and social skills, develop interests, and assist with accessing community facilities. Activities in these groups are designed to be fun and age appropriate. Social skills are modelled, encouraged, and positively reinforced.

Emphasis is also placed upon increasing the young person's knowledge of psychosis through informal psychoeducation discussions. Balancing structured activities with unstructured time as well as carefully considering group configuration are key considerations. Group programme workers actively attempt to develop group cohesion.

Due to client interest and the age appropriateness of vocational and educational pathways, the EPPIC Group Programme offers the Vocational/ Educational Stream. This stream is facilitated collaboratively between group programme workers and teachers trained in special education from the Travancore School, which is a local government special school catering for the educational needs of young people in the mental health service. Activities in these groups can be carefully graded and thus can be specifically tailored to meet individual participant's needs. The groups are designed to help young people return to school, further their education, choose a career pathway, develop work skills, and find a job. Horticulture and catering groups are currently on offer. These groups are linked with local educational facilities and allow participants opportunities to enrol in a course and complete modules of accredited educational certificates.

A recent addition to the programme was the Victorian Certificate of Applied Learning (VCAL). This is a senior secondary education certificate that has a focus upon applied learning. It is widely utilized throughout the secondary education sector in the state of Victoria, Australia and offers a pathway to further vocational training or employment. Groups include Work It Out, designed to explore school work and training options. Participants in this group are provided with opportunities to develop resumés and practise job interview and work skills. Linking with employment support services and providing opportunities for work experience may also be organized as a stepping stone towards employment. Participating in a group environment encourages peer support and shared learning, and encourages the practice of social skills required within the classroom and workforce.

In keeping with the overall objectives of the EPPIC service, the group programme offers the Psychoeducation/Personal Development Stream. This stream complements the work offered by outpatient case managers. Groups include Get in the Know (psychoeducation for psychosis), Chill (a combination of stress-management, relaxation techniques and CBT for managing anxiety symptoms), Straight Up (communication skills and assertiveness training), Pound Dog (relaxation, CBT and graduated exposure utilizing dog walking to assist with reducing social anxiety and phobia) and Get on Up (CBT for managing depression).

Emphasis in the groups is placed upon peer learning and sharing. Internal audits conducted within the EPPIC Recovery Group Programme indicated that attendance is lower at these discussion-based groups compared with activity-based groups. Non-attendance may be due to stigma, privacy concerns, and aversive experiences in previous peer or group relationships. There may also be a perception that attending a group is similar to going to school, or a fear that participating will require divulging innermost thoughts. When attendance to these discussion-based groups is low, group workers maximize opportunities for psychoeducation by including informal discussions within the activity-based groups.

Finally, young people often request opportunities for creative pursuits. The Creative/Expressive Stream provides group members with opportunities to learn new skills. This stream provides outlets for expression other than verbalizing. Group members are also given opportunities to redevelop interests in activities that they may have pursued before becoming unwell. Some group members join creative and expressive groups to participate in a shared activity, to relax and have fun. Groups offered include music, art and creative writing.

Group programme engagement

One of the biggest challenges for group programme workers is engaging clients. Woodhead (2004) presented a literature review that highlighted some of the issues of engaging youth with mental health services. Factors identified that decrease engagement include being in the adolescent or young adult age group, lack of insight, concern with privacy, stigma, and past negative experiences of peer groups. Factors seen to assist with engagement include a good relationship between the client and the group therapist, continuity of care, a short period between inpatient stay and first outpatient appointment (including group attendance), availability of fun and activity-based groups, the provision of food, reminder telephone calls, and a youth-friendly environment. To ensure an environment is youth friendly, it is important to consider the physical setting and have an awareness and respect for young people's issues and culture (Woodhead, 2002).

Group case studies

A description of three groups recently offered at the EPPIC Group Programme is provided here. Each group has multiple objectives and can be adapted to meet the individual goals of clients. Club 21, a drop-in style social and recreational group, is utilized to assist with engaging new clients. This group is strategically scheduled midday on Mondays to catch up with participants after the weekend. The group includes lunch as an incentive for attendance.

The group aims to enhance self-confidence through the provision of support, a safe environment, and participation in achievable and fun activities. Staff encourage and positively reinforce peer support, and model appropriate social skills. Emphasis is also placed on increasing the young person's knowledge of psychosis through informal psychoeducation discussions. In this informal environment, staff can assess progress of recovery, individual skills and any signs of relapse.

The content of Club 21 may vary each week; however, the basic group structure that occurs over a two-hour period is consistent. The format of the session includes an initial warm-up period where new participants are introduced, welcomed, and orientated to the facilities and the group. Following this, workers focus on inviting all clients into small group activities of the group members' choice. Halfway through the group session, with the assistance of both workers and clients, lunch is prepared and served, and everyone is encouraged to eat together. Group programme workers use this time to enhance group cohesion by asking open-ended questions and initiating discussion to address common themes and interests. Clients are encouraged to interact, share their personal stories and support one another. Opportunities for psychoeducation regularly arise at this time. To encourage wider group cohesion, workers often suggest a large group activity after lunch. Emphasis is placed on the inclusion of new clients and strengthening connections between group members. The session closes with discussion about the group and a review of any issues that may have arisen.

As part of routine quality assurance and to gain some understanding of the popularity and impact of this group, over a twelve-month period staff asked clients to reflect on their experience of attending through responding to a written questionnaire. Thirty-five forms were completed. The format consisted of both open and closed questions and allowed group members to remain anonymous. In summary (see Table 14.1), 76 per cent of participants stated that they attended the group to be with others who were in similar situations to themselves. Some described a loss of friendships since they became unwell, while others wanted a more understanding peer group. About 70 per cent said that the group gave them something to look forward to each week, including a reason to get out of bed in the morning. Up to 60 per cent attributed some symptom relief and other personal benefits to attending,

Table 14.1 Reasons for attending Club 21 from participants' questionnaire (n = 35)

Reasons for attending	%
Chance to catch up with friends	79.5
People who go are in similar situation to me	76.5
Chance to make new friends	75.0
Something to look forward to each week	70.6
Fills in time	66.7
Improves self-confidence	60.0
Feel more confident around other people	55.8
Helps me relax	52.9
Case manager told me to attend	34.4

including increased feelings of relaxation and self-confidence in social situations. Many members reported that they made new friends within the group and continued to see them outside of group time; 71 per cent reported feeling more confident in social situations outside of the group environment (see Table 14.2).

This evaluation seems to support previous data which indicated that participating in interesting, age-appropriate activities and socializing with other young people going through similar experiences is valued. Club 21 provides an opportunity to practise the social and coping skills discussed in individual therapy. It allows group members to share experiences, learn more about psychosis, and to support one another in a therapeutic group environment. The encouragement of participants to make decisions about activity choices within Club 21 also aims to enhance a sense of empowerment.

Catering is a vocational and educational group that aims to assist young people to commence or return to education, work placement, training or employment. The group runs up to five hours each session for two days per week and requires participants to undertake a variety of professional catering responsibilities for the ORYGEN Youth Health Service cafeteria. Tasks include meal preparation, counter service and cleaning duties. As this group occurs in a commercial kitchen safety precautions are essential, so group facilitators carefully assess mental state and the safety risks of prospective participants. Clients presenting with safety risks will not be included into the group until individual management plans including strategies for managing symptoms and behaviours are developed. As always, careful consideration is given to group composition.

Participants begin their tasks working one-to-one or in small groups. At various intervals throughout the group, members take breaks to review their progress, discuss issues with group leaders, and eat lunch together. These breaks provide opportunities for staff to initiate discussion and enhance group cohesion.

Activities in the group are carefully graded to meet the individual goals and abilities of participants. Aims vary depending on individual level of function and the specific stage of recovery. Objectives include increasing attention, concentration, organization and motivation, learning basic domestic living

Table 14.2 Benefits of Club 21 – results from participants' questionnaire (n = 35)

Benefits	%
More confident in social situations within Club 21	94.4
More confident in social situations outside Club 21	71.0
Made new friends outside group meetings	94.4
Saw Club 21 members outside group meetings	55.6

skills, improving social interaction and relationship skills within a work environment, developing strategies to deal with the demands of a workplace, and developing specific knowledge and skills for working in a commercial kitchen.

Participants do not have to be specifically interested in working in the hospitality industry to join this group, but it is an option to all those interested in the task and is encouraged for all wishing to return to school or to improve their general pre-vocational skills. Group leaders point out to prospective members the similarities and challenges inherent in most working environments and how participating in Catering will assist with overcoming these.

As an added incentive to participate, group members can enrol in VCAL subjects and work toward specific educational accredited certificates. Participants can also move on to voluntary catering settings or more advanced training. Opportunities for paid employment have also arisen on occasions. General feedback from participants is positive, with most indicating an improvement in their individual goals.

Outdoor adventure is another social and recreational group which aims to promote recovery through engaging participants in carefully graded outdoors activities in a supportive environment. Specific objectives for participants focus on increasing self-esteem and improving social and communication skills. Because some of the activities selected are very challenging, participants are carefully screened to ensure that they will be safe and can manage the tasks successfully. Group rules, expectations and individual goals are developed in the first session. Participants are encouraged to step outside their comfort zones, support one another, try new activities and have fun.

This group runs for one day per week over eight consecutive weeks and is facilitated by two group programme workers along with specialized outdoor adventure trainers. Activities are carefully graded so that participants can experience success and can build on achievements from previous sessions. Each week the challenge progresses in three domains: personal, social and physical. Hiking is a possible initial session. This activity rates relatively low as a challenge and group facilitators can easily grade it to achieve a successful outcome. For example, hiking provides low levels of personal anxiety, requires minimal social interaction and is relatively easy to achieve physically. By week 4 group members participate in caving or abseiling. At week 6 they are encouraged to participate in a high ropes activity. This session can be both anxiety provoking and difficult physically. It requires group cohesion, trust and social skills as participants belay and encourage one another. The group culminates in a three-day white water rafting camp, which can be highly challenging. The setting geographically is remote and activities can be difficult. Emphasis is placed on shared learning and team support. Throughout the weeks some group time is dedicated to the sharing and processing of the experience. This includes discussing what was learnt and achieved and how this relates or impacts on recovery. The Rosenberg Self-esteem Scale (Rosenberg, 1965) and qualitative questionnaires are utilized at the commencement and completion of programmes to evaluate the overall impact (Luxmoore et al., 2004).

Future directions

Collaboration between service providers in the development of groups is an important future direction for all mental health services to consider. Collaborative groups are an effective way of maximizing staff resources, ensuring a larger client membership, and provide new and challenging opportunities for young people. At EPPIC a social and recreational group called The Tribe is offered to both young people attending the group programme and those attending a local psychiatric disability rehabilitation service. Young people can choose to attend this group even after discharge and up until the age of 30. Attendance offers a variety of social and recreational opportunities including supported extended recovery. Both services share costs and other responsibilities associated with the group.

Some early psychosis services in regional Victoria are also developing collaborative group programme. These groups share staff, costs and transport. Clinicians organizing these groups report this to be an effective way of working. It is practical and provides extended opportunities for peer supervision and support.

Collaboration has also developed between the EPPIC Group Programme and local artists. Funding through local government arts grants has enabled young people to work with a variety of artists, including a filmmaker and a wood sculptor. Collaboration with a local circus troupe is currently being planned. As with all groups, careful planning is required around tasks, individuals' goals, suitability for attendance and group configuration. Group programme clinicians work closely with each artist to manage the therapeutic environment.

The EPPIC Group Programme receives research and philanthropic grants to evaluate specific groups such as Blazing Saddles (a horse-riding group), and outdoor adventure programmes. However, empirical research in the area of mental health group therapy is limited. This is another important future direction for mental health services. The information and data highlighted in this chapter supports the inclusion of therapeutic group work within clinical programmes. Research into group work is a complex task, but ongoing exploration of the effectiveness of approaches is essential. It is only through further research that the value of group work programmes in clinical mental health settings can continue to grow in recognition.

References

Albiston, D., Francey, S., and Harrigan, S. (1998). Group programmes for recovery from early psychosis. *British Journal of Psychiatry*, *172*, 117–121.

Birchwood, M. and Macmillan, F. (1993). Early intervention in schizophrenia. *Australian and New Zealand Journal of Psychiatry*, *27*, 374–378.

Chovil, I. (2005). First psychosis prodrome: Rehabilitation and recovery. *Psychiatric Rehabilitation Journal*, *28*, 407–411.

Edwards, J. and McGorry, P. D. (2002). *Implementing early intervention in psychosis: A guide to establishing early psychosis services*. London: Martin Dunitz.

EPPIC Statewide Services (2000). *Group work in early psychosis*, vol. 3. Melbourne: Department of Human Services.

Francey, S. (1999). The role of day programmes in recovery from early psychosis. In P. D. McGorry and H. J. Jackson (Eds.) *Recognition and management of early psychosis: A preventive approach* (pp. 407–433). Cambridge: Cambridge University Press.

Harper, C. (2003). Facilitating a group. In S. Pepper (Ed.) *A sense of belonging: Groups at work* (pp. 27–31). Melbourne: New Paradigm Press, an imprint of Psychiatric Disability Services of Australia (VICSERV) Inc.

Luxmoore, M., Turner, T., and Cotton, S. (2004). Taking risks and overcoming challenges: Outdoor adventure group therapy for first episode psychosis. Poster presented at International Conference on Early Psychosis, Vancouver, Canada, September.

McCay, K., Ryan, K., and Amey, S. (1996). Mitigating engulfment: Recovering from a first episode of psychosis. *Journal of Psychosocial Nursing*, *34*, 40–44.

McDermott, F. (2003). Group work in the mental health field: Researching outcome. *Australian Social Work*, *56*, 352–363.

Macdonald, E., Sauer, K., Howie, L., and Albiston, D. (2005). What happens to social relationships in early psychosis? A phenomenological study of young people's experiences. *Journal of Mental Health*, *14*, 129–143.

Mackrell, L. and Lavender, T. (2004). Peer relationships in adolescents experiencing a first episode of psychosis. *Journal of Mental Health*, *13*, 467–479.

Miller, R. and Mason, S. (1998). Group work with first episode schizophrenia clients. *Social Work with Groups*, *21*, 19–33.

Miller, R. and Mason, S. (2001). Using group therapy to enhance treatment compliance in first episode schizophrenia. *Social Work with Groups*, *24*, 37–51.

Penn, D. L., Waldheter, E. J., Perkins, D. O., Mueser, K. T., and Lieberman, J. A. (2005). Psychosocial treatment for first-episode psychosis: A research update. *American Journal of Psychiatry*, *162*, 2220–2232.

Rosenberg, M. (1965). *Society and the adolescent self-image*. Princeton, NJ: Princeton University Press.

Toseland, R. and Siporin, M. (1986). When to recommend group treatment: A review of the clinical and the research literature. *International Journal of Group Psychotherapy*, *36*, 171–201.

Turner, T., Luxmoore, M., Cotton, S., Schotten, H., Woodhead, G., Albiston, D., and Johnson, T. (2004). Group programs in early psychosis: Preliminary data from EPPIC group programme database. Poster presented at International Conference on Early Psychosis, Vancouver, Canada, September.

Woodhead, G. (2002). Physical attraction: The physical environment as a tool for engagement. *Acta Psychiatrica Scandinavica, 106* (Suppl. 413), 102.

Woodhead, G. (2004). Decreasing the drop out with drop-in: Engaging young people with first episode psychosis in groups. Unpublished manuscript.

Woodside, H., Schell, L., and Allison-Hedges, J. (2006). Listening for recovery: The vocational success of people living with mental illness. *Canadian Journal of Occupational Therapy, 73*, 36–43.

Chapter 15

Systemically speaking
Integrating multi-family group work

Grace Couchman

Introduction

Each of us is embedded in the interwoven threads of community. Like a textured cloth, its basic substance is a weft and weave that has been consistently integrated with time and effort. A cloth's patterning can be both subtle and bold, and while often delicate in its minute structures, the careful integration of a cloth's components can lend it a strength that prepares it for robust purposes and times of tough wear and tear. Community, like the cotton and linen in our daily lives, is sometimes taken for granted in its capacity to provide comfort and protection and also underestimated in its need for maintenance. Increasingly, the mental health care agenda emphasizes the support and improvement of family and community as it becomes clear that families and communities need assistance to repair the social wear and tear wrought by family trauma and mental illness.

Mental health management has increasingly focused on the development of social community as central to people's mental health (WHO, 2001). The adoption of the biopsychosocial framework for illness assessment and intervention by mental health services has encouraged mental health practitioners to take a systemic lens to mental health management. The framework broadens the factors which are considered when exploring individual mental health and encourages the inclusion of family and community as sites of challenge and intervention.

The notion of using community development to improve mental health has been, since Durkheim's study of suicide and social structure (Durkheim, 1952), a significant aspect of mental health care, especially within the disciplines of social work and social psychiatry. Sometimes arising by design and sometimes by accident (McFarlane et al., 2003), psychiatric services have, to some degree, included families and worked with context. Discrete family pathology concepts such as the psychopathogenic family and the schizophrenogenic mother have been largely superseded by the more general stress vulnerability model, which embraces both social and biological stressors and acknowledges the impact of the advent of mental illness on family functioning. Current models suggest that the way families and communities behave and position themselves does influence mental health outcomes for individuals. This can be in terms of contributing to or offsetting the impact of trauma (Morrison et al., 2003; Read et al., 2001), participating in or changing stressful family relationships (Barrowclough et al., 1994; Leff, 1999), and being variably informed about recovery management (Anderson et al., 1986; Falloon et al., 1984; McFarlane, 2002).

Multi-family group models of mental health intervention have developed from systemic psychiatric models, some accidents of inclusion, and a growing body of evidence that families play a strong role in the wellness of family members. The McFarlane model is one that has been applied to the treatment of serious mental illness such as psychosis and depression. Its strength lies in its capacity to embrace biological, social and psychological knowledge while engaging families in an egalitarian systemic process which amplifies family resources and skill. The programme, in practice, provides mental health service users and their families with a community of families which serve as a microcosm of wider society, and support social reintegration and recovery. This chapter will describe the evolution of a Melbourne-based multi-family group programme. The dilemmas of implementing the intervention in an Australian context will be discussed, and some important features of therapeutic clinical research and family inclusion in service provision will be highlighted.

Programme development

The Melbourne-based Inner West Multi-Family Group Project arose from a number of intersecting interests. In 1996, the Inner West Area Mental Health Service area manager, a former family therapist, encouraged a number of senior clinicians to participate in the McFarlane-style family intervention training developed conjointly by a Melbourne-based academic institution and a mental illness advocacy organization. Following this initial exposure, the clinical service manager and her staff initiated a multi-family group programme and, when internal resources were not adequate, successfully obtained external funding in collaboration with a specialist family therapy organization, the Bouverie Centre. The external funding provided experienced clinical and research staff for a four-year programme involving two Mental Health Services and two local Psychiatric Disability Support Services in the urban region of Melbourne.

Families were recruited from the pool of current service users and both English and Vietnamese-speaking families were invited to participate. The programme was open to those in both acute, and rehabilitation parts of the service with the stipulation that they were able to engage in a group programme and had regular contact with a family member or friend who was willing to participate. This, at times, excluded families where there was low family interest, current violence or severe drug issues, and/or low levels of language proficiency. Acute anxiety or psychosis was not regarded as grounds for exclusion. In general, the service users who attended the group had moderate to severe mental health vulnerability and a number of the participants experienced acute illness during their project participation.

The multi-family intervention

The programme was based on the McFarlane multi-family group intervention (McFarlane, 2002). The original McFarlane model recommended a 24-month programme which spanned acute and rehabilitation phases of service involvement. The Melbourne programme spanned 12 months given that recruitment was mostly of post-acute service users who were attending the continuing care component of the service. In accordance with the McFarlane model, families were engaged carefully over one to three single-family sessions. They subsequently entered the group programme where they were provided with fortnightly meetings, of one and a half hours and additional support as required. Two trained facilitators conducted meetings in both community and mental health service settings. In brief, the first four meetings of the programme focused on the sharing of up-to-date illness information, and storytelling by each family about both their experience of illness and their life aside from illness. In subsequent meetings the families, sequentially socialized, caught up with the events of the two previous weeks, used a group process to find solutions to day-to-day problems, and further socialized. The families were encouraged to network, to socialize outside the group and to share their resources. In addition, funded social outings were organized for each group. These varied from a night barbecue to a day visit to a health resort. Within-group reviews were held at both 6 and 12 months.

Evaluation

Quantitative and qualitative data was obtained for the purposes of programme evaluation. The research study took the form of a randomized, controlled trial which compared multi-family group intervention to usual case management. In a Melbourne mental health setting, case management consists of biological, social and psychological intervention on a 2–4 weekly basis mostly provided by post-graduate trained clinicians. The quantitative findings suggested multi-family groups were effective in reducing relapse and psychiatric symptomatology (Bradley et al., 2006). The study also revealed that the multi-family group intervention promoted a sense of community, provided access to strategies and resources, improved family relationships, and helped families to manage emotional distress. The reduction of families' isolation, and anxiety facilitated their better use of new family perspectives, new knowledge and the skills offered by social and clinical services (Couchman, 2004a).

The quantitative data consisted of standardized measures taken both pre- and post-intervention. These measures included the Brief Psychiatric Rating Scale (BPRS: Ventura et al., 1993), the Quality of Life Scale (Heinrichs et al., 1984), the Scale for the Assessment of Negative Symptoms (Andreasen, 1989), and the Family Burden Scale (Pai and Kapur, 1981). Relapse was also monitored. In comparison to their case-managed counterparts, the multi-family group participants showed a statistically significant lower level of clinical relapse, over both one and two years, as well as less psychiatric symptoms, particularly cognitive disorganization, over the same period measured by the BPRS (Bradley et al., 2006). These differences were similar for English-speaking and Vietnamese-speaking families and were consistent, and even enhanced, six months later.

The qualitative aspect of the study consisted of the analysis of data drawn from 16 interviews with the service users, other family members, and mental health clinicians. The data was derived from semi-structured interviews conducted in either English or Vietnamese with skilled translation. The data was analysed using a grounded theory methodology (Punch, 2005). This consisted of identifying conceptual codes, theoretical codes and finally core concepts using a recursive process of comparison. Data was organized using a data display method (Hurworth, 1998).

Four major concepts

Four major concepts were derived from the data. The first was that of *social connection*. In reference to this, participants described the social marginalization of their families and the profound impact of group connection. Feelings of normality and being part of a community were pivotal aspects. A second core concept was *tackling the problems of mental illness*. In relation to this, participants described the importance of receiving and sharing information and of finding solutions to their problems. This was particularly enhanced by being with people who had experienced similar difficulties. Interestingly, while professional mental illness information was viewed as useful, families identified the disclosure of family feelings and experience to be just as important. *Equality and responsibility* was a third concept, which referred to changes in the families' relationship with the group, family members and service providers. The families' struggle for equal relationships and fairness in sharing responsibility was articulated. The group provided a forum for discussing and enacting changed relationships. The concept of *coping life with illness* was a fourth concept, which referred to the families' need to acknowledge the enormity and nature of their burden and to disclose their emotional pain and grief. The multi-family group provided hope and examples of coping through exposure to the courage and strategies of the families.

The interviews also revealed two collective ideas of the group which expressed the nature of the families' group bond. The first, 'being in the same boat' consisted of notions of families being 'at sea', 'shipwrecked' and being on a courageous journey. It framed families as collectively adrift and engaged in a chronic struggle for survival. A second idea was of the multi-family group as 'an extended family' where one was unconditionally accepted and supported in the long term no matter how bizarre or difficult was one's behaviour. This highlighted the complexity for families of managing psychotic episodes while, at the same time, providing an accommodating home where all were welcome.

The Melbourne programme highlighted the success and understanding that can be achieved through the careful development, implementation and evaluation of a family inclusive approach. An orientation toward systemic practice and family inclusion assisted its genesis. The availability of supportive scientific evidence enhanced the model's credibility at a service-development level. Supportive management structures and external funding were fundamental to the project's development and completion. The dual quantitative and qualitative elements ensured a rich and rounded account of family and service change, and provided important insight into the therapeutic processes associated with positive clinical outcomes. While the programme was a relatively close replication of the McFarlane multi-family group model, it was modified to suit an Australian environment and to take advantage of therapeutic techniques from solution-focused and narrative therapies. The process of programme development yielded useful insights into functional adaptations and avenues to programme success.

Working systemically with families: challenges and adaptations

The practice of multi-family group interventions had developed over 20 years in a variety of international locations in services which had, in their own way, captured the unique needs of their target community. International multi-family group programmes observed in Norway, USA and Belgium were observed to differ in their relative emphasis on various programme elements (Couchman, 2004b). However, close examination revealed a number of stable principles that underpinned the work. All these programmes were characterized by careful and respectful engagement of families, a practical group approach to mental health issues, a systemic view of mental illness causality, and an emphasis on optimizing family and social relationships. The McFarlane model was defined as much by its underlying principles of respect, non-blame, egalitarianism, and practicality as it was by its structures and techniques.

The structure of the programme was relatively simple and accessible, and promoted a group process rather than specific meeting content. Its emphasis on the interactions of families at a number of levels reflected a number of systemic concepts and family therapy practices (Goldenberg and Goldenberg,

2000). The simple structure and interactive emphasis gave the model a capacity to meet the needs of a range of mental health populations, such as people diagnosed with depression, psychosis, borderline personality disorder as well as those with general health difficulties. The basic structure ensured some flexibility about the specific aspects of mental health that could be discussed so that two multi-family groups could have the same basic structure, but targeted the specific mental health concerns raised by their respective group families.

The inclusion of families in mental health service provision

We're lucky there are carers as well as people who have once been sick in the group. It's like you talk and your family member listens to you as well as to other people.

(J., partner-carer)

In general, the idea and practice of working in a family-sensitive way was challenging to service providers, service users and families. This section explores practical strategies for facilitating family inclusion and the conduct of ethical research. It also addresses ways to provide relevant mental health information, and the use of problem solving as an accessible group process for all family members.

Engaging case managers

In an Australian mental health service system, the level of clinician contact with families ranges from low to medium. Family inclusion in mental health services is recommended by government guidelines, but the actual extent of family inclusion largely depends on the therapeutic orientation and skill of individual case managers. Most Australian mental health clinicians are postgraduates from a range of allied health disciplines and hold variable levels of training in family sensitive practice. The Inner West Multi-Family Group Project was met with a mix of local excitement and curiosity. It also raised a number of concerns for those clinicians with minimal exposure to family work or beliefs that family inclusion would be to the detriment of service users. Some clinicians were concerned that the involvement of families would be hard to manage and contain and that they would be overwhelmed by family needs. It was largely by way of exposure that clinicians came to view family inclusion as time-effective and productive for their clients.

Some clinicians regarded the problem-solving idea as too simple, and/or were doubtful that Australians would be comfortable with a group problem-solving format. There was concern that the model challenged usual Australian customs of moderate to high levels of personal privacy between family members, and reluctance to discuss mental health issues. However, families appeared to enjoy the practical focus that problem solving created. While non-ill family members often preferred a more free floating discussion format, service users reported finding the problem-solving structure supportive. Similarly, doubts were raised about the model's suitability for an Australian-Vietnamese population. There was frequent reference to the idea that Asian families were strongly emotionally private and averse to psychological concepts of mental illness, and that this would hamper programme participation. One clinician suggested that mental health discussions would be more likely through a Vietnamese cooking or social group. However, the cultural factors did not preclude group participation, but did require the careful fostering of the families' sense of safety and their understanding and trust of confidentiality rules. Reluctance to speak about mental illness appeared to be an international phenomenon that transcended culture, and required general but assertive handling. The Vietnamese families, in practice, valued the inclusion of family and drew upon the group for guidance and the regulation of family members. It appeared that collectivist cultural values were, in fact, quite compatible with the multi-family group process. Throughout the project, wherever possible, case managers were included in the engagement and work with families. This served the purpose of providing support to the referred families and also enhanced case manager exposure to family inclusive practice.

Engaging families

At the outset, families responded with curious surprise when invited to take part in the project and, potentially, a group. Vietnamese families generally required a longer engagement period with more active outreach as they rarely perceived themselves as relevant to mental health service provision. Around 20 per cent of the families stated they had not previously spoken to a service clinician because of either language or work constraints, or the failure of services to invite them. The Vietnamese families also required considerable reassurance about the boundaries of confidentiality. In general, most participating families expressed positive interest, even though initial approaches to them yielded mixed responses. Occasionally, families interpreted an invitation to participate as evidence of the service's view of them as pathological rather than as a positive resource for their relatives' recovery and support. Some family members became tearful as they revealed their hardships for the first time and expressed fear of being overwhelmed by pent-up emotion. Others worried that a focus on themselves might detract from the service given to their ill relative. The service users occasionally were reluctant to involve their families. Some worried that inclusion would create further burden for the family. Some feared the session might leave them feeling objectified or excessively pathologized by both their family and the service provider. In general, families were nervous about talking about mental health issues with their families. Most described only rare discussions about illness in the home, and some were concerned that discussion might cause illness or conflict. Families required reassurance that the facilitator had some experience of working with families and groups and that the sessions would be sensitively conducted, and consultative. Each family was offered individual or joint engagement sessions, however all families elected to be seen together.

The engagement sessions provided an opportunity to establish the working model. It was useful, for successful engagement, that the facilitator was familiar with the family and social context of mental illness as well as being knowledgeable about the dynamics that commonly develop between service providers, service users and families in the context of an illness diagnosis. Families were encouraged to relate their experiences. These included survival, family self-discovery, losses and disappointments, accumulated trauma, social marginalization, self doubt, and the, at times, ill-fit of mental health services. Facilitators were able to connect with families while also actively curbing the worst of the common and destructive illness dynamics. For example, service providers and families easily reverted to talking about the service user in the third person, in their presence. The facilitator actively modelled direct engagement and shared consultation. Similarly, family members' conversation often descended into unproductive blaming. In this instance, the facilitator was able to educate the family about the attractiveness but unhelpfulness of blame when families are feeling hopeless and helpless. Families rarely acknowledged their victories and strengths when faced with chronic problems, and also tended to define themselves, narrowly, in terms of illness. Curiosity and persistence on the part of the facilitator often revealed a rich and often unexpected account of family life which countered the families' often pathologizing descriptions of themselves. Expanded descriptions were an asset for ongoing work. They provided clues of the families' motivation and values, and highlighted future goals for illness recovery.

A significant proportion of each family's conflict and distress arose in the engagement sessions and often required careful listening and intervention so that the family's participation could continue, and they felt their family and sensitivities were understood. Intra-family conflict was largely manageable and then mostly quite constrained in the ongoing group meetings. It seemed that overt conflict was somewhat dampened by both the demands for social propriety, inherent to any group activity, and the frequent opportunities to discuss conflictual issues across families rather than within them.

Engaging service providers

The inclusion of families in the project had an impact beyond the changes for individuals and families. Service providers gained significant insight into the experience of families through greater client disclosure and project-related feedback and training. At a statewide level, two participating families provided training to other mental health services at the end of their project involvement. The mother of one service user achieved formal funding for her carer support group. A second carer-mother designed and implemented a website to be used as a resource and support for family members living with mental health problems. Two of the service users became involved in consumer consultancy within the Melbourne mental health service system.

The productive provision of illness information

Our son is like that and her [another carer] daughter is like that also. Some are more sick, some are less. We never understood what was wrong. We had to learn about the degrees of illness from our son's behavior and from the other people who came to the group. Practical is always better. Reading books never helped. Practical you can see.

(S., father-carer)

Qualitative analysis of the families' experience of the multi-family group suggested that, while families appreciated having access to scientific knowledge, they equally valued the examples and wisdoms provided by their own and other family members. The McFarlane model emphasized the sharing of up-to-date mental health information. This included the common theories, precipitants and manifestations of illness, as well as the full range of strategies and interventions which individuals and families find useful. The model advocates adherence to a stress vulnerability model and scientific evidence-based criteria for the selection of suitable professional information for families. However, it also placed high value on the real-life accounts and wisdoms of experienced families and clinicians. Therefore, a range of materials was provided. Up-to-date information was provided about biological, social and psychological factors which had been associated with psychosis, trauma and poor family coping (Anderson et al., 1986; Dixon et al., 2003; McFarlane, 2002; Morrison et al., 2003). Family accounts of effective family strategies and remedies were provided from the real-life experiences of families. Accounts of managing mental illness symptoms and lifestyle were also drawn from published compilations of service users' strategies (Watkins, 1993), and recordings such as a video produced by a local psychologist which detailed his own hospitalization and relapse experience. Combined with the accounts of the participating families, these educational materials provided a rich introduction to theories, interventions and possibilities. The Vietnamese and English-speaking groups differed to only a small degree. The Vietnamese group was conducted entirely in the Vietnamese language and the biomedical information was simplified because the families largely had no formal science education. Material was also incorporated which recognized spiritual and culturally specific understandings of illness such as karma, heat and cold, and ghost possession.

A number of clinicians were concerned about the overt discussion of biological models of illness and the potential that service users would feel pathologized, especially in the context of biological models being highly dominant in the psychiatric system. This raised two issues, one being how to deal with the dynamics of theory adherence and the other being what constituted legitimate evidence.

In terms of the dominance of particular theories of illness, the facilitators were mindful of the need for a broad-ranging approach which engaged families, while providing them with useful and practical ideas in a cohesive framework. This was especially difficult in the area of mental illness due to the fact that a definitive cause remains elusive (Lukens and McFarlane, 2002). Systems theory, developed from the study of biological systems, highlighted the importance of systems being receptive to new information despite their inherent need to maintain stability, and the tendency of systems to engage in active homeostatic correction in the face of challenges to the system's integrity (Goding, 1992). Applied to the psychiatric knowledge system, these assertions imply that psychiatric paradigms can theoretically dominate even when new information provides a challenge and that there is a necessity to maintain an organized openness to a range of knowledge. In terms of providing education about mental illness, it followed that a flexible approach to epistemology was necessary in order that a balance was attained. This respected family knowledge and current psychiatric models but was also prepared to entertain new information as well as acknowledge areas of uncertainty.

The programme's commitment was to harness biological, social, cultural, spiritual and psychological information in the interests of recovery. This required the facilitators to be familiar with current research and theory and to be discriminating about the evidence that was drawn from the research domain. Facilitators were most effective when they displayed respect for broader philosophical and spiritual thinking and were familiar with grass-roots family experience. The facilitators applied an empirical approach to selection of published real-life family accounts, seeking stories which contained evidence of constructive mental health change and where the detail of the story was sufficient to provide adequate context. Mostly, the family accounts added to, rather than detracted from, the scientific data and the families benefited from exposure to a range of theoretical and practical ideas. Ultimately, families adopted the scientific, lay knowledge and/or group wisdom that fitted with their own understanding of their circumstances.

The discussion of the causes or precipitants of mental illness presented a dilemma in that the advantage of identifying specific precipitating factors and targeted treatment was sometimes offset by the narrow focus which it encouraged. For example, a biomedical diagnosis of psychosis due to biological factors created certainty and a way forward for families. However, such a narrow account of illness obscured other central factors such as family behaviour, environmental stress, or drug use. It was not only biological explanations that could become constraining. For example, a narrow trauma explanation for illness similarly provided constraint by encouraging a focus on primary emotional injuries at the expense of dealing with ongoing lifestyle issues. Our approach was that educating families about illness and recovery required facilitators to remain curious about what families wanted to know and why (Fadden, 2005), an inclusive rather than exclusive approach to causality, and a knowledgeable and discriminating approach to mental health research and evidence.

Problem solving and solution finding

Being with people in the same boat means you are compelled to find solutions.

(A., service-user)

Initially, the idea of using problem solving as a group process sat awkwardly with service providers. In addition, the project coordinator had enjoyed using both problem-focused and solution-focused methods for promoting change (Berg, 1993; De Shazer, 1982). However, the methods fitted well together and proved most productive in combination.

In solution-focused approaches, analysis of problems, solely, has been viewed as reinforcing the problem system, amplifying failure, and limiting possibilities for change. The underlying notion has been that problems are problems largely because people already have a notion of an alternative situation and that these alternative situations should be examined and utilized in the therapy. Both problem-solving and solution-finding methods are practical, and action oriented. A combination of the two ensured that problems received full consideration and that a wide and innovative range of solutions were created. The multi-family group model was easily adapted to a partially solution-focused format but had tended to be adopted in the problem-focused format due to the readiness of mental health services to take it up in that form in the early stages of the model's development (W. McFarlane, personal communication, October 2003). During the Melbourne project, families were encouraged to use both problem-focused and solution-focused formats although, fundamentally, the structure of the group changed little.

The solution-focused format tended to create a more positive tone and so the problem-solving/solution-finding formats were used alternately or when one or the other seemed more suitable. Solution-focused questioning could shift the orientation of the exercise in helpful ways.

For example, when T. presented the problem that 'getting out of bed is too hard', she was prompted to consider what she would be doing if this was not a problem. She then spoke of having a job that made her feel 'part of the world'. In response to this, the group worked on ways that T. could 'be part of the world' and, maybe, get herself a job.

Some questioning techniques were also drawn from Narrative Therapy (White and Epston, 1990) such that the process of problems definition was gently expanded. For example, a problem such as alcohol use might have been explored as a relational or externalized concept using questions such as 'What does it take for you to give in to drink?', 'How do you know when drinking has the upper hand?', or 'What does drink think about your efforts to get it under control?' This type of questioning often led to an understanding of relevant underlying issues and more effective problem solving given that it was sometimes the case that the presenting problem was not necessarily the most important one to work on.

For example, M., an elderly parent of a service user, P., told the group that she was concerned about P.'s frequent conversations with himself and 'his voices'. However, when M. was further questioned about the relationship between herself and P.'s 'voices', she revealed that the 'voices' left her feeling extremely lonely and distant from her son P., and that she was feeling extremely socially isolated. The problem solving and solution finding conducted in relation to this issue focused on helping M. feel more 'in touch' with P., her family, and her community.

The modifications made to the McFarlane model were largely additions of simple clinical techniques to the basic multi-family group structure. It was noted that international programmes also reflected the theoretical and clinical orientation and skills of their project managers and group facilitators (Couchman, 2004b). Service users reported finding both formats simple, useful and easy to follow and enjoyed the narrative style techniques. Some non-ill family members found the simple structured formats a little 'school-like'. However, they were maintained, to ensure equitable participation given that service users were overwhelmed and silenced by fast-moving, free-flowing conversations, due to illness and medication side effects, and found the more structured approach to be supportive. Occasionally, the format was changed to a more free-flowing discussion of general issues for example, dealing with grief or finding work.

There were many problem-solving and solution-finding sessions, in the various groups, dealing with managing symptoms and side effects, general relaxation, improving sleep, making friends, and increasing one's independence. On some occasions, service users sought help from the group to actively manage acute relapse.

For example, A. was becoming restless, not sleeping; he was starting to wear clothing connected with a destructive set of beliefs (that he was part of a famous band), and was spending long hours reading existential philosophy. Apart from directing him toward medical consultation, the group generated a range of options such as that A. reduce his intense reading, be active in walking at the local park twice daily, meet up with a group member for coffee the next day, and establish a more regular daily routine.

At times, non-ill family members sought assistance through problem solving and solution finding.

For example, G., a care giver, was revealed by her son to engage in problematic gambling. The group generated solutions which included G. attending gamblers anonymous with another group member who revealed having a similar problem.

Over the course of the group the conversation expanded from being primarily focused on mental illness symptoms and the service user, to being focused on the maximization of mental health for the whole group.

Vietnamese families preferred oral rather than written tasks because their level of literacy was low. However, the general problem-solving/solution-finding structure was maintained. Vietnamese families were remarkable for their level of disclosure once the parameters of confidentiality were understood; they then revealed a wide range of very personal concerns. It appeared that collectivist-type culture actively encouraged the use of the community for establishing rules, solving problems and exerting influence on individuals.

Ethical research strategies

But they're not really going to listen to what I think . . . are they?

(S., service-user)

The inclusion of quantitative and qualitative research components in the project ensured that family experiences could be articulated beyond responses to researcher-derived quantitative questionnaires. The combination of methodologies enabled the dissemination of findings in both phenomenological and empirical form.

Service clinicians were initially concerned about their clients and families being involved in research and undergoing processes such as assessment interviews, random allocation to treatment and control conditions, and identification as research participants. One major concern was that families may refuse to take part and miss out on a potentially useful clinical programme. There was also a concern that families would feel poorly serviced when allocated to a control condition, and would feel objectified by the research process.

From the outset, a commitment was made to conduct the research in a way that was open, prioritized the needs of families, and provided accurate and representative research findings. To this end, the research staff were clinically trained and engaged with families in a therapeutic manner even where simple assessments were being conducted. The assessor was often generous with her time and listened to the extent of the information that the families wished to provide. Where families were allocated to a control condition, they were invited to subsequently attend a group programme after their control group participation was complete. All families received usual case management services and case managers were informed of any pressing family concerns, for any family engaged in the project.

The evaluation of the project provided opportunities for families to articulate their experience. Reviews were conducted during the treatment groups to maximize family input, and the qualitative interviews were largely unstructured to enable families to generate content on their own terms. The quantitative and qualitative findings were presented to the families at a service-funded dinner to which all the participating families were invited.

Conclusion

Systemically speaking, family-inclusion and multi-family group participation were shown to be clinically effective and healthy additions to mental health service provision. The project created opportunities to examine the interface between service users, providers and families. It also provided a forum to discuss the dynamics of care, being accountable for others, and the responsibilities of case managing or caring for someone who is seriously disabled.

The Melbourne multi-family group project revealed that many families generally struggled alone with illness problems, as well as with their own negative perceptions of themselves and their family. Isolation provided a potent genesis for poor self-perception, family pathologizing, as well as strong feelings of being 'not normal' and of being marginalized by the general community.

As T. described it, 'You feel like a freak. Your whole family is cast out of society and you need people who can pull you back to normality.'

The group appeared to serve as an anchor for family normality, even if that was a different kind of normal. Families valued the length of the programme and described important processes such as 'seeing how things go over time', and learning from the practical wisdoms of other families in response to emerging events.

The project research findings demonstrated that while families welcomed professional knowledge, they equally valued the opportunity to offer advice, listen to other members of their own families and work with other families. Professional knowledge was reported as being reassuring, lowering anxiety, and promoting both a sense of hope and a way forward. It was noted, however, that families often held on to their own beliefs about the underlying causes of illness, but used additional information in an eclectic 'do what works' model of strategic action. Professional biopsychosocial knowledge appeared to create a sense of security which reduced anxiety and distress, enough that families could then turn their thinking to devising assertive plans of practical and effective action. The finding that effective family education occurred in programmes of ten sessions or more (Cuijpers, 1999) may have reflected the interaction of the professional knowledge framework, within which families then examined their own problems from a range of viewpoints, and generated their own clever and culturally suitable solutions.

A little discussed aspect of multi-family group involvement is the challenge that it provides to the dynamic of caring. This is a sensitive issue which is complicated by high levels of carers' burden, the dependence of service users, and the general socioeconomic dependence which mental illness generates. While it was challenging for a small group to tackle the illness dynamics, this happened naturally within the process of multi-family group interaction and information sharing.

The need for families to find solace, comfort and hope can be sorely underrated, despite our understanding of the extent to which family stress and distress can disrupt constructive functioning. While mental health services are not necessarily in the best position to provide therapeutic support for all family members, this project suggested that family inclusion by services could reduce family distress, improve family relating, and improve service user's mental health outcomes.

The key to creating family inclusiveness and a multi-family group programme was the engagement of service users, case managers and families. All parts of the system both needed and had relevant knowledge. Multi-family groups provided a forum where that knowledge could be constructively shared and utilized.

References

Anderson, C., Reiss, D., and Hogarty, G. (1986). *Schizophrenia and the family*. New York: Guilford.

Andreasen, N. (1989). The Scale for the Assessment of Negative Symptoms (SANS): Conceptual and theoretical foundations. *British Journal of Psychiatry*, *155* (Suppl. 7), 49–52.

Barrowclough, C., Johnston, M., and Tarrier, N. (1994). Attribution, expressed emotion and patient relapse: An attributional model of relatives' responses to schizophrenic illness. *Behavior Therapy*, *25*, 67–88.

Berg, I. (1993). *Family based services: A solution-focused approach*. New York: Norton.

Bradley, G., Couchman, G., Perlesz, A., Nyugen, A., Singh, B., and Riess, C. (2006). Multiple family group treatment for English and Vietnamese-speaking families living with Schizophrenia. *Psychiatric Services*, *5*, 521–530.

Couchman, G. (2004a). *Multi-family group work: The inner west experience*. Melbourne: Victorian Association of Family Therapy Research Forum.

Couchman, G. (2004b). *An exploration of the use of multi-family groups in direct mental health practice: An overview of multi-family group work in U.S.A., Belgium, and Norway*. Melbourne: Department of Human Services.

Cuijpers, P. (1999). The effects of family intervention on relatives' burden: A meta-analysis. *Journal of Mental Health*, *8*, 275–285.

De Shazer, S. (1982). *Patterns of brief therapy: An ecosystemic approach*. New York: Guilford.

Dixon, L., Curtis, A., and Lucksted, A. (2003). Update of family psychoeducation. *Schizophrenia Bulletin*, *26*, 5–23.

Durkheim, E. (1952). *Suicide*. London: Routledge and Kegan Paul.

Fadden, G. (2005). *Meriden family behavioural intervention training program*. Melbourne: Northwestern Health Care Network.

Falloon, I., Boyd, J., and McGill, C. (1984). *Family care of schizophrenia: A problem-solving approach to the care of mental illness*. New York: Guilford.

Goding, G. (1992). *The principles of family therapy*. Melbourne: Victorian Association of Family Therapists.

Goldenberg, I. and Goldenberg, H. (2000). *Family therapy: An overview*. Monterey, CA: Brooks/Cole.

Heinrichs, D., Hanlon, T., and Carpenter, W. (1984). The Quality of Life Scale: An instrument for rating the schizophrenic deficit syndrome. *Schizophrenia Bulletin*, *10*, 388–398.

Hurworth, R. (1998). *Qualitative analysis training program*. Melbourne: Victoria University.

Leff, J. (1999). *The unbalanced mind*. London: Weidenfeld and Nicolson.

Lukens, E. and McFarlane, W. (2002). Families, social networks and schizophrenia. In W. McFarlane (Ed.), *Multifamily groups in the treatment of severe psychiatric disorders* (pp. 18–35). New York: Guilford.

McFarlane, W. (2002). *Multifamily groups in the treatment of severe psychiatric disorders*. New York: Guilford.

McFarlane, W., Dixon, L., Lukens, E., and Lucksted, A. (2003). Family psychoeducation and schizophrenia: A review of the literature. *Journal of Marital and Family Therapy*, *29*, 223–246.

Morrison, A., Frame, L., and Larkin, W. (2003). Relationships between trauma and psychosis: A review and integration. *British Journal of Clinical Psychology*, *42*, 331–353.

Pai, S. and Kapur, R. (1981). The burden on the family of a psychiatric patient: Development of an interview schedule. *British Journal of Psychiatry*, *138*, 332–335.

Punch, K. (2005). *Introduction to social research: Quantitative and qualitative approaches*. London: Sage.

Read, J., Perry, B., Moskowitz, A., and Connolly, J. (2001). The contribution of early traumatic events to schizophrenia in some patients. *Psychiatry: Interpersonal and Biological Processes*, *64*, 319–345.

Ventura, J., Green, M., Shaner, A., and Liberman, R. (1993). Training and quality assurance with the Brief Psychiatric Rating Scale: 'The drift busters'. *International Journal of Methods in Psychiatric Research*, 3, 221–224.

Watkins, J. (1993). *Hearing voices: A self-help guide and reference book*. Melbourne: Richmond Fellowship of Victoria.

White, M. and Epston, D. (1990). *Narrative means to therapeutic ends*. New York: Norton.

WHO (2001). *Mental health: New understanding, new hope*. Geneva: WHO.

Index

Note: page numbers in *italics* refer to information contained in tables; page numbers in **bold** refer to diagrams.

abstinence 152, 157
abuse 21; *see also* childhood abuse; childhood sexual abuse; sexual abuse
Adams, J. 174
Addington, D. 162
Addington, J. 54, 61, 162
adherence 152, 157, 161, 163; to antipsychotics 155–6, 157; Insight-Adherence-Abstinence model 152, 157, 161, 163; to pharmacotherapy in bipolar disorder 169, 171, 172–3; to psychosocial approaches 173; and the treatment alliance 172–4; *see also* compliance; non-compliance
adoption studies 37
adrenaline 7
advocacy 218, 220–1
agency, sense of 63
aggression 145, 158
Alanen, Y. 38
Alanen, Y. O. 18, 25, 30–1, 80
Albiston, D. 225, 230, 231
alcohol use 108, 111, 156–7, 226, 251; binge drinking 103, 105
alien control/intrusion 48, 56
aloneness, psychological 191
American Expert Consensus Guideline Series for schizophrenia 38
American Journal of Insanity 200
American Psychiatric Association 202; treatment guidelines 203
amphetamines 176
ancestors 104, 193
Anderson, C. M. 214
Andreasen, Nancy 54

anger 161
antidepressants 122, 172
antipsychotics 3; adherence issues 75–6, 155–6, 157; on an integrated treatment program for first-episode schizophrenia 152, 153, 159; changing 159; ineffective 78, 79, 80, 159; long-term use of 82; Norwegian guidelines on 79–80; PORT study on 77; use in the pre-psychotic stage 122; second-generation 202; side effects 76, 122, 159, 160; TIPS programme 79, 82; *see also* neuroleptics; *specific drugs*
anxiety 83, 121, 126, 142
Appraisal Guideline Research and Evaluation Europe (AGREE) 203
Arieti, S. 20
artists 237
Asian people 186; *see also* Vietnamese families
assertiveness 41, 42, 43
assessment 214
asylums 92
attachment systems theory 58–9
attitudes 169, 172–3
attributions 55, 56–8, 65
attunement 169
Auckland, New Zealand 197
Australia 3, 18, 93, 94, 112, 117, 122–4, 225, 227–8, 230–7, 241–54
authoring 188, 189–90, 194–5
autism 56–7
autonomic hyperactivity 6, 7, 9
autonomy 29, 110
awareness-raising 142, 217, 218, 219–20